THE TEXANS

THE OLD WEST

THE TEXANS

By the Editors of

TIME-LIFE BOOKS

with text by

David Nevin

TIME-LIFE BOOKS / ALEXANDRIA, VIRGINIA

Time-Life Books Inc.
is a wholly owned subsidiary of

TIME INCORPORATED

Founder: Henry R. Luce 1898-1967

Editor-in-Chief: Henry Anatole Grunwald
President: J. Richard Munro
Chairman of the Board: Ralph P. Davidson
Executive Vice President: Clifford J. Grum
Chairman, Executive Committee: James R. Shepley
Editorial Director: Ralph Graves
Group Vice President, Books: Joan D. Manley
Vice Chairman: Arthur Temple

TIME-LIFE BOOKS INC.

Editor: George Constable
Executive Editor: George Daniels
Board of Editors: Dale M. Brown, Thomas H. Flaherty Jr.,
William Frankel, Thomas A. Lewis, Martin Mann, Philip W.
Payne, John Paul Porter, Gerry Schremp, Gerald Simons,
Nakanori Tashiro, Kit van Tulleken
Art Director: Tom Suzuki
  Assistant: Arnold C. Holeywell
Director of Administration: David L. Harrison
Director of Operations: Gennaro C. Esposito
Director of Research: Carolyn L. Sackett
  Assistant: Phyllis K. Wise
Director of Photography: Dolores Allen Littles

President: Carl G. Jaeger
Executive Vice Presidents: John Steven Maxwell,
David J. Walsh
Vice Presidents: George Artandi, Stephen L. Bair,
Peter G. Barnes, Nicholas Benton, John L. Canova,
Beatrice T. Dobie, Carol Flaumenhaft, James L. Mercer,
Herbert Sorkin, Paul R. Stewart

THE OLD WEST

Editor: George Daniels
EDITORIAL STAFF FOR "THE TEXANS"
Picture Editor: Jean Tennant
Text Editor: Valerie Moolman
Designer: Bruce Blair
Staff Writers: Carol Clingan, Lee Greene, Frank
Kappler, Kirk Landers, Robert Tschirky, Eve Wengler
Chief Researcher: June O. Goldberg
Researchers: Loretta Britten, Thomas Fitzharris,
Harriet Heck, Mary Leverty, Archer Mayor,
Mary Kay Moran, Vivian Stephens,
John Conrad Weiser
Design Assistant: Faye Eng
Copy Coordinators: Barbara H. Fuller, Gregory Weed
Picture Coordinator: Marianne Dowell

EDITORIAL OPERATIONS
Production Director: Feliciano Madrid
  Assistants: Peter A. Inchauteguiz, Karen A. Meyerson
Copy Processing: Gordon E. Buck
Quality Control Director: Robert L. Young
  Assistant: James J. Cox
  Associates: Daniel J. McSweeney, Michael G. Wight
Art Coordinator: Anne B. Landry
Copy Room Director: Susan Galloway Goldberg
  Assistants: Celia Beattie, Ricki Tarlow

THE AUTHOR: David Nevin is a Texan. The son of a veterinary officer of the United States Army, he spent much of his boyhood living on Army posts that had garrisoned Indian-fighting soldiers half a century before. He served in the United States Navy and the Merchant Marine, worked as a newspaperman in Texas and became a writer for *Life*. He has also written for *The Saturday Evening Post* and *McCall's*. He now devotes himself to writing books, which include a volume of his own called *The Texans*, *Muskie of Maine* and three other volumes of the Old West series, *The Soldiers*, *The Expressmen* and *The Mexican War*.

THE COVER: A detail from *Dawn at the Alamo* (shown in full on pages 76-77) discloses the climax of the battle that burned the date March 6, 1836, into the hearts of Texans. In the foreground Major Robert Evans is making a futile attempt to touch off the fortified mission's powder magazine before the defenders are overwhelmed by Mexican troops. Artist Henry A. McArdle, who was born in Ireland the year the battle was fought, emigrated to the United States, where he served in the Confederate Army. He became enamored of Texas history and executed this meticulously detailed painting seven decades after the fact. It hangs in the Texas Senate.

CORRESPONDENTS: Elisabeth Kraemer (Bonn); Margot Hapgood, Dorothy Bacon, Lesley Coleman (London); Susan Jonas, Lucy T. Voulgaris (New York); Maria Vincenza Aloisi, Josephine du Brusle (Paris); Ann Natanson (Rome). Valuable assistance was also provided by: Karin B. Pearce (London); Carolyn T. Chubet, Miriam Hsia, Christina Lieberman (New York); Mimi Murphy (Rome); Martha Green (San Francisco).

Other Publications:

PLANET EARTH
COLLECTOR'S LIBRARY OF THE CIVIL WAR
LIBRARY OF HEALTH
CLASSICS OF THE OLD WEST
THE EPIC OF FLIGHT
THE GOOD COOK
THE SEAFARERS
THE ENCYCLOPEDIA OF COLLECTIBLES
THE GREAT CITIES
WORLD WAR II
HOME REPAIR AND IMPROVEMENT
THE WORLD'S WILD PLACES
THE TIME-LIFE LIBRARY OF BOATING
HUMAN BEHAVIOR
THE ART OF SEWING
THE EMERGENCE OF MAN
THE AMERICAN WILDERNESS
THE TIME-LIFE ENCYCLOPEDIA OF GARDENING
LIFE LIBRARY OF PHOTOGRAPHY
THIS FABULOUS CENTURY
FOODS OF THE WORLD
TIME-LIFE LIBRARY OF AMERICA
TIME-LIFE LIBRARY OF ART
GREAT AGES OF MAN
LIFE SCIENCE LIBRARY
THE LIFE HISTORY OF THE UNITED STATES
TIME READING PROGRAM
LIFE NATURE LIBRARY
LIFE WORLD LIBRARY
FAMILY LIBRARY:
  HOW THINGS WORK IN YOUR HOME
  THE TIME-LIFE BOOK OF THE FAMILY CAR
  THE TIME-LIFE FAMILY LEGAL GUIDE
  THE TIME-LIFE BOOK OF FAMILY FINANCE

For information about any Time-Life book, please write:
Reader Information
Time-Life Books
541 North Fairbanks Court
Chicago, Illinois 60611

Library of Congress Cataloguing in Publication Data
Time-Life Books.
  The Texans/by the editors of Time-Life Books; with text by
  David Nevin.—New York: Time-Life Books, c1975.
  240 p. : ill. (some col.); 28 cm.—(The Old West)
  Bibliography: p. 236-237.
  Includes index.
  1. Texas—History—To 1846. 2. Texas—History—Revolution,
  1835-1836. 3. Texas—History—Republic, 1836-1846.
  4. Texas—History—1846-1865.
  I. Nevin, David, 1927-   II. Title.
  III. Series: The Old West (Alexandria, Va.)
F389.T55 1975   976.4   75-15450
ISBN 0-8094-1502-X
ISBN 0-8094-1501-1 lib. bdg.
ISBN 0-8094-1500-3 retail ed.

*This volume is one of a series that
chronicles the history of the American West
from the early 16th Century to the end of
the 19th Century.*

CONTENTS

1 | A special breed in a bountiful land

The lure of a new life in fabulous Texas, with land and riches thrown in, proved irresistible to thousands of Americans in the decades after 1822, the year when pioneer land developer Stephen Austin began the fulfillment of his grandiose promise "to redeem Texas from its wilderness state by . . . spreading over it North American population, enterprise and intelligence."

It was Austin's dream to settle Mexican Texas with wholesome, strait-laced colonies where "no drunkard, no gambler, no profane swearer, no idler" would be tolerated. But if Austin had strict ideas about who could or could not be a Texan, there were no such proscriptions once other colonizers arrived in Texas and discovered what an incredibly bountiful land it was.

Americans came in droves—from everywhere, and for every reason imaginable. There were hardscrabble farmers from Kentucky, cotton growers from Georgia, soldier-adventurers from Tennessee, entrepreneurs and artisans from New York. Some came seeking fortunes in land or cattle; others had no plan, but merely sought refuge from unpaid bills or unhappy marriages. A few of them were criminals. Many were strapping figures, well suited to the frontier. And many were sickly—with tuberculosis and other maladies—searching for health in the clean air.

In 1836 alone, 5,000 immigrants swarmed into Texas from Louisiana via a single Sabine River ferry crossing to help boost the infant republic's population to 35,000. By 1847, shortly after Texas was annexed to the United States, the number was 140,000. And to the stream of Americans were added thousands of Europeans.

The faces of the men and women on these pages represent a sampling of that mix. Some played historic roles; others left behind little more than their portraits. But as prototypical Texans, all shared the fiercely independent spirit that caused them to reject all established orders in favor of molding an exciting land of their own. They formed a loosely knit band worthy of the sobriquet of "maverick"—a term passed into the language by one of their number: lifelong nonconformist Sam Maverick.

Thomas McKinney's firm lent $150,000 to the Texas rebels.

Adolphus Sterne was Nacogdoches' German-born mayor in 1833.

James Brown, a former New York brick mason, arrived in Galveston around 1842 and built a cathedral, a jailhouse and a show-place home—all of brick, naturally.

Mary Adams Maverick, Sam's wife, is circled by five of her 10 children in 1855. Her 36 grandchildren included Congressman Maury Maverick, New Deal crusader of the 1930s.

Henry Kinney, a founder of Corpus Christi, tried unsuccessfully in 1854 to carve a 30-million-acre empire in Nicaragua.

Gail Borden *(with son John)* helped establish Texas' first successful paper in 1835 and surveyed the site of Houston before striking it rich with a condensed-milk process.

Robert Hancock Hunter, son of a pioneer doctor, witnessed the capture of the Mexican general Santa Anna by Texas militiamen after the Battle of San Jacinto in 1836.

Henry Hedgecoxe, British-born agent of a Texas land firm, settled near Austin after the Hedgecoxe War of 1852, a land-rights spat that saw settlers chase him from his office.

Ben McCulloch followed his friend Davy Crockett to Texas in 1836 and remained there to serve as a Texas Ranger and federal marshal.

David Burnet, a onetime New Jersey accountant, turned up in Texas as a land speculator, led the separatist movement and in 1836 became the first president of Texas.

Celima DeBlanc, a member of the aristocratic Creole community that came to Liberty in 1845, married William Duncan and settled down to a life of servants and soirees.

11

Alphonso Steele, a Kentuckian who went to fight for Texas at 18, was wounded at San Jacinto and lived to tell about it until he died at 94 — the last survivor.

Benjamin Long, elected as one of the first mayors of Dallas in 1868, originally emigrated from Switzerland with his family to a 300-member French colony, La Réunion.

Edward Burleson, A North Carolinian, went to Texas in 1830, took part in the siege of San Antonio and led a regiment at San Jacinto. He was later vice president of Texas.

Memucan Hunt, Texas' envoy to Washington, D.C. in 1837, urged annexation of his nation. Later he promoted a railroad from Galveston Bay to the Red River.

13

Beginning anew beyond the River Sabine

An aura of legend, tinctured with improbability, hangs over the Texans. Of all the Americans who went west in the 19th Century, none held a stronger claim to singularity than the pioneers who boldly planted their roots in the soil of Texas. They were the first Americans ever to settle the immense land west of Missouri. They were the only Americans ever to settle in force in a land ruled by a large and unfriendly power. And they created the only American state ever to join the union as a prosperous and populous nation, after which they proceeded to make it infinitely more prosperous and populous. All this the Texans accomplished with spectacular flourish, in barely four decades, under circumstances that would certainly have defeated a less daring and ambitious people.

Theirs was an unlikely sweep of history, replete with Texas-sized phenomena: frontiering on a colossal scale, fantastic business deals, incredible battles, larger-than-life heroes. And to make it all the more astounding, most of it took place when the West was a virgin half-continent, scarcely known in the East. The Texans established a flourishing society in the 1820s, when trappers pushing into the Rockies thought that pelts would last forever. The Texans won a bitter war of independence in 1836, two years before the United States began to make a systematic survey of the Western wilderness. A decade later, they took Texas into the Union as a state, just four years after the first wagon train made it to Oregon. In 1850, when there were only about a dozen white men in Colorado, the census in Texas showed a population of 212,592. By 1860, the state was home to more than 600,000 boisterous, venturesome, maverick Texans.

Yet of all the extraordinary things about the Texans and the making of Texas, none was more remarkable than the circumstances under which their story began.

In 1820, Texas was merely a terrible temptation for Americans. Glowing reports from reputable travelers — and disreputable renegades — painted an exciting picture of Texas' unexploited potential: the rich soil of the central plains and the dense forests of eastern Texas, natural harbors on the Gulf of Mexico and navigable rivers leading into the interior, a salubrious climate and tremendous wild herds of horses and longhorned cattle. But Texas was a wilderness property of the King of Spain, and the Spanish, who suspected the United States of aggressive intentions, had ruled it off limits for all Americans. For the Spanish conquerors, Texas had been a broad highway leading into the heart of North America. For land-hungry Americans it was now a giant stumbling block to continental ambitions.

The scheme that would break this frustrating impasse was concocted in the summer of 1820 by a bankrupt 59-year-old Missourian named Moses Austin. It seemed mad, an idea that flew straight in the face of reality. Moses planned to apply to the Spanish rulers for a large Texas land grant — and then dispense acreage to American pioneers at a handsome profit. He proposed his scheme to his son Stephen, a 26-year-old bachelor who shared his bankruptcy but not his desperation. Stephen thought so little of its chances for success that he resisted it politely for almost a year and finally joined it against his better judgment. In fact, Stephen Austin would never have become the "Father of Texas" had he not been a fond and dutiful son.

The stage was set for their Texas venture by epochal developments on two continents. The old colonial nations, weakened in Europe by wars and in-

---

Missourian Stephen F. Austin was only 27 when he embarked on the dream of settling Americans in Texas. But he was well suited to lead, having already served as a bank director, militia officer and judge.

ternal upheavals, were on the retreat in North America at the same time that the United States, young and vigorous, was expanding willy-nilly. In the first two decades of the 19th Century, the United States more than doubled its land area, acquiring some 800,000 square miles in the Louisiana Purchase of 1803 and 58,560 square miles more in the form of Florida. Significantly, both of those great regions had once been Spanish property.

In 1800, Spain, no longer able to sustain its government in Louisiana Territory, had ceded the region to France, which in turn had sold it to the United States in 1803. The ink on the purchase contract had barely dried when a Spanish statesman noted the flood of immigrants into the territory: "The Americans are already spreading out like oil on a cloth."

The United States acquired Florida from Spain by a more direct route. In the second decade of the 19th Century, Indians from Florida staged damaging raids on American settlements across the border. Vengeance was swift, as Americans led by Andrew Jackson mounted an unauthorized invasion of Florida to punish the marauders. So overwhelming was the American presence, and so loose the Spanish hold on the area, that Spain decided to cede the territory to the United States for five million dollars under the Adams-Onís Treaty of 1819. Still, the affair left a sour taste in Spanish mouths. The United States could not be accused of deliberate aggression: its border citizens were merely protecting themselves. But the distinction was not appreciated by the Spaniards.

That was the crux of Spain's problem in the case of Texas: whenever Americans appeared in numbers, the United States government, for whatever reason, was never far behind. Between 1800 and 1820, close to two million Americans had streamed westward across the Appalachian Mountains, and they were fast closing in on the borders of Texas—the Sabine River in the east and the Red River in the north. By contrast Spain, in 300 years of colonial endeavor, had managed to settle Texas with only a token population—about 3,500 in 1820. Spain had only a few people to spare from the beleaguered homeland, and its colonial authorities in Mexico could persuade very few Mexicans to occupy and farm their dangerous northern province —which was the only real way to hold it. Weakness

made the Spanish fearful, defensive and xenophobic.

As part of the 1819 treaty, the United States had disavowed any claim to Texas and pledged to hold the Texas border inviolate. But the Spanish in Texas had already had some experience with Americans, all of it cautionary. As early as the 1790s, a ruthless young rustler named Philip Nolan was practically commuting across the border on commercial horse-stealing expeditions; Spanish soldiers finally caught up with his band, shot him dead and sent his ears as trophies to the Texas Governor. But other freebooters swept into Texas in increasing numbers, and though they were beaten off, their forays undid whatever progress the Spanish had made. The East Texas community of Nacogdoches—one of only three towns in Texas —boasted more than 1,000 inhabitants in 1811, but was ravaged by repeated raids and abandoned in 1820.

Americans with less violent designs were just as troublesome in a subtler way. No treaty was strong enough to keep out the ubiquitous American frontiersmen. Audacious, stubborn, self-reliant, they simply squatted in Spanish territory and turned obnoxious when "foreign" officials tried to eject them. These trespassers—indeed all Americans—were earnestly urged by President James Madison to stay out of Texas. But the Spanish knew they would not comply, and assumed that the United States government would, as usual, follow close on their heels.

This troubled background was taken carefully into account by Moses Austin when he planned his Texas real-estate venture. He knew that Spanish manpower could not hold Texas for long against the land-hungry American trespassers, and he believed that as an *empresario*—the proprietor and promoter of a colony—he would help the Spanish authorities do just that. In his petition for the land grant he planned to argue that *his* Americans would be different. In the first place, they would no longer be Americans, but Spaniards who had sworn allegiance to the King of Spain. They would all be responsible, law-abiding men. And with legally titled farms of their own to protect, they could be counted on to defend Texas against illegal Americans and hostile Indians as well.

Moreover, Moses considered his own experience with the Spanish a convincing illustration of how successfully he could operate under Spanish rule. A Con-

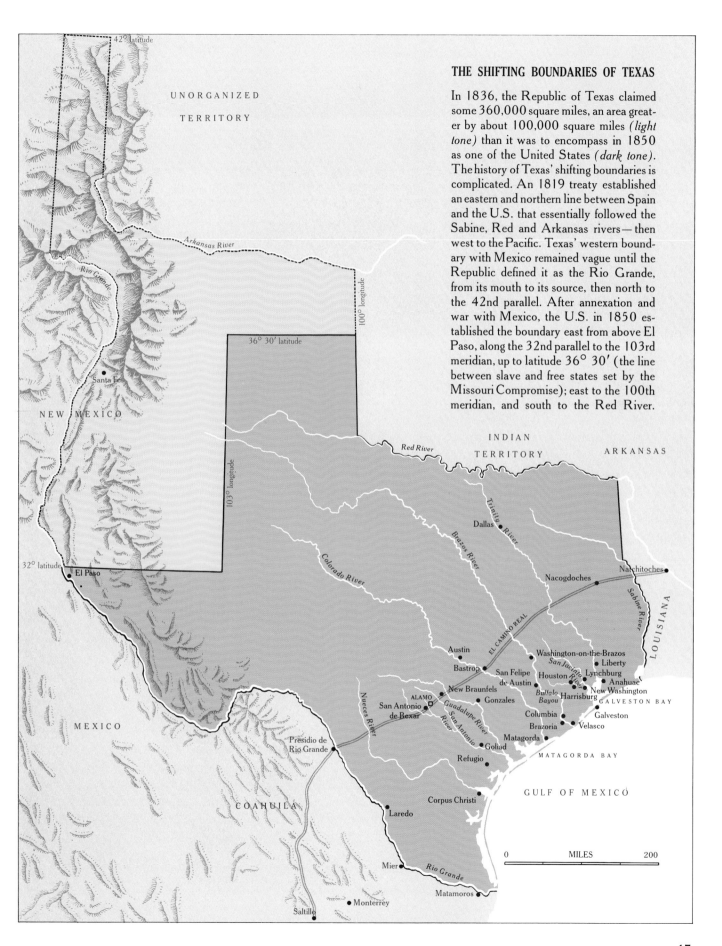

THE SHIFTING BOUNDARIES OF TEXAS

In 1836, the Republic of Texas claimed some 360,000 square miles, an area greater by about 100,000 square miles *(light tone)* than it was to encompass in 1850 as one of the United States *(dark tone)*. The history of Texas' shifting boundaries is complicated. An 1819 treaty established an eastern and northern line between Spain and the U.S. that essentially followed the Sabine, Red and Arkansas rivers — then west to the Pacific. Texas' western boundary with Mexico remained vague until the Republic defined it as the Rio Grande, from its mouth to its source, then north to the 42nd parallel. After annexation and war with Mexico, the U.S. in 1850 established the boundary east from above El Paso, along the 32nd parallel to the 103rd meridian, up to latitude 36° 30′ (the line between slave and free states set by the Missouri Compromise); east to the 100th meridian, and south to the Red River.

UNORGANIZED TERRITORY

42° latitude

Arkansas River

Rio Grande

100° longitude

36° 30′ latitude

103° longitude

Santa Fe

NEW MEXICO

32° latitude

El Paso

MEXICO

COAHUILA

Presidio de Rio Grande

Laredo

Mier

Matamoros

Monterrey

Saltillo

Rio Grande

Nueces River

Colorado River

Corpus Christi

Refugio

Goliad

Matagorda

Brazoria

Columbia

Velasco

San Antonio River

Guadalupe River

San Antonio de Bexar

ALAMO

New Braunfels

Gonzales

Bastrop

Austin

San Felipe de Austin

EL CAMINO REAL

Washington-on-the-Brazos

San Jacinto

Houston

Buffalo Bayou

Harrisburg

Liberty

Lynchburg

Anahuac

New Washington

GALVESTON BAY

Galveston

Brazos River

Trinity River

Dallas

Red River

INDIAN TERRITORY

ARKANSAS

Nacogdoches

Natchitoches

Sabine River

LOUISIANA

MATAGORDA BAY

GULF OF MEXICO

0   MILES   200

Four colonists thread their way through an eastern Texas canebrake, whose arching reeds blot out the sun. The awesome vegetation was proof of the soil's fertility: starting as green shoots each spring, the reeds would tower 25 feet before toppling and decaying, to start the cycle over again.

necticut native, he had settled his family in Missouri in 1798, while that raw frontier was still part of Spanish Louisiana. Being an eminently practical man, intent on doing business, he cleared his way by pledging his loyalty to the Spanish king. It worked out well. Spanish officials returned his cordial cooperation, and he began to prosper under their aegis. Moses was less than overjoyed when the Louisiana Purchase of 1803 restored his American citizenship. With the arrival of the United States government came such encumbrances as taxes, militia duty and stiffer land laws.

It is not known exactly when Moses Austin first conceived of his plan to colonize Texas. As early as 1813 he thought of applying for a license to trade in Texas, but nothing came of it, presumably because his Missouri business was doing so well at the time. Actually, his financial interests—a lead mine, real estate, eventually a bank in St. Louis—made him rich by frontier standards. And in all of it, Moses was helped greatly by Stephen, the elder of his two sons, who took over as his general factotum in 1817, and whose managerial talents and efficiency complemented his own freewheeling ways. At that point, Moses lacked a strong motive for the Texas land scheme.

That motive was supplied in 1819, when a financial panic wiped out the Austin business. From then on, Moses was deep in debt and never more than a step ahead of his creditors. He dashed frantically about the frontier in vain efforts to relieve his financial plight.

For the same reason, and with the same results, Stephen tried various ventures in Arkansas Territory, then drifted to New Orleans to seek gainful employment. But times were hard and opportunities scarce. In spite of his college education (Transylvania University in Kentucky), his business background and his political experience (six years in the Missouri House of Representatives), Stephen could find nothing better than a low-paid job helping the editor of a Louisiana newspaper. Stephen was so disheartened that he began a new career in law. But his studies meant—as he worriedly wrote home—that "I shall earn nothing to help you with for at least 18 months."

Through the summer of 1820, the Texas idea slowly took shape in Moses' mind, helped along by recent changes on the frontier. Wild land speculation had been a major cause of the panic of 1819, and to prevent a re-

The Napoleonic exiles of Champ d'Asile

Although most early Texas settlers were Americans, land-hungry immigrants from other nations also sought to build a better life for themselves from the vast opportunities there. Among them was a group of Frenchmen who, in March 1818, chose a site on the Trinity River, about 30 miles north of Galveston. The settlers, mainly supporters of Napoleon who had fled to the United States after the Emperor's downfall, called their Texas home Champ d'Asile, or Field of Asylum. There, according to General Charles Lallemand, their leader, they intended to transform into rich farmland a vast territory until then "uninhabited by civilized mankind" and peopled by "Indian tribes, who, caring for nothing but the chase, leave the broad acres uncultivated....We ask peace and friendship from all those who surround us and we shall be grateful for the slightest token of their goodwill."

But while Lallemand's proclamation avowed that Champ d'Asile was to be "purely agricultural and commercial in principal," its very presence was alarming to the governments of the United States and Spain, both of which had laid claim to Texas. It was rumored that the French settlers were well armed and spent as much time at military drills as in tilling the soil. The rumor gained credence from a known plot of French refugees to invade Mexico, then on the verge of revolt against Spanish rule, and to establish a Mexican empire with Napoleon's brother, Joseph, on the throne.

In June 1818, John Quincy Adams, Secretary of State during President Monroe's administration, sent his agent George Graham to Texas with instructions to "ascertain the precise and real object" of the suspect French colony. When Graham finally found the Champ d'Asile settlers they were not on the Trinity River at all but rather on Galveston Island, and they were neither prosperous farmers nor aggressive militarists. Instead he was greeted by the pitiful survivors of a doomed venture—a sickly collection of some 115 men and women, living a hand-to-mouth existence among Jean Lafitte's pirates.

The colonists had lasted only five months at their original river location, during which span they built huts and fortifications but planted few crops. Then suddenly, on hearing that a Spanish force was on its way from Mexico to drive them out, they had abandoned Champ d'Asile.

The abrupt flight from their Field of Asylum seems to have been merely one disaster among many. In summing up their reverses, one colonist wrote: "About half of our companions had perished either on [Galveston] island or in Texas, from disease, overwork, hunger, misery, duels, and assassinations; two others were taken and eaten by the hordes of savages who sometimes land at Galveston."

Meanwhile, in France, the press had been carrying glowing, but entirely fanciful accounts of a flourishing colony on the Trinity. Even when the sad truth was out, some writers and artists refused to believe it, and for years continued to picture Champ d'Asile, as at right, as a glorious episode in the early history of Texas.

Splendidly caparisoned, Napoleonic officers carve the

Champ d'Asile colony from the Texas wilderness in this 1830 French color engraving, made 12 years after the ill-fated settlement actually was abandoned.

the Louisiana town of Natchitoches, the jumping-off point for the Texas border.

Carrying his old Spanish passport as evidence of his good faith and accompanied by a slave and two prospective settlers, Moses set out in late November for San Antonio de Bexar, the provincial capital of Texas. Their route, a meager traders' trail with the pretentious name *El Camino Real* (Royal Road), began on the far side of the Sabine River and took them 400 miles to San Antonio in the heart of Texas. As Austin rode along in warm December weather, he saw a country fairly begging for settlers. He forded many streams running clean over sandy bottoms. Along their banks he found giant pecan trees that showered the ground with nuts of surprising sweetness. The tall prairie grass would support stock, and the rich brown earth beneath would produce good crops. There was game everywhere, especially deer. Austin noted that the air was dry, which meant this would be healthy country.

On December 23, the party topped the hills overlooking San Antonio and rode wearily downslope toward the century-old town. They passed an abandoned mission, formerly known as San Antonio de Valero and soon to be called the Alamo. Entering the Military Plaza at the center of town, they picked their way past idle groups of townspeople, strolling musicians, Franciscan friars in brown robes and sandals.

Civilized life in Spanish Texas — what there was of it — was obviously easy but not nearly so bountiful as the countryside suggested. For the most part, the citizens were shabbily dressed, and their houses, built in a maze of crooked alleys, were made of rough logs filled in with mud. For all its 800 inhabitants San Antonio was just an overaged frontier town. It bespoke lassitude, failed efforts and fading dreams.

Moses caused consternation among the Spanish functionaries when he appeared without invitation at the residence of Texas Governor Antonio de Martinez. Discovering that Moses was an American, the Governor refused even to examine his papers, and ordered him to leave Texas with all possible speed.

Moses stumbled out into the plaza, his grand scheme apparently in ruins. But then blind chance offered a reprieve: he encountered an old friend, the Baron de Bastrop, whom he had known as a large landowner in Louisiana Territory during the last days of Spanish

currence the government tightened its regulations for making the public domain available to settlers. No longer did the claimant have four years to pay for his land; full payment had to be made upon taking title. And the price—$1.25 an acre—was no bargain in cash-poor times. If Moses could offer Texas land at a lower price or on easier terms, he was sure he would find American customers eager to swear allegiance to Spain.

By October 1820, Moses had definitely decided, in spite of Stephen's cautionings, to risk an exploratory trip to Texas. If Moses had hoped that Stephen would offer to go along, he was sadly disappointed. Moses completed his preparations in Missouri, then went to

To the settlers in Austins settlement.

FELLOW CITIZENS,

After an absence of sixteen months I have the pleasure of returning once more to the settlement which it has been the labor of the last three years of my life to establish in the unsettled deserts of this province. Nothing but the interest of the settlers, and the general welfare of the settlement could have induced me to make the sacrifices of time, of fatigue and money, which this enterprize has cost me; but feeling in honor bound never to abandon those who had embarked with me, and animated with the hope of rendering an important service to the great Mexican nation, and particularly to this Province, by the formation of a flourishing colony within its limits, I have persevered through all the difficulties created by the political convulsions of the last year, and now have the satisfaction of announcing that every necessary power relative to the formation of the colony is granted to me by the Supreme Executive power and Sovereign Congress of Mexico; and that I shall immediately commence in conjunction with the Baron de Bastrop, the governmental Commissioner appointed for this purpose, to designate the land for the settlers, and deliver complete titles therefor.

It will be observed, by all who wish to be received into this colony, that the conditions indicated by me in the first commencement of the settlement must be complied with, and particularly that the most unquestionable testimony of good character, and industrious and moral habits will be required. No person can be permitted to remain in the settlement longer than may be absolutely necessary to prepare to prepare for a removal who does not exhibit such testimony. This regulation is in conformity with the orders of the Superior Government, and will be enforced with the utmost rigour.

Being charged by the Superior Government with the administration of justice, the punishment of crimes, and the preservation of good order and tranquility within the settlement, it will be my study to devote that attention to those subjects which their transcendant importance requires, and I confidently hope that with the aid of the settlers we shall be able to present an example of industry and good morals equally creditable to ourselves and gratifying to the government of our adoption.

The Alcaldes appointed on the Colorado and Brazos in the month of November last will continue to exercise their functions until the year for which they were elected expires, at which time a new election for those officers will be ordered. The administration of justice by the Alcaldes will be subject to my inspection; and appeals from their decisions will be decided by me. Fixed regulations will be established on this subject, and made known to the settlers as soon as time will permit.

I beg every individual in the establishment to be impressed with the important truth that his future prosperity and happiness depends on the correctness of his own conduct. Honest and industrious men may live together all their lives without a law-suit or difference with each other. I have known examples of this kind in the United States: so it must be with us—nothing is more easy: all that is necessary is for every one to attend industriously to his own business, and in all cases follow the great and sacred christian rule, *to do unto others as you wish them to do unto you.* As regards the suppression of vice and immorality, and the punishment of crime, much depends on yourselves. The wisest laws and the most efficient administration of justice, in criminal cases, avails but little, unless seconded by the good examples, patriotism and virtues of the people. It will therefore be expected that every man in the settlement will at all times be willing to aid the civil authority whenever called on to pursue, apprehend or punish criminals, and also, that the most prompt information will be given to the nearest civil officer, of any murder, robbery, breach of the peace, or other violation of the laws.

Being also charged with the Commission of Lt. Colonel Commandant of the Militia within the settlement, I shall, as soon as possible, organize a battalion of militia, in which every man capable of bearing arms must be enrolled and hold himself in readiness to march at a moment's warning, whenever called on to repel the attacks of hostile indians or other enemies of the Mexican nation.

I am limited to the number of 300 families for the settlement on the Colorado and Brazos. The government have ordered that all over that number who are introduced by me, must settle in the interior of the province, near the ancient establishments.

As soon as the necessary information can be procured, a town will be established as the capital of the settlement, and a port of entry will be designated on the coast for the introduction of all articles required for the use of the settlers All town scites are reserved, and no person will be permitted to locate them.

Fellow Citizens, let me again repeat that your happiness rests with yourselves; the Mexican Government have been bountiful in the favors and privileges which she has granted to the settlement, in return for which all she asks is that you will be firm supporters and defenders of the Independence and Liberty of the Mexican Nation; that you should industriously cultivate the soil that is granted you, that you should strictly obey the laws and constituted authorities, and in fact, that you should be good citizens and virtuous men.

STEPHEN F. AUSTIN

Province of Texas, July, 1823.

power there. Unbeknownst to Moses, the baron's title was his own idea; he had actually been a town tax collector in Holland, until he had absconded with a year's revenues. Bastrop's booty had long since been exhausted in the New World, but his polished manners had gained him admittance into government circles, an effete little world where he lived by his wits.

Moses blurted out his woes to the baron, who was quick to see that Austin's plan might indeed profit the Spanish—and himself as well. Volunteering to intercede, Bastrop took Moses' papers and cornered his friend the Governor. After outlining Moses' proposal, Bastrop produced the American's Spanish passport, and it carried the day. Martinez agreed to reconsider.

In his formal presentation a few days later, Moses explained that he represented 300 American families, all sympathetic to Spain, who wanted to settle permanently in Texas and cultivate cotton, sugar and corn. Martinez was impressed. He informed Moses that he would forward his petition, and recommend its approval, to the commandant general in charge of Texas.

Moses departed San Antonio at the end of December, and arrived back in Potosi, Missouri, on January 15, 1821. Working feverishly to settle his affairs, he dashed off progress reports to Stephen in New Orleans, and his increasing enthusiasm gradually wore down his son's resistance to the venture. Finally, around the middle of May, Moses got word from Texas: the commandant general had approved his petition; he would be granted 200,000 acres of his choice. Jubilantly Moses wrote Stephen: "I now can go forward with confidence, and hope and pray you will Discharge your Doubts as to the Enterprise. Raise your spirits. Times are changing. A new chance presents itself."

At last Stephen bowed to his father's greater drive and more urgent need. He made no strong commitment to the venture. But he agreed to accompany Moses on his next trip to select the site for the colony. Stephen was waiting for Moses in Natchitoches when he was greeted instead by word of his father's death.

A letter from his mother explained the mournful circumstances. Moses, exhausted by his trip back from Texas and his frenzied preparations to return, had caught pneumonia and weakened steadily. Just before he died on June 10, Moses made certain that his plans would not perish with him. "He called me to his bed-side," Mrs. Austin wrote, "and with much distress and difficulty of speech he begged me to tell you to take his place, and if god in his wisdom thought best to disappoint him in the accomplishment of his plans formed for the benefit of the family, he prayed him to extend his goodness to you and to enable you to go on with the business in the same way he would have done."

Stephen, ever the loyal son, could not deny his father's deathbed request and only legacy. For better or worse, he was locked into Moses' Texas venture.

In fact, the change in command was much for the better. Stephen was not the dynamic, decisive leader his father would have been, and he was too frail for the hard work of frontiering. But the compensating qualities that Stephen did have—patience, tact, propriety and quiet determination—would succeed where Moses' aggressiveness might well have failed.

Stephen Austin closed the door on the past when, on July 15, 1821, he entered Texas with a few Americans and headed for San Antonio. As Austin later recalled, "I bid an everlasting farewell to my native country, and adopted this, and in so doing I determined to fulfill rigidly all the duties and obligations of a Mexican citizen." In this resolve he never weakened.

On reaching San Antonio, Austin was cordially received by Governor Martinez, who accepted him as heir to his father's grant. He met and was befriended by the self-styled Baron de Bastrop. After 10 days, Austin had worked out a plan for distributing land in his colony; it called for allotting 640 acres to each man, with additional acreage for his wife and children. Martinez approved the plan and forwarded it to his superior, reporting that Austin "gave the impression of being a man of high honor, of scrupulous regard for formality, and of desiring to learn how to discharge faithfully the duties proposed by his late father."

With Martinez' permission, Austin and his pioneers headed southeast to select the land for his colony. He paused at La Bahia, the only real town in Texas besides San Antonio, and wrote announcements of his colony, which eastbound travelers took to Louisiana. Then his party struck out to explore the lower reaches of the Colorado and Brazos rivers.

Austin found it "the most favored region I had ever seen," and decided to request the area for his colony.

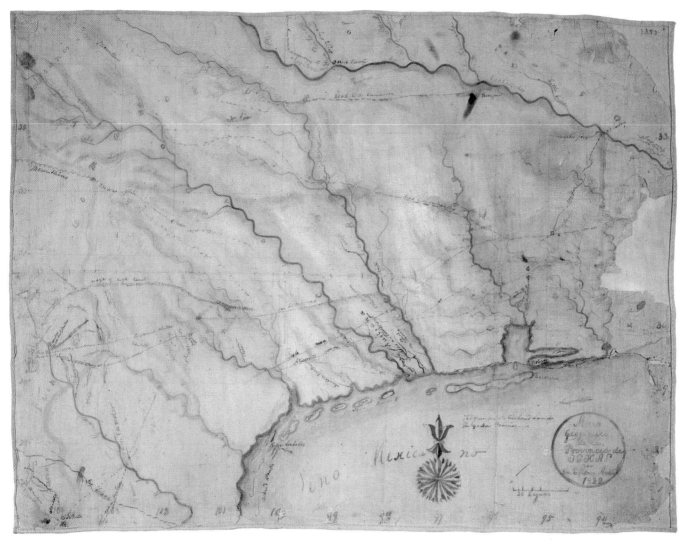

On September 20, while exploring along the Brazos River, Austin found what he described in his journal as "a most beautiful situation for a town or settlement. The country back of this place for about 15 miles is as good in every respect as a man could wish for, land all first rate, plenty of timber, fine water." On that bluff, a safe 15 miles from the malarial swamps of the Gulf Coast and 175 miles from San Antonio, Austin would build his town, San Felipe de Austin.

But first he had to return to Louisiana to prepare to move permanently onto his grant. From Natchitoches in October 1821 he sent Governor Martinez an exact description of the boundaries he desired for his colony; actually, Austin was asking for an immense grant estimated at 18,000 square miles—some 11 million acres. He also found and answered nearly a hundred letters from would-be settlers who had read or heard of his announcement. Austin guessed that he could recruit 1,500 families just as easily as the 300 required to fulfill his agreement as *empresario*. Because several settlers wanted to precede him to the grant, Austin sent ahead Josiah Bell, a former business associate in Arkansas Territory, to act as his deputy.

In November, Austin traveled to New Orleans on errands that would cost him dearly—in worry as well as money. To raise operating capital, he signed away a half interest in his colony to a lawyer friend, Joseph Hawkins, for the sum of $4,000. Austin then bought a small sloop named *Lively,* and filled the hold with tools and provisions for his settlers. He instructed the crewmen to put in at the mouth of the Colorado River and to wait for him to come overland and guide them to the colony. But, as Austin later learned, *Lively* mistakenly landed at the Brazos River, and when no one showed up, the ship returned to New Orleans. On its second voyage, *Lively* ran aground on Galveston Island—a total loss along with her cargo.

Austin started overland to his grant in the middle of December and arrived in January 1822. Several settlers were already on hand. Because farmers had to move between crops, a man usually took in his harvest in his old home; hurried ahead to clear land and plant in Texas; then built a cabin to prepare for his family's arrival. Most of Austin's settlers came from nearby Southern states and frontier territories, but their journeys were long nonetheless, and timing was crucial.

The first settler to reach the grant was Andrew Robinson, who arrived in late November, 1821, and camped on the west bank of the Brazos River. Robinson was soon joined by three brothers and their families—Abner, Joseph and Robert Kuykendall from Arkansas. In December, after several others had arrived, Joseph Kuykendall and a Daniel Gilleland moved farther west and started the first settlement on the Colorado River. Though Austin had sent Josiah Bell ahead in October, the agent had tarried and did not turn up until early January. By then, men were coming in steadily increasing numbers.

Through January and February, Austin dashed about the wilderness, trying to put his colony on a sound footing. He took a party to the mouth of the Colorado and searched in vain for the crew of *Lively.* Forced to make do without *Lively*'s provisions and equipment, the settlers struggled to survive those first few months. Flour for bread ran out by the end of January, and the settlers did not dare make any from the corn they had brought for planting. Fortunately, a high-protein diet was there for the taking. According to Abner Kuykendall's son Gibson, "Deer and turkies were abundant. The deer were lean but the turkies were fine and fat and constituted for several months the most valuable part of our subsistence."

It was sometimes easier to shoot game than to get it home for the table. Jesse Burnham, who came from Tennessee with his family, had killed a deer and was butchering it "when an Indian came up and wanted to take

Early settlers pole their rafts down the Pedernales River in the Texas "Hill Country" to the north of San Antonio. Although the rolling terrain was well watered, it was much too rocky for extensive farming. Eventually, however, it turned out to be first-rate ranch land for herds of sheep and cattle.

Sketched in southeast Texas by a British traveler, an early farmstead stands among stumps of the trees used in constructing it. Writing above the drawing identifies most of the smaller cabins as slave quarters.

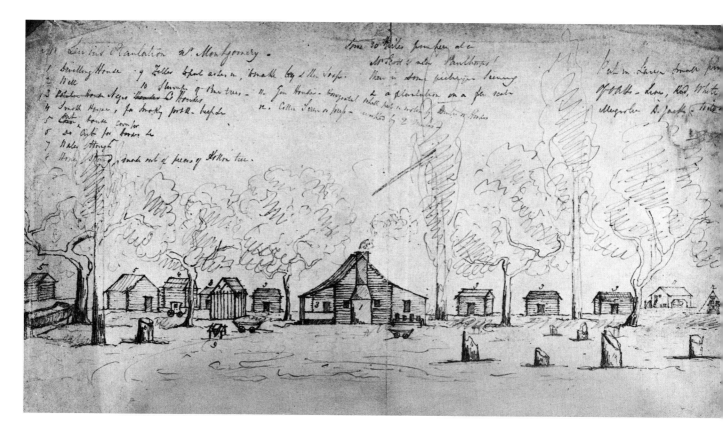

it from me. I would not let him have it, but got it on my back and started for camp. I walked along as fast as I could, he pulling at the deer and making signs that he wanted it on his back. Oh, but I was mad! When I got to camp it was full of Indians and every one had been dividing meat with them. I told them that I would not give them a piece of meat to save my life, and if that Indian came about me I'd kill him."

The Indians were Karankawas, one of the many small tribes living in southern Texas. They naturally resented the settlers' intrusion on their hunting grounds, and small bands soon began thieving raids. In the deadly little skirmishes neither side gave quarter, and in the first year a number of settlers were killed.

The colonists were on their own. How true that was came clear in the case of Jesse Burnham's neighbor, a certain Mr. Parker. "His leg was terribly diseased," wrote Burnham, "and he begged us to cut it off two months before we consented. Tom Williams, Kuykendall, Bostick and I undertook the job with a dull saw and a shoe knife, the only tools we had. I was to have the management of it, and hold the flesh back, Tom

Williams was to do the cutting of the flesh, Bostick to saw the bone, and Kuykendall to do the sewing. I took his suspenders off and bandaged the leg just above where we wanted to cut. I put a hair rope over the bandage, put a stick in it, and twisted it; then I was ready to begin operations. When Mr. Kuykendall began to sew it he trembled, so I took the needle and finished it. Parker rested easy for several days; but the eleventh day he died."

To meet the needs of his settlers, Austin had only one resource available—land—and he used it liberally in a constructive program. For example he offered William Kincheloe, a settler from Louisiana, an extra 640 acres and a town lot in exchange for building a mill on the Colorado River. And he allotted no less than 44,000 acres to Jared Groce, a man who became practically a public utility to the colony. Groce, a wealthy 39-year-old planter from Alabama, arrived in January 1822, with an enormous caravan of 50 covered wagons and 100 slaves. To maintain his retinue and wrest a huge plantation from the wilderness, Groce imported great quantities of supplies, which he offered to share with other settlers. Groce was the first of Texas' big operators and the founder of an important dynasty.

On March 3, Austin gave up his search for *Lively* and concentrated on the implementation of his colonization plan. He had been dispensing land in an informal manner. Besides the eight complete families who had already arrived, 100 men on the Colorado and 50 more on the Brazos were building cabins to prepare for their women and children—all on acreage to which they had no clear legal title. To settle the matter and report on his progress to Martinez, Austin anxiously set out for San Antonio.

Disastrous news awaited him. The Governor informed him that the Mexicans had staged a revolution in Mexico City and ousted their long-time Spanish masters. As a result, Austin's grant had been wiped out, and he would have to reapply to the new revolutionary government in Mexico City. In dismay, Austin sent word to Josiah Bell to carry on for him at the colony, then hurried off on a 1,200-mile journey to the south. The road was infested with bandits, and in the hopes of decoying them Austin traveled disguised as a beggar. The masquerade worked, but nothing in Mexico City did.

"I arrived in the City of Mexico in April," Austin wrote his colonists, "without acquaintances, without friends, Ignorant of the Language, of the Laws, the forms, the dispositions and feelings of the Government, with barely the means of paying my expenses for a few months. Added to all this I found the City in an unsettled state, the whole people and country still agitated by the revolutionary convulsion, public opinion vacillating—Party spirit raging."

Austin gradually learned the nature of Mexico's political turmoil. After the Spanish were ejected, two main political parties contended for power: the liberal Federalists, who wanted to invest the states (formerly called provinces) with a good deal of autonomy; and the conservative Centralists, who demanded a strong central regime and who, in May 1822, proclaimed General Agustin Iturbide Emperor of Mexico. To make matters truly confusing, both parties contained several rival factions, and opportunists would change factions—and even parties—for momentary gain. Austin had no political bias; he sought out everyone—from wealthy Centralists to Federalist clerks—who might

help him. But week after week, month after month, his best efforts came to nought.

Austin's first and most pressing need was a general colonization law which would permit Americans to settle in Texas. He petitioned the provisional Congress for such a law, citing his father's old argument that responsible Americans would defend Texas for Mexico. The Federalists, who were eager to develop the area, favored his view, and the Centralists opposed it with the old charge that Americans formed the vanguard for United States conquest. While the debate dragged on, Austin wrote worried letters to his settlers in Texas. He hoped that they were "in peace and happiness, with *Bread* in abundance and contentment in every breast." He urged them "not to be discouraged. A short time will change the scene and we shall enjoy many a merry dance and wedding frolic together."

In October, Emperor Iturbide dissolved the Congress and created a military junta to do its work. Finally, in January 1823, Iturbide heeded Austin's petition and signed a colonization law. For a moment, Austin thought that he had won his battle. But then power slipped from Iturbide's grasp, and his colonization law was canceled by a new Congress. Doggedly, Austin began petitioning the Congress all over again.

At this juncture, Austin had been in Mexico City for 11 months, struggling to build a foundation of trust among the Mexicans. His well-bred civility, his lively interest in local problems and, perhaps most important, the pains he took to learn fluent Spanish, flattered the sensitive Mexicans, who bitterly resented the contempt that most Americans showed for them and their culture. Important politicians and influential aristocrats welcomed him socially, admired his persistent dedication to legal process, listened with fascination to his shrewd but modest suggestions for solving their political dilemma. Moreover his advice was eagerly sought by other would-be *empresarios,* who had come to appeal for land grants of their own. Austin was—and he would remain for nearly a decade—the only man with the knowledge and diplomatic skills to guide the American Texans through the maze of Mexican politics.

At last, on April 11, 1823, Austin triumphed, and it was a victory to savor. The Mexican Congress approved his colony under terms more favorable than he had requested. Most settlers were to receive 4,605

The Mission of San José, five miles from San Antonio, was one of 20 constructed by Franciscan friars in Spanish Texas around 1700. Their campaign to proselytize the Indians was unsuccessful, and by the 1830s many of the churches, abandoned by the fathers, were crumbling into ruins.

acres, and Austin's land commissioner—none other than Baron de Bastrop—was empowered to issue clear title to each claim. The Mexican government waived taxes for six years and asked no payment for the land, only a small fee for registering individual titles. Austin was authorized to charge his settlers 12 1/2 cents per acre to cover his costs, including surveying and military defense, and he was awarded 100,000 acres for his own use. Because Mexican leaders lacked the funds and personnel to create a government for his grant, they appointed him their chief official in the colony and gave him the title of Civil Commandant.

The Mexicans had preserved two Spanish preconditions for land ownership: every settler must become a Mexican citizen and a Roman Catholic. Neither requirement worried Austin, though he knew that many Americans were harshly anti-Catholic. Austin had received assurances from Mexican officials that Catholic rites would not be enforced. Protestant conscience would be tolerated so long as it was not flaunted publicly. Austin quoted with bemusement a cynical Mexican proverb that covered the situation perfectly: "God punishes the exposure more than the crime."

Austin left Mexico City full of confidence and arrived at the colony in August 1823, to find it on the brink of collapse. The first corn crop, planted back in April of 1822, had withered during a severe summer drought, and attacks by the Karankawas had killed more settlers. No one had come forward to rally the colonists in their time of distress, and a dozen or so families had returned to the United States. Prime acreage was abandoned; one Missourian traded his property for a mule to ride back to Missouri. Though most of the settlers stuck it out through the 17 months of Austin's absence, they were badly in need of reassurance.

Austin, like a kind but stern father, told the survivors what they wanted to hear: their troubles would soon be over if they worked hard and followed his counsel closely. He then published some rules to guide the colony, and, as he had done so often in the past few years, picked up the pieces and started over again.

The reappearance of the *empresario* stopped the exodus from Texas, and word that his colony was legal and its land policy was liberal reversed the tide, attracting old deserters and many more newcomers. By September of 1824, Baron de Bastrop had issued 272 titles, and 25 more followed soon afterward. Actually, Austin fell three families short of the 300 families he had contracted to introduce. All the same the 297 were quickly dubbed the Old Three Hundred to distinguish them from new colonists whom Austin brought in to fulfill later contracts for supplementary land grants.

From each incoming settler Austin demanded written testimony "that his character is *perfectly unblemished,* that he is a moral and industrious man, and absolutely free from the vice of intoxication." Because Austin was personally responsible to the Mexican government for the conduct of his people, he spared no effort to keep out the ordinary run of uncouth, lawless frontiersmen, whom he called "leatherstockings." Only four of the Old Three Hundred could not sign their names, and practically all were law-abiding. There was truth in what Austin wrote to a prospective settler: "You will be astonished to see all our houses with no other fastening than a wooden pin or door latch."

If a man's references were acceptable, Austin next required him to swear allegiance to Mexico, and reminded him of his obligation to the Catholic Church. Then Austin issued the settler a permit that gave him 30 days to choose his land from what was available. Austin's surveyor—Horatio Chriesman, a young Missourian—then hustled out to plat the claim, and Bastrop issued title promptly.

Austin divided his grants so that each 4,605-acre property consisted of two units: a plot of farming land, about 177 acres, and a tract of grazing land, about 4,428 acres. Whenever possible, each property was given frontage on water and was at least four times as deep as it was wide, thus giving the maximum number of families direct access to cheap river transportation.

Conditions improved rapidly after Austin's return from Mexico City. The crops planted that year and the next were good, and they included not only corn but also cotton, which would soon become Texas' main cash crop. John Jenkins, who arrived as a boy in 1828 after his father had made advance preparations, found 10 acres of corn, with a good starter crop of 10 to 12 rows of cotton. As for the family's new home, it was "half-covered log cabin with a dirt floor." John considered the cabin comfortable, and admired the skill and energy of newcomers who were building similar houses of cedar logs and pine boards, "all of which had to be cut, hewn, brought to hand, and built in shape, without wagons, nails or any kind of machinery."

The Jenkinses and everyone else continued to plant corn for bread, and a number of settlers had a cow for milk. But according to Noah Smithwick, who arrived from Tennessee in 1827, domestic animals were in such short supply for years that "Possession of any number gave notoriety and name to the possessor. Thus there were 'Cow' Cooper and 'Hog' Mitchell." Smithwick also noted that flour was $10 a barrel and "few people had any money to buy anything more than coffee and tobacco, which were considered absolutely indispensable." Of necessity, the forest still supplied the mainstay of the Texas diet, and the quality and care of firearms were basic to life itself. Of course the men enjoyed hunting for its own sake and for the escape it gave them from hard labor, but the women had practically no relief from grinding drudgery. "The women," Noah Smithwick said, "there was where the situation bore heaviest. As one lady remarked, 'Texas was a heaven for men and dogs, but hell for women and oxen.' They—the women—talked sadly of the old homes and friends left behind, of the hardships they were undergoing, and the dangers."

The men quickly volunteered for local defense groups that Austin organized to repel Indian attacks. These militia companies soon switched from static defense to wide-ranging horse patrols, which staged attacks on Indian encampments. Hence they came to be called "ranging companies"—the precursors of the Texas Rangers, who fought Indians and outlaws with equal relish. To Austin, the attacks on the Indians were not only a practical necessity but a contractual duty he owed to the Mexican government. Indeed he personally led one of his Indian campaigns on direct orders from a Mexican general.

On such missions, any Indians were fair game. Pursuing a band of horse thieves, Abner Kuykendall found another Indian group and attacked it, killing several men. Kuykendall's son Barzillai noted that these Indians "were well provided with ropes and bridles and doubtless had come on a stealing expedition." The action satisfied the settlers. They were tired and their horses were worn out, so "Father was constrained to

forego the pursuit of the thieves and return home."

Austin's militia was only one product of his continuing struggle to set up a self-sustaining organization in his colony. Using Mexican forms, he permitted the settlers in each area to elect an *alcalde,* who combined the functions of mayor, judge and sheriff. Discreetly, Austin Americanized and modified Mexican laws to help his *alcaldes* and settlers understand them, and to put up with their intervention in what Americans considered their own private affairs.

By 1825, the colony was populous enough for Austin to have created four districts, each with its own *alcalde.* Austin was the only link between the districts and between his colony and the Texas government. He duly reported to the Governor and expressed his settlers' need for more government services—connecting roads, public schools and other items Americans had come to expect from their government. But the Governor lacked the funds and personnel for those needs, and Austin was reluctant to push the matter.

Conditions changed radically in 1825, after the liberal Federalists, who then controlled the Congress in Mexico City, passed two well-meaning laws designed to give the states greater authority to meet the problems of increased immigration. One law consolidated Mexico's northern frontier, combining Texas with its western neighbor Coahuila, and gave the new entity a representative government of sorts. However, the capital of "Coahuila y Texas" was established at Saltillo, nearly 500 miles from San Felipe, and all of Texas was given only one seat in the state legislature.

The second law gave the states the power, heretofore exercised by the national government, to enact their own colonization policy. Coahuila y Texas opened wide the floodgates of immigration, issuing land grants to *empresarios* and even to individual settlers.

In the next decade, some 25 land grants were made under *empresario* contracts similar to Austin's; Austin himself received several new grants. The result was a patchwork of colonies *(map, page 59)* that stretched from the Louisiana border to the Nueces River and engulfed the Mexican settlements in the San Antonio area. The *empresarios* agreed to import 100 to 800 families within six years; they were promised a land bonus of about 23,000 acres for every 100 families they introduced, and were allowed to charge each fam-

The original "Old Three Hundred"

Among the most cherished documents of early Texas history is Stephen Austin's record of the first venturesome Americans to settle in his colony centered on the town of San Felipe de Austin. Between 1824 and 1827, Austin assigned tracts of land to 297 families, who came to be known as the Old Three Hundred—the number that was specified in Austin's contract with Mexico. To claim descent from these hardy pioneers became as much a matter of pride to Texans as Jamestown ancestry was to a Southerner or the Mayflower to a New Englander.

In compiling his list of original colonists, Austin gave only the dry facts—names, title dates and acreage granted, along with its location. His ledger conveys no hint of the excitement with which the Old Three Hundred took possession of their land nor of the ritual that accompanied the great event. But the papers legalizing the grant, which Austin filed with Mexican authorities, reveal that the occasion was a mixture of solemnity and high spirits.

The full record of a typical grant, made in 1824 to Arthur McCormick, describes how a party—including Austin and his land commissioner, Baron de Bastrop—"repaired to the tract we have granted. We put the said Arthur McCormick in possession of said tract, taking him by the hand, leading him over it, telling him in loud and clear voices that in the name of the Government of the Mexican nation, we put him in possession and the said Arthur McCormick in token of finding himself in real and personal possession shouted aloud, pulled up grass, threw stones,

fixed stakes, and performed the other ceremonies fixed by custom"—which traced to land laws of the 1600s.

McCormick had the misfortune to die a year or so later, but many of the Three Hundred went on to shout aloud

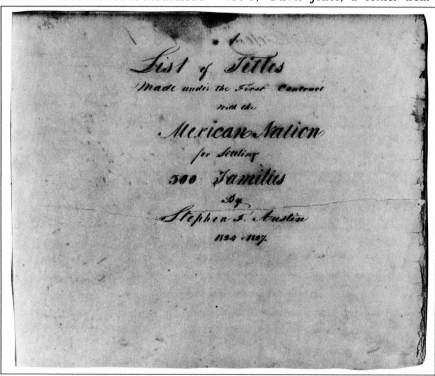

The original cloth cover protects Austin's roster of the "first families" of Texas.

and fix stakes in the great uprising that shaped Texas as an independent nation. One such man was Clement C. Dyer, from Tennessee. In October 1835, when a convention of Texans met to consider secession from Mexico, Dyer—by then owner of a plantation—was a delegate. Another Tennessee-born colonist, John H. Moore, led the Texans in the skirmish at Gonzales that sparked the Texas revolution. Jared E.

Groce, raised in Virginia, organized and maintained a hospital for the citizen army and from his large plantation supplied food for the fighting men.

After Texas won independence in 1836, Oliver Jones, a settler from Connecticut, was appointed chairman of a committee to recommend a flag and seal for the new republic. Jones himself is said to have designed the flag with the great Lone Star that epitomizes the unity and caliber of the Old Three Hundred who first colonized Texas. They were, declared Austin, "as good men as can be found in any part of the United States, and certainly more so than ever settled a frontier."

Austin's ledger reveals that Clement Dyer *(below)* was granted 4,428 acres for ranching and one and a half *labores,* 265 acres, for farming. The thin paper allowed writing on the reverse side to show through.

Clement C. Dyer and his wife, Sarah, were charter members of Austin's colony. She was the daughter of William Stafford, a settler whose plantation Dyer managed.

ily a service fee of $60 for its basic allotment of 4,428 acres. Most *empresarios* signed their contracts in good faith, and several spent lavishly to recruit settlers. But most were plagued by Indians, boundary disputes and their own ineptitudes, and even with Austin's help, failed to fulfill their contracts. Their grants were rescinded, then passed on to new *empresarios* or divided up among neighboring colonies. To make matters worse, the well-meaning *empresarios* were given a bad name by a number of feckless speculators who sold their grants for a quick profit without introducing a single settler. A few *empresarios* were outright swindlers. It was up to the buyer to beware, and many did not.

Yet even speculators and failed *empresarios* spread news of Texas, and the influx of immigrants rose sharply. By 1830, Austin's colonies had some 4,000 settlers, and there were 16,000 Americans in Texas —about four times the Mexican population. The Americans were making progress, albeit spotty.

By 1830, a dozen-odd American villages had cropped up, and a few were growing into towns. The old Mexican town of Nacogdoches was resettled and by the end of the decade it had about 800 inhabitants. In Austin's colonies, Bell's Landing and Mina were founded, and Austin's cousin, Mary Austin Holley, reported from Brazoria that she was "surprised to see brick stores and frame dwelling houses," with nearly 300 townspeople and "a busy, prosperous air."

Austin's own San Felipe boasted some 200 people, 50 houses and two general stores as early as 1828. Noah Smithwick, who opened a blacksmith shop there that year, said that the buildings were all "of unhewn logs with clapboard roofs," and described Austin's house as "a double log cabin with a wide 'passage' through the center." Austin lived in one cabin and conducted the affairs of his colonies from the other. That made it virtually the capitol of American Texas.

Predictably, the economic gains of the colonies were uneven at best. Well into the 1830s the most important crop was corn—used for bread, liquor and stock feed. Cotton, raised by slave labor on Southern-style plantations, was definitely the crop of the future; exports reached 4,000 bales in 1833, and jumped to 10,000 bales the next year.

Texas' foremost cotton grower, and one of its leading stock raisers, was Jared Groce, the beneficent supplier of Austin's first colony. Groce enlarged his huge original property of 44,000 acres by buying up land from neighbors, and in 1825 he began processing his cotton harvest in his own gin. Lesser growers were also doing well: one man with a good-sized plantation was said to have realized the equivalent of $10,000 on one cotton crop. Most trade was barter, for cash was still woefully short. An observer reported in 1832, "There are in these districts many good citizens, many good livers, men of property, who do not handle five dollars in a year." Those who happened to have cash could lend it at 25 per cent per annum.

The more Texas changed, the more Stephen Austin remained the same. Just as he had been a dutiful son, now he was the dutiful father to all his colonists, whom he actually referred to as his family; he kept so busy tending to their needs that he never got around to taking a wife and siring children of his own. And Austin remained a dutiful servant of the Mexican government. His abiding loyalty and gratitude were neatly summed up in a letter he wrote in 1829 to his married sister, who was planning to move to the colony: "This is the most liberal and munificent Government on earth to emigrants—after being here one year you will oppose a change even to Uncle Sam."

In moments not pre-empted by work, Austin led a frugal, lonely, almost ascetic life. He described his lot as "coffee, corn bread, milk and butter, and a bachelor's household, which is confusion, dirt and torment." His brother came to the colony but took sick and died; his mother died as she was preparing to come; and when his sister and her family arrived, their cheerful presence pointed up the emptiness of Austin's life until then. Austin could be convivial enough. He enjoyed good talk, music, dancing and parties; but there was little social life in the early days of the colony, and, as he put it, he developed the "habit of taciturnity."

Joseph C. Clopper, a brash young newcomer from Cincinnati, met Austin in 1828 and described him, with some surprise, as a "small, spare little old bach-

Stephen Austin reaches for a rifle as a wounded scout bursts in with word of an Indian raid on San Felipe, Austin's first colony. The men, gathered in 1824 to map boundaries before issuing title to a parcel of land, included Austin's land commissioner, Baron de Bastrop *(left edge of painting)*.

The turbulent, short-lived Republic of Fredonia

One of the wildest incidents in the early settlement of Texas was the strange affair of the Fredonian Rebellion. It had a cast of characters straight out of fiction: disreputable entrepreneurs, outraged landholders, disgruntled Indians, mistrustful Mexicans. And it had a scenario to match, featuring an alliance of Mexican soldiers and American colonists pitted against another group of Americans who had seized a Mexican fort and were claiming all Texas as their own.

It all began in September 1825, with the arrival from Mississippi of an arrogant and shady land *empresario,* Haden Edwards, and his hotheaded brother, Benjamin. The Mexican government had given Haden Edwards a grant of more than 300,000 acres near the East Texas village of Nacogdoches, on which he planned to settle 800 American families. There was just one problem: parts of his grant were already occupied by American squatters and Mexican settlers, some of whom held legitimate titles under Spanish grants, which Mexico continued to honor.

The government must have assumed that Edwards' grant was large enough for all. But Edwards soon issued an ultimatum: all who hoped to stay must "immediately present themselves to me and show me their titles or documents, if any they possess, so that they may be received or rejected and if they do not do this, the said lands will be sold to the first person who occupies them."

Not surprisingly, this harsh injunction outraged the earlier settlers. Bitterly resentful of an *empresario* who

Empresario Haden Edwards

threatened to confiscate their land or extort payment for what they felt was already theirs, the settlers complained to the Mexican government.

In June 1826, while Haden Edwards was on a visit to the United States, leaving brother Benjamin in charge, word reached the colony that the President of Mexico had revoked Edwards' empresario contract and ordered the brothers out of the country. At that point, the triumphant first settlers of Nacogdoches started reclaiming the land on which Edwards' initial group of 50 families had just settled.

Now it was the newcomers' turn to be outraged. Most of them rallied to the side of the irascible Benjamin, who issued a call for revolt against a Mexican government that invited in American colonists and then allowed their rights to be violated.

All this was deeply worrisome to Stephen Austin, who knew that any uprising might turn Mexico against his

own colony and Americans in general. He urgently advised the Edwards brothers to seek a peaceful solution with Mexican authorities.

However, on December 16, with Benjamin in the lead, 30 colonists rode into Nacogdoches carrying a red-and-white banner emblazoned with the motto "Independence, Liberty and Justice." There they seized an old fort and proclaimed the "Republic of Fredonia"—a name designed to stress their independence of Mexico.

It was as harebrained a move as it was brazen. However the Fredonians thought they had a hole card: before revolting they had signed a treaty dividing up Texas with Cherokee Indians who had migrated into the region and were angry because Mexico would grant them no land. The treaty was as muddle-headed as the rest of the rebellion. The Indian who signed it had no authority and was disavowed by the tribal council, and the Fredonians were on their own.

On January 28, 1827, a force of 250 Mexicans set out to crush the Fredonians. With them were 100 of Austin's colonists, as anxious as the Mexicans to be rid of the Fredonians. But there was no one to crush. When the expedition reached Nacogdoches, the fort was deserted. Hopelessly outnumbered, and deserted by the Indians, the Edwards brothers and their followers had fled to safety in the United States. The Republic of Fredonia had lasted barely six weeks.

A resident of the Nacogdoches region later wrote its epitaph in a letter to Austin: "There never was a more silly, wild, quicksotic scheme."

elor"—this at the age of 35. The same year Noah Smithwick pictured him as careworn and unassuming: "There was little in Austin's outward appearance to indicate the tremendous energy of which he was possessed." Austin's unselfish labors were wearing him down, and his sister-in-law thought that "if he does not quit his desk, ride about and take more exercise, his life will be but short."

Whatever the risk, Austin continued his multitudinous duties, disbursing land, answering letters from prospective immigrants, translating official Mexican papers into English and American petitions into Spanish, advising other *empresarios,* guiding the business ventures of new enterprisers, settling disputes and commanding the militia. As the years went on, he also began accusing the colonists of ingratitude for all he was doing in their behalf.

The cause of Austin's irritation was an unfair opinion held by some colonists and crudely put by a settler named James Gaines, who wrote Austin in 1824: "Your people say you slight them by reserving to yourself all the Good Land, they say you are never Governed Two days by the Same Rule nor Law." More specifically, the malcontents maintained that Austin showed favoritism in awarding huge properties to men like Jared Groce, and that since Austin himself received great tracts for bringing in settlers, his 12 1/2 cents per acre charge to them was a double profit and a gouge. In rebuttal, Austin explained that the income from great holdings like Groce's benefited the colony as a whole; that he lacked the time to work his own acreage and was forbidden to sell it to raise operating expenses for the colony's essential business. "The settlers do not reflect," wrote Austin bitterly to a Mexican friend, "that I cannot live on lands; that I cannot eat them, make clothes of them, nor sell them; and that I have spent all that I had in their service."

Austin realized that "it is innate in an American to suspect and abuse a public officer whether he deserves it or not." But Austin did not fully understand the underlying cause of the settlers' grievances. While his colonists respected him and relied heavily upon him, they also resented him—not just because his land policies seemed arbitrary but because he was really a one-man government. To be sure, Austin permitted his settlers to elect their *alcaldes,* but it was a privilege he bestowed, not a right they possessed. The Americans' ingrained determination to run their own affairs had expressed itself eloquently in the American Revolution; in the years ahead it would express itself again against the Mexican government.

But as the second decade began, American settlers in Texas had no real provocation to revolt. The government had levied no taxes, conscripted no Americans as soldiers, and made no effort to ram down American throats its requirement of the Catholic faith.

The religious question was a strange, imponderable matter. Practically all prospective immigrants knew that nominal acceptance of Catholicism was a prerequisite for land ownership in Texas. Americans who were anti-Catholic or who believed irreconcilably in the American doctrine of the separation of church and state, did not come to Texas for this reason. Those who came doubtless shared the view of a Missourian who wrote Austin, "I know I can be as good a Christian there as I can here. It is only a name anyhow."

An itinerant priest, Padre Michael Muldoon, occasionally appeared to baptize people, but since this ceremony made one eligible for land ownership, Americans considered it a business matter rather than a religious problem. The real difficulty was that, for American settlers in Texas, there was no organized religion whatsoever, and in time this state of affairs grew irksome even to people not notably religious. In many areas Americans were born and buried without benefit of clergy, and as for worship, one settler said indignantly, "The people of this country seem to have forgotten that there is such a commandment as 'Remember the Sabbath.' This day is generally spent in visiting, driving stock and breaking mustangs; there is no such thing as attending church."

Couples were frequently married in a civil ceremony, which Padre Muldoon willingly reinforced for a fee when he came by on his rounds. Noah Smithwick, who attended a civil wedding at Bell's Landing, reported that Thomas Duke, then the *alcalde* at San Felipe, "tied the nuptial knot in good American style, but the contracting parties had in addition to sign a bond to avail themselves of the priest's services at the earliest opportunity." This bond was not nearly as binding as it sounded. Couples who fell out after their civil wedding could cancel it by simply tearing up their

GALVESTON BAY & TEXAS LAND COMPANY

Nº 3573.

This Certifies,

177 136/1000 Acres.

That the Subscribers as the Trustees and Attorneys of **LORENZO DE ZAVALA, JOSEPH VEHLEIN,** and **DAVID G. BURNET,** have given and do hereby give to *George Curtis* and his legal representatives the bearer hereof, their consent to the location of and holding in severally: **ONE LABOR** of Land within the limits of four adjoining tracts of Land in **TEXAS,** heretofore severally granted to the said Lorenzo De Zavala on the 12th of March 1829, Joseph Vehlein on the 21st December 1826, and 17th November 1828; and David G. Burnet on the 22nd December 1826, as **EMPRESARIOS,** for **COLONIZING** the same according to the terms of the said grants, and the **LAWS** of the **UNITED STATES** of **MEXICO,** and the **STATE** of **COAHUILA** and **TEXAS,** which said ——— in one common interest, and placed under the direction and management of the Subscribers, as the **ATTORNEYS** and Trustees of the said **EMPRESARIOS,** by virtue of and according to their several **DEEDS** of Indenture, dated the 16th October 1830, and to the articles of Association of said Company.

The four tracts of Land aforesaid, comprehend all the **LAND** not settled according to **LAW,** and the terms of said grants, lying within the following limits (excepting the town of Nacogdoches, Beginning at the Westerly boundary of the **UNITED STATES** of **AMERICA** on the Gulph of **MEXICO,** thence running Northerly on the Westerly side of the Sabine River to the road leading from **NATCHITOCHES** to **NACOGDOCHES;** thence running Westerly along said Road a distance of Twenty Spanish Leagues from the boundary line to the suburbs or Vicinity of Nacogdoches, then proceeding from said Town of Nacogdoches Northwardly a distance of fifteen Spanish Leagues, where leaving free on one side the Twenty Boundary leagues in a parallel with the River Sabine, and the dividing line of the **UNITED STATES** of the North, shall be placed a **LAND MARK,** and from which a right line shall be drawn to the West until it strikes the Rivulet named Navasoto, from thence the line shall descend upon the left margin of the said Rivulet, following its course until it meets the Road leading from **BEXAR** to **NACOGDOCHES;** thence running along said Road till it comes to a point thereon being due North of the source of the Waters of the Rivulet St. Jacinto; thence running due South to the source of the Waters of the said River, thence it shall follow the left bank of the St. **JACINTO** to **GALVESTON BAY,** thence by the Westerly side of said **BAY** to the **GULPH** of **MEXICO,** excluding the **ISLAND** of St. **LOUIS,** and thence by the said **GULPH** of **MEXICO** to the place of beginning.

The location of said land is to be made under the **SUPERVISION** and direction of the Agent of the Trustees and Attorneys of the **EMPRESARIOS** aforesaid residing on the land, who, after making a record of the same shall make report thereof to the Commissioner appointed by the **GOVERNMENT,** to the intent that the holder of this Scrip upon the surrender thereof may have his land **SURVEYED,** and receive his title thereto in severalty from said Commissioner, according to Law. **SUBJECT** to the payments required by the **LAWS** of the **STATE.** This scrip being Indorsed by the original holder is Transferable by delivery. Copies of the Original **GRANTS** and subsequent conveyances and articles of association of the **COMPANY** as well as the Colonization laws before referred to, will be exhibited upon application to either of the Subscribers hereto

New York 16th October 1830

Trustees & Attorneys.

Sec.

SCRIP Nº 3573 for ONE LABOR, containing 177 136/1000 English Acres.

bond, for only Roman Catholic marriages were considered legal in Texas.

In any case, Padre Muldoon was a good drinking companion and highly sympathetic to Americans, and they made his every appearance a Roman holiday. Henry Smith, who later served briefly as Governor of Texas, said, "All who wished to marry, as well as those who had been bonded for years, had now to come forward and have the slip knot made fast. A number of these old married people determined to save trouble by having one grand wedding and give the padre an opportunity to do a wholesale business. The day was fine and every countenance seemed to brighten with the prospect of the anticipated enjoyment, not for the pleasure of seeing the old people married over again entirely, but the baptism, the wine, the dinner, the dance and the sight of a Roman Catholic Priest—was equal to a rare show in Texas."

Americans could wait for proper churching, but their need for adequate government was genuinely urgent, especially in the areas of law enforcement and the administration of justice. Local courts were virtually powerless to act because almost every case had to be referred for decision to Saltillo, 500 miles away. What is more, the forms of referral were so complicated that case papers, laboriously drafted in the Spanish language, were often sent back several times for redrafting —while the issues and litigants languished in limbo month after month. In exasperation, Austin once declared that a Mexican-style criminal trial, which was conducted without a jury, "amounts to no tryal at all," because the "formula required in the prosecution of criminals is so difficult that most of the courts in Texas have long since ceased to attempt its execution."

Criminal acts were no novelty even among Austin's solid, responsible colonists, and they demanded prompt justice. In a celebrated case in San Felipe, a lawyer with an evil reputation was killed in a street fight, and two men were held for trial for 18 months, much of that time in chains, while the case papers drifted back and forth between Saltillo and San Felipe. The case had a chilling effect on the Texans, for almost any self-respecting man could be forced into a street fight.

To make matters worse, the success of Texas in general and Austin's colonies in particular was attracting more of the very people whom Austin tried so hard to keep out—the "leatherstockings," the "turbulent frontiersmen." A few were fugitives from justice, the letters "G.T.T."—meaning "Gone to Texas"—became a sneering reference to shady characters who had to leave the United States to stay out of jail. But for the most part, they were not lawbreakers; they were merely willful, independent and opportunistic.

Compared to Austin's hand-picked colonists, the newcomers were much less tolerant of the Mexican government with its inefficiency, its failure to provide democratic process, its religious requirement. They saw no reason why they should give up the rights they had enjoyed in the United States; and they believed that foremost among their rights as Americans and free men was resistance to injustice and tyranny in any government. Austin's colonists had willingly repressed their American credo in exchange for land, but the newcomers—hordes of individualists on the make—were much less patient.

Moreover, the passage of a decade had altered Austin's original settlers. They were now substantial landowners on their way to becoming an elite. They had interests to protect, and were perfectly right in fearing that the impatient newcomers would roil the waters. Austin, always conservative and loyal to Mexico, was naturally the archchampion of peaceful, gradual progress. As such, he would remain a force to reckon with for several years to come. But he failed to realize that the aggressive newcomers were the wave of the future, and this failure made him the wave of the past. Like his father, Moses, before him, he had gone as far as he could with the "Texas venture," and now the leadership of the Americans was slipping into other hands.

LAND CERTIFICATES AT FIVE CENTS AN ACRE

Operating in New York as agent for a group of *empresarios*, the Galveston Bay and Texas Land Company in 1830 sold "land certificates" to would-be settlers for five cents an acre. But the certificates merely allowed investors to join an *empresario's* colony; title to the land could only be secured from the Mexican government, which imposed other fees and conditions (among them becoming a Roman Catholic). Furthermore, from 1830 to 1834 Mexico forbade American immigration; and although the company noted the prohibition in a pamphlet (suggesting it would be temporary) many prospective settlers, unaware of the law, arrived in Texas only to be rejected by the authorities.

2 | A capital gilded and remote

Few Texans in the early days of colonization ever set foot in Mexico City, capital of their adopted land. What little they knew about it came from Stephen Austin and the handful of other *empresarios* who made pilgrimages to the metropolis in pursuit of land grants. Yet even such worthy observers could scarcely convey all the facets of the city, one of the oldest and certainly the grandest in the New World.

Founded in the 14th Century as the seat of the Aztec empire, razed and rebuilt by Cortez as the heart of New Spain in the 16th Century, Mexico City by the 1830s had become a stunning metropolis of almost 200,000 people. It was a city of stupendous ruins and magnificent cathedrals, of imposing fortifications and vast open air markets. Broad avenues led to regal plazas, and behind the stone facades were elegant homes with fountained courtyards and cool gardens. There were also slums, fetid and sprawling; Austin wrote that their inhabitants were "most miserably poor and wretched."

Though nominally the capital of a young republic, Mexico City exuded, in the words of one observer, an aura "as anti-republican as one could wish to see." With the transfer of power from Spain came the assumptions of domestic wealth, and Mexico's officers, politicians and businessmen paraded it conspicuously. Ladies of position wore diamonds and satin slippers on their morning social calls; gold chains fell from their necks to their knees. Formal invitations were often ornamented with spun-silver lace and sterling tassels, and daily life unraveled in a leisurely procession of concerts, receptions, theater performances and bullfights.

The Texas colonists, living in rude log cabins and working the soil with their hands, could never be a part of this gilded world. And soon they could not live in peace with its masters. For beneath the gala atmosphere of Mexico City, political forces were building that would lead to civil war in the outlying states, and invest an ambitious general with the powers of a brutal dictator.

Mexico City's cathedral, the biggest church in the Americas, which was in construction for two centuries, looms over Liberation Plaza.

The resplendent elite of Mexico City turn out for a promenade in the shaded confines of Alameda Park. The park was also the traditional scene of a dizzying courtship ritual in which marriageable young women circled the fountain (*center*) in one direction, hopeful swains in the other.

Cloaked aristocrats and Indian vendors intermingle in the Plaza de Santo Domingo. The Church of Santo Domingo (*background*) was established by Dominican priests in 1571, and won infamy as a courtroom in which accused heretics were tried during the bloody Mexican Inquisition.

48

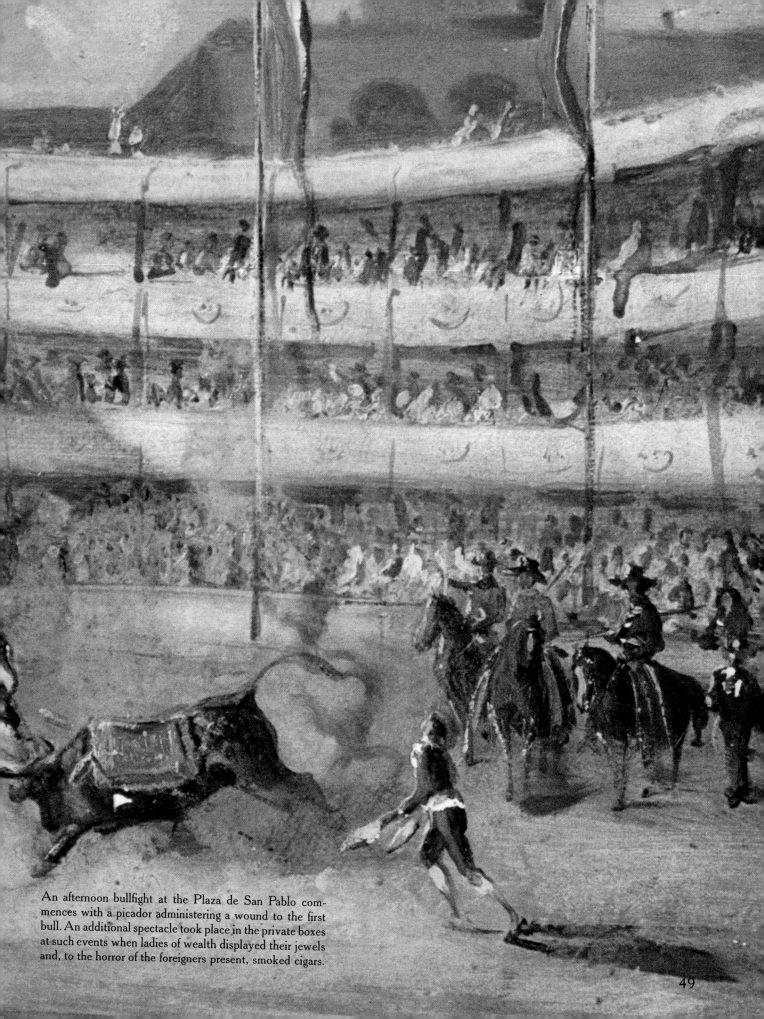

An afternoon bullfight at the Plaza de San Pablo commences with a picador administering a wound to the first bull. An additional spectacle took place in the private boxes at such events when ladies of wealth displayed their jewels and, to the horror of the foreigners present, smoked cigars.

"Let the brave rally to the standard"

On December 2, 1832, astride a sleek, broom-tailed mare, Sam Houston splashed into a shallow stretch of the Red River and crossed from Indian Territory into Texas. He rode alone, his bedroll lashed behind. In his pocket he carried a special passport issued on orders of the President of the United States, who directed him to confer with certain Comanche chieftains; he would find them near San Antonio and would seek to persuade them to make peace with neighboring tribes on United States soil.

As his mount climbed the river bank onto a broad plain of grass burned russet in winter's frost, Houston looked up and saw an eagle circling effortlessly overhead—as if to salute his arrival. A good omen. Like the Indians among whom he had spent so many years, Sam Houston was much drawn to signs and portents.

The mission was scarcely a pressing one. Houston had his own reasons for going to Texas, and his close friend, Andrew Jackson, had provided him with a pretext. The document he bore was more a means of introduction to xenophobic Mexican authorities than an emblem of his mission's importance. It was significant that the directive was from the President—an indication of the position Houston enjoyed. He had been a general of militia, a Congressman and the Governor of Tennessee; and though his fortunes had been reversed in a single cruel stroke, he retained the confidence of President Jackson—a confidence that had once spawned talk of him as heir to Jackson's mantle.

Houston was 39 when he rode into Texas—a tall, powerfully muscled buccaneer of a man. Volcanic of temper, brave beyond measure, possessed of profound notions of patriotism and honor, he was ready to fight at the first summons of a trumpet or at the mere whisper of an insult. On his body he bore battle scars that he displayed like the rosettes of honor earned by his contemporaries on the battlefields of Europe. Baring his torso, he was wont to declare himself "a humble republican soldier who wears his decorations here!" Yet this rough-and-tumble warrior could exhibit infinite patience when it suited his mood or seemed to advance an inner-directed design.

Again and again Houston had proved himself a political savant and magnetic leader, a powerful orator and clever debater. And in his personal life, though abysmally unlucky in love, he remained unfailingly courtly to women. Once, when a pretty young cousin asked him to write in her memory book, he dashed off a poem on the spot: "No matter where my bark be tost on Life's tumultuous, stormy sea; my anchor gone, my rudder lost, Still, cousin, I will think of thee."

Houston's verse was a fair assessment of his life. Storm-tossed he was, and sometimes rudder-lost; but as he left the Red River behind him and headed south, he was fated for an epic role in the destiny of Texas.

Sam Houston's forebears had arrived in the New World from Scotland in 1730 and had gradually acquired considerable wealth as Virginia plantation owners. Sam's father failed to inherit this business acumen, or any interest in working a plantation. Deciding that a military life was more appropriate for a gentleman, he left the estate to look after itself while he pursued an uneventful Army career. But the place would not look after itself, nor could his wife supervise it while raising the family. Over the years the plantation ran down and accumulated debts. Each time Captain Samuel Houston came home he sold off slaves and parcels of land; and when he died in 1806, the family fortunes were

Sam Houston had already proved himself a courageous soldier and shrewd politician when he assumed the role of Texas' liberator. This watercolor on ivory, painted in the 1840s, is attributed to George Catlin.

gone. His widow, Elizabeth, and nine children, of whom Sam was the fifth, were left with little except debts. Mrs. Houston, a tall, handsome woman of great courage, loaded her brood into two wagons and struck off across the Alleghenies into Tennessee. Not far from Knoxville she took a grant of 419 acres and, with the aid of her sons, cleared the land for a farm.

Sam was 14 when his mother took him to Tennessee. Even then he was a restless spirit, chafing at family chores and schoolwork—except for the classics, which he adored. At 17 he slipped away from home to explore the little island of Hiwassie in the Tennessee River. There he wandered into a camp of Cherokee Indians, who warmed to the tough, free-spirited youth. The clan's chief, known to white men as John Jolly, conferred on Sam the Indian name Co-lon-neh,

the Raven—a bird honored by the Cherokees for its far-sightedness, sagacity and boldness. Before long the chief had adopted Sam as a son.

Weeks passed. Sam's mother was distraught; family and neighbors scoured the woods. Eventually Sam's older brothers, James and John, found him on Hiwassie. He was seated under a tree, reading Alexander Pope's translation of the *Iliad*. Marking his place, he coolly informed them that he "liked the wild liberty of the Red men better than the tyranny of my own brothers"—and added that he preferred to read in peace. James and John returned home to tell their mother that her wayward Sam was at least safe.

For the better part of three years Houston lived with the Cherokees—"wandering," as he later wrote, "along the banks of streams, side by side with some Indian maiden, sheltered by the deep woods . . . running wild, sleeping on the ground, chasing game, living in the forests, making love and reading Homer's *Iliad*."

In 1813, young Sam's idyl came to an abrupt end. The Red Sticks, a bloodthirsty faction of Creek Indians, were on a rampage in what is now Alabama, and United States forces were marching to put an end to their atrocities. For a young man with Houston's zest for action, it was a call to arms. At 20, he enlisted in the Army to join the campaign against the Creeks. In 1814, as a third lieutenant, he came under General Andrew Jackson's command at the Battle of Horseshoe Bend, where the Red Sticks made their last stand *(pages 54-55)*. It was his first meeting with Jackson, already a well-known public figure in both war and peace; and, because of Houston's exemplary conduct in the battle, it was to shape his life.

Houston was wounded three times, yet fought on so gallantly that Jackson never forgot his bravery. Houston's courage and leadership earned him promotion to second lieutenant, and he seriously considered making the military his career. But then he found himself involved in an incident that turned him completely away from the regular United States Army.

In October 1817, when Houston was in Nashville on Army duty, he was appointed subagent to the Cherokees. Since the War Department administered Indian affairs and needed the services of a man who understood the Cherokees, Houston was a natural and—for the Indians—a fortuitous choice. His Cherokee friends immediately enlisted his aid in righting a wrong. They complained they had not received annuities promised them by the War Department in exchange for their ancestral land. Gravely, Houston acknowledged the injustice and on February 5, 1818, he arrived in Washington leading a delegation of tribesmen.

Never in the annals of the United States Army had an officer appeared before the Secretary of War quite so conspicuously out of uniform. When the group was ushered into the office of John Calhoun, there was Houston at its head, dressed in nothing but a breech-cloth and blanket. Calhoun heard him out—and then angrily demanded to know what a United States Army officer meant by appearing before him in savage garb. Houston explained that he thought it only courteous to his Indian friends to dress as one of them, since he was their spokesman and appointed subagent. But his answer did nothing to mollify his outraged superior.

A few days later Calhoun unexpectedly sent for Houston to demand another explanation—this time for something infinitely more serious. Houston was under suspicion of slave-smuggling, the Secretary informed him; charges by unnamed individuals had reached his ears, and it was up to Houston to account for them. Houston was utterly taken aback, but he did have some inkling of the truth. Through his Indian friends —he told Calhoun—he had learned that bands of smugglers were transporting black slaves from Florida through the Indian reservations to the border settlements. Far from being involved in such traffic, he had attempted to break up the sordid trade. But exactly who the smugglers were he did not know. So straightforward was Houston's story that Calhoun somewhat reluctantly promised to open an investigation. It was found, in the course of his perfunctory inquiries, that the slave smugglers' own friends in Congress had lodged the accusation to divert suspicion from the true culprits and prevent further interference by Houston. Houston himself was found to be completely innocent. But Calhoun, having learned all this, never so much as offered an apology. In disgust, Houston resigned his commission and turned his sights to law and politics.

Returning to Nashville, he read 18 months of law in half a year, passed the Tennessee bar examination, set up his own law practice—and began his spectacular rise to political fame. The people of Tennessee were impressed by Houston's splendidly commanding presence and quick grasp of local politics. They elected him Attorney General of Tennessee in 1819, a commander of Tennessee militia in 1821, and, two years later, United States Congressman.

"I am satisfied that there must be a conducting Providence!" wrote Houston when he was a 30-year-old Congressman-elect. "Five years since I came to this place—without friends—without cash—and almost without acquaintances—consequently without credit. And here among talents and distinction, I have made my stand! or the people have made it for me."

Houston had received a great deal more help than he cared to admit. His self-congratulatory attitude was most ungenerous, but typical of his tendency to exaggerate. In truth, the odds had been stacked in his favor. He was not without friends in Tennessee; and if there was a conducting Providence, its name was Andrew Jackson.

A national war hero, revered for his victory over the British at New Orleans in 1815 and his invasion of Spanish Florida in 1818, Jackson was the most powerful man in Tennessee. Houston often visited his former chief in Nashville, and from him obtained much encouragement and counsel. It was Jackson who had used his considerable influence to put Houston in national politics as a Democratic candidate for Congress.

Jackson himself was elected to the Senate in 1823. Next year he ran for the Presidency with Sam Houston as one of his most active campaigners. Jackson won the popular vote by a large margin, but failed to get the required majority in the Electoral College. The election was thrown into the House of Representatives, which chose John Quincy Adams.

Undaunted, Houston and a number of other partisans plunged into action to keep Jackson's candidacy alive for the next election, operating what Houston called a "literary bureau" to churn out speeches and pamphlets in support of their candidate. No less was Houston politicking on his own behalf. Late in 1827 he was elected governor of Tennessee, giving him a new platform from which to promote Jackson's candidacy. In the election of 1828, Jackson defeated Adams resoundingly. His champion, Houston, was now a man with direct access to the White House and in an ideal position to advance his own ambitions. ◉

The making of a career at Horseshoe Bend

Sam Houston earned his first battle scars as a 20-year-old infantry lieutenant under Andrew Jackson in the Creek Indian War of 1813-1814. The war, which raged across Alabama, grew out of civil strife among the Creeks themselves. Though many of the natives were friendly to white settlers, one faction, known as the "Red Sticks" for their crimson war clubs, was violently opposed and attacked both the whites and their own brethren.

On August 30, 1813, a thousand Red Sticks overwhelmed Fort Mims, a white settlement near Mobile, and massacred several hundred men, women and children.

Six weeks later, Andrew Jackson, then a commander of Tennessee militia, marched south with an army to put an end to the "horrid butcheries perpetrating on our defenceless fellow citizens." After sustaining a number of defeats, the Red Sticks under a half-blood chief, Menewa, made a last stand at Horseshoe Bend on the Tallapoosa River on March 27, 1814. There, Jackson's army, including 100 friendly Creeks and reinforced by the 39th Infantry Regiment of the United States regular army—Sam Houston's regiment —confronted Menewa's 1,000 men barricaded behind a log breastwork.

The 39th spearheaded the attack, and Houston's thigh was pierced by an arrow. Later he took two rifle balls in the shoulder. Some 800 Indians died in the battle; Jackson lost 49 men.

The Red Sticks were crushed. Menewa escaped, but their principal war chief, William Weatherford, gave up. A few months later, the Creeks ceded to the United States 20 million acres of what Andrew Jackson called "the best unsettled country in America."

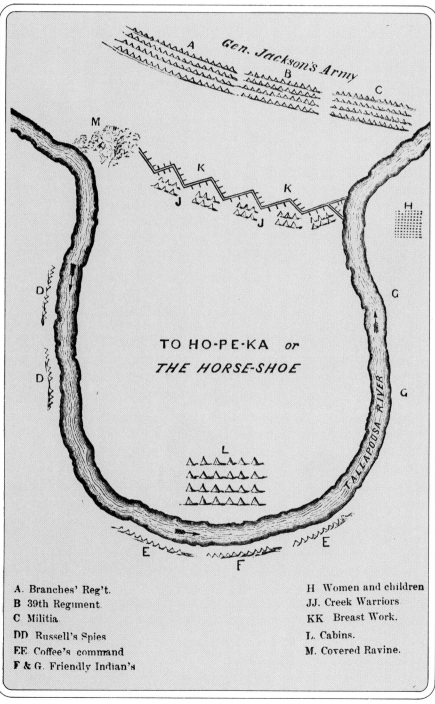

A. Branches' Reg't.
B 39th Regiment.
C Militia.
DD Russell's Spies
EE Coffee's command
F & G. Friendly Indian's

H Women and children
JJ. Creek Warriors
KK Breast Work.
L. Cabins.
M. Covered Ravine.

This 1855 battle plan records the disposition of Jackson's troops against the Creeks.

William McIntosh, a Creek chief who opposed war with the whites, fought gallantly for Jackson against his own tribesmen in the battle at Horseshoe Bend. The chief's costume reflects his Scottish and Indian parentage.

In an 1855 engraving, Lieutenant Sam Houston fights heroically on top of the Creeks' breastwork, calling to his troops to follow him, oblivious of an arrow embedded in his thigh and of the efforts of a companion-in-arms to remove it.

Menewa, known as Crazy War Hunter for his daring, led the Creeks in their final stand. Wounded seven times, and with most of his warriors dead, Menewa escaped across the Tallapoosa River.

Andrew Jackson's Indian guide and adviser during the Creek War was Selocta, a chief favoring peaceful coexistence with white settlers. At the surrender of William Weatherford, the half-blood leader of the Red Sticks, Selocta acted as Jackson's interpreter.

In this 1843 engraving, Chief William Weatherford extends a peace pipe to General Jackson signifying an end to hostilities. "If I had any warriors left, I would still fight," he said. Impressed by the chief's courage, Jackson set him free, warning that he would be hanged if he attacked again.

To make it all complete, in 1829 Houston took a bride. He was 35, a man of the woods and the world, a bullet-scarred soldier and a political climber. Eliza Allen of Gallatin, Tennessee, was 20, sheltered and shy, persuaded by her ambitious parents that marriage to the great Governor Sam would be most advantageous.

The result was catastrophe. Within three months the marriage was broken. Eliza returned to her parents; Houston went into dark seclusion in the Nashville Inn. And the gossip began. Eliza's friends pointed to Houston's drinking and suggested that the blame lay there. Houston's friends believed that Eliza was still in love with a former suitor—possibly a young lawyer, Will Tyree. A widely credited story held that Houston had caught her sobbing over old love letters, and had erupted into a jealous rage.

Neither Eliza nor Houston offered any explanation. Whispers of speculation built into open questions, and street corner gossip turned the episode into a major scandal. Houston might have put the matter to rest with some sort of statement. But he was too proud a man to bare his personal life, and he refused: "This is a painful, but it is a private affair. I do not recognize the right of the public to interfere."

But interfere the public did. In Nashville, placard-bearing crowds demanded an explanation and vilified him as a coward. But still he kept his silence. Finally, after five days, deeply humiliated and stunned by the public attitude, he threw his career to the winds and sent a letter of resignation to the Speaker of the Tennessee Senate. "As I am overwhelmed by sudden calamities," he wrote, "it is certainly due myself and more respectful to the world, that I should retire from a position which, in the public judgment, I might seem to occupy by questionable authority." Embittered and desperately unhappy, Houston decided to go home to the Cherokees.

His Indian friends had been moved by government treaty to Arkansas Territory, and on April 23, 1829, he departed from Tennessee aboard the Arkansas River packet *Red Rover* to join them. Two of Eliza's relatives visited him aboard and attempted to elicit a reason for his behavior. With stubborn gallantry, Houston would only say that "if any wretch ever dares to utter a word against the purity of Mrs. Houston I will come back and write the libel in his heart's blood."

A demoralized and unkempt Houston drank his way through the trip. At one point in the journey, as he later wrote in his memoirs, he "was in an agony of despair and strongly tempted to leap overboard to end my worthless life." But at that moment came the first omen: "An eagle swooped down near my head, and then, soaring aloft with wildest screams, was lost in the rays of the setting sun. I knew that a great destiny waited for me in the West."

Houston may also have been prompted to a more positive outlook by the presence on board of Jim Bowie, the famed knife fighter (*page 60*), who had settled in Texas the year before and was given to extolling the richness of the land with contagious enthusiasm. Inspired by Bowie's tales, Houston in his more garrulous moments spun boozy dreams of new glory to another dedicated drinker aboard, a jovial but injudicious Irishman named H. Haralson, who tended to repeat—with embellishments—whatever he heard.

By the time Houston reached Little Rock, Arkansas, word of his babblings on *Red Rover* had reached a good many interested ears. Speculation has it that the stories started with the gossipy Haralson. The known facts are only that Tennessee Congressman John Marable, an acquaintance of both Haralson and Houston, broadcast a tale that Houston was scheming to "conquer Mexico or Texas," crown himself emperor of the West, "and be worth two millions in two years." Word of mouth spread the story like a brush fire. Two of Houston's old Nashville friends with interests in Texas, John and William Wharton, caught wind of it and wrote him. "I have heard you intended an expedition against Texas," said John Wharton. "I suppose, if it is true, you will let your Nashville friends know of it. Texas is a fine field for enterprise. You can get a grant of land, be surrounded by your friends, and what may not the coming of time bring about?"

Eventually the stories came to the attention of Andrew Jackson in the White House by way of the meddling Congressman Marable. In sharp alarm, he wrote his protégé: "It has been communicated to me that you had the *illegal enterprise* in view of conquering Texas. . . . I cannot believe you have any such chimerical visionary scheme in view. Your pledge of honor to the contrary is a sufficient guarantee that you will never

This 1837 map of Texas, based on one drawn by Stephen Austin, outlines each land grant plus an open area *(gray)*. The list at bottom left totals 14,050 families, of which 11,300 were on Austin's land.

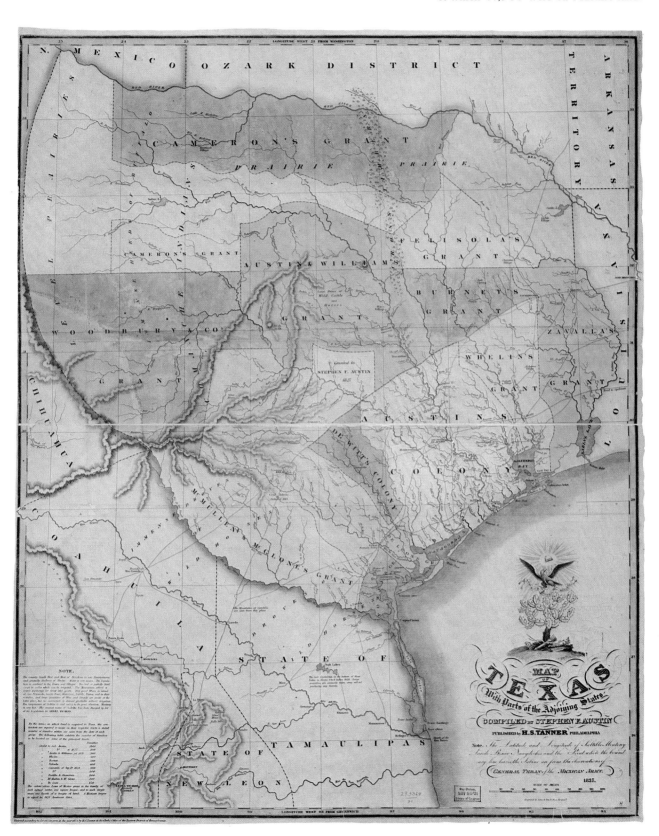

"Greater than Caesar, nearly equal to Thor!"

Even as a youth Jim Bowie was the sort to inspire awe. Born to a rugged frontier family in 1796, he grew up on the Louisiana bayous, and by the time he was 18—raw-boned big and rawhide tough—he was already riding alligators and stalking deer with a lasso. Over the next two decades Bowie made a fortune in slave-smuggling and land speculation, courted society ladies and fought Indians with equal flourish—before he went to a hero's death in the defense of the Alamo. But it was as a knife fighter that Bowie became a legend in his time.

In the early 1800s the knife was the preeminent sidearm—more efficient by far than the muzzle-loading pistols of the day. Men carried everything from pocketknives to butcher knives. But the favorite combat knife was the blade designed in 1830 by Jim Bowie to stab like a dagger, slice like a razor and chop like a cleaver.

The foundation for Bowie's fame as a fighter rests on two battles. The first took place on a Mississippi River sand bar near Natchez in 1827 when two pistol duelists faced off to settle a grudge. After the duelists fired at each other twice, missing both times, fighting broke out among the

Jim Bowie, about 35 years old

10 opposing seconds. One was Bowie, armed with a butcher knife (he had yet to design the Bowie knife).

In the melee, Bowie was shot in the hip and shoulder, stabbed in the chest and beaten on the head. But before he collapsed he disemboweled one assailant, slashed another to ribbons and helped his comrades put the opposing seconds to rout.

The second battle—in which Bowie first tested the weapon that bore his name—took place in Texas in

1830. Bowie was ambushed by three knife-wielding assassins hired by a saloon-keeper he had once wounded in a fight. The first antagonist to reach Bowie was nearly beheaded by one stroke of Bowie's heavy blade. The next inflicted a slight wound on Bowie's leg before Bowie ripped open his belly. The third tried to flee, but Bowie, according to one overenthusiastic account, "split his skull to the shoulders" with a single blow.

Not all of Bowie's storied confrontations were bloody. Henry Clay was witness to one incident and enjoyed recounting it ever after. Clay was on a stagecoach ride in 1832, during which an obnoxious fellow ignored a lady's request to extinguish his pipe —and suddenly found another passenger, by the name of Bowie, holding a monstrous knife to his throat. He reconsidered.

Clay later celebrated Bowie as "the greatest fighter in the Southwest." But Clay's appraisal was pale compared to that of British historian Thomas Carlyle, who, hearing about Bowie, exclaimed: "By Hercules! The man was greater than Caesar—nay, nearly equal to Odin or Thor! The Texans ought to build him an altar."

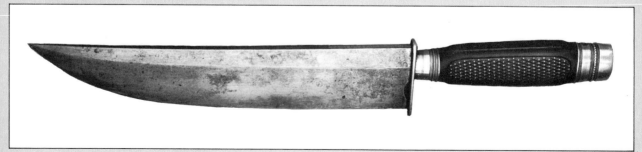

The Bowie knife, in this 1839 model, weighs almost one pound, and has a 12-inch blade that tapers down to a double-edged point.

engage in any enterprise injurious to your country."

Houston, who was stopping over in Little Rock for a few days before resuming his journey, wrote Jackson, giving him his oath. Hotly he added that he did not "distinctly understand the extent of the information, or its character, but I suppose it was intended to complete my ruin." Depression engulfed him again. Ill with fever as well, he made his way to the Cherokee camp near Fort Smith on the Arkansas River.

Houston was not to emerge for nearly three years. Most of the time he was drunk. Despondent over his ruined marriage and career, he drank so heavily that the Indians rechristened him Oo-tse-tee Ar-dee-tah-skee, or Big Drunk. For months at a stretch his mind was a blur of dreams and schemes, dark fancies and visions of Texas. Twice he sobered up enough to travel to Washington with the Cherokees to complain to Secretary of War John Eaton about the dishonesty of the Indian agents. On the second trip, he got himself into a jam that could have completed his destruction—but in the end it brought him roaring back to life.

On March 31, 1832, Ohio Congressman William Stanbery slurred Houston on the floor of the House, hinting broadly that the Tennessean had fraudulently attempted to obtain a contract to supply Indian rations. The attack, like the Calhoun charge 14 years before, was unfair in the extreme. It was true that Houston had tried to get a contract back in 1830, but only after learning that a group of corrupt agents had been supplying the Indians with insufficient, inferior rations and pocketing vast profits themselves. As Houston stated in his memoirs, "They had been contractors for furnishing Indian rations; and through their injustice or delinquency, some of the Indians had died of starvation, and to multitudes only a scanty and insufficient supply had been issued."

Therefore, when the War Department publicly requested bids for the award of new ration contracts, Houston submitted one of his own. It was not the lowest bid, for his proposal was based on raising the quality of the rations and improving their distribution.

When Secretary of War John Eaton refused to let the contracts go to the lowest bidder, he was charged with favoritism toward Houston. Accusations of corruption were flung at Eaton, Houston and even President Jackson. The upshot was that Eaton refused

to consider all bids, and the furor died down—until Congressman Stanbery resurrected it in the House after Eaton's resignation. "Was the Secretary of War removed," the Congressman demanded rhetorically, "in consequence of his attempt fraudulently to give to Governor Houston the contract for Indian rations?"

Eaton made no public reply, but the thinly veiled accusation was too much for Sam Houston. One evening he waylaid Stanbery on a Washington street and beat him into submission with a hickory cane.

"MOST DARING OUTRAGE AND ASSAULT," cried the *United States Telegraph,* in Washington, D.C. Stanbery's fellow Congressmen were almost as upset as Stanbery himself; Congressional remarks were privileged, and in any event not to be answered so rudely. Former Congressman Sam Houston was forthwith ordered to stand trial in the House for contempt of Congress and breach of privilege.

The trial lasted a month. Houston was represented by Francis Scott Key, better known for writing "The Star-Spangled Banner" than for his legal talent. His performance was so bad that Houston took over his own defense. On the night before his summation, he sat up drinking with friends, and in the morning felt poorly. "I took a cup of coffee but it refused to stick," he later wrote. "After something like an hour had passed, I took another cup and it stuck, and I said, 'I am all right,' and proceeded to array myself in my splendid apparel"—bought with money from Jackson.

Houston's speech was masterful: "When a member of this House, entrenched in his privilege, brands a private citizen in the face of the whole nation, as a fraudulent villain he renders himself answerable to the party aggrieved. . . . It is not my rights alone, but the rights of millions that are involved here." He spoke for nearly an hour, leavening his discourse on the perils of legislative tyranny with fragments of his own verse. At the end, he pointed to the American flag, and cried: "So long as that flag shall bear aloft its glittering stars, so long shall the rights of American citizens be preserved safe . . . till discord shall wreck the spheres—the grand march of time shall cease—and not one fragment of all creation be left to chafe the bosom of eternity's waves."

The oration brought down the House. Houston, of course, had to be found guilty as charged. But his sentence was the merest of wrist taps. Speaker Andrew

Stevenson paid him a number of handsome compliments, then concluded: "I forebear to say more than to pronounce the judgment of the House which is that you be reprimanded at this bar by the Speaker, and I do reprimand you accordingly."

Years later, Houston told a journalist for *Harper's Magazine:* "I was dying out, and had they taken me before a justice of the peace and fined me ten dollars it would have killed me. But they gave me a national tribunal for a theatre, and that set me up again."

Fully alive once more and burning with enthusiasm, Houston turned his thoughts to Texas. Surely there, in that great, raw land about which his friends, the Whartons, still wrote him, he would find scope for his energy and a chance to recover from his great reverses. He called on his old friend in the White House, and Jackson gave him the opportunity to make his comeback: a Presidential mission to Texas.

A new mood was emergent in the Texas colonies. The turbulent frontiersmen and mountaineers—the "leather stockings" whom Stephen Austin had tried in vain to keep out—were becoming impatient with Austin's conciliatory ways and complaisant attitude toward Mexico. What they wanted was, in effect; an America in Texas, and they wanted it soon. Inevitably, this put them on a collision course with the Mexican government.

Under the liberal Constitution of 1824, Mexico was ostensibly a democracy with power distributed among the states. But for eight years, in a paroxysm of political maneuvers and revolts, the government had swung between liberal Federalism and Centralist dictatorship. The Texans, with their democratic American heritage, favored the liberal policies of the Mexican Federalists, who at least had some concept of states' rights. But in the early 1830s, Mexico's government was in the hands of a dictatorial Centralist, Anastacio Bustamante, who distrusted the self-willed Texans and had no intention of granting reforms in state government. Indeed, he was moving against them.

The Texans traced their troubles with Bustamante to 1828, when the alarmed Mexican government sent General Manuel de Mier y Terán to investigate reports of the growing Americanization of Texas. Terán confirmed Mexico City's worst fears. Only in and around San Antonio were Mexicans predominant. East of that city and Goliad, Americans outnumbered Mexicans by 10 to 1. The few Mexicans scattered throughout East Texas were generally poor, illiterate farmers and laborers. The Americans, on the other hand, were industrious, relatively affluent, and—according to Terán—overweeningly ambitious. It was inevitable, he felt, that they would seize control unless swift and decisive action was taken. In his report to the government, Terán advocated the establishment of a chain of military posts, and urged that substantial numbers of Mexicans be settled in Texas to balance the Americans. "Either the Government occupies Texas now," he warned, "or it is lost forever."

Bustamante's Centralist government reacted by passing a law on April 6, 1830, that went beyond Terán's recommendations. It not only provided for the military occupation of Texas, with garrisons to be manned by convict soldiers who were to remain as settlers upon completion of their terms, but it also decreed an absolute end to all American immigration.

Just as Texan hopes for fair treatment seemed at their nadir, a new champion of Federalism came upon the scene. He was General Antonio López de Santa Anna; and the Texans saw him as their savior from an intolerable situation. Instead he was to become not only the ultimate dictator of Mexico but a powerful and vicious adversary to both Texas and Houston.

Santa Anna was tall and theatrically handsome, spare but wide in the shoulders, given to enhancing his appearance with gaudy, bemedaled uniforms and Napoleonic cocked hats. He was a womanizer, an opium eater, a phobic so terrified of water that he could barely

---

INCIDENT AT GONZALES—THE TRIGGER TO WAR

The shots that touched off Texas' war of independence were fired at the town of Gonzales on October 2, 1835, by Texas volunteers who refused to surrender a cannon to a Mexican detachment. The Mexicans were routed, and the engagement—sometimes called the "Lexington of the Texas Revolution"—provided immediate ammunition for those who argued that open rebellion was the only alternative to dictatorial Mexican rule. Among the most prominent of the rebels was William Harris Wharton, a militant lawyer, who returned from the camp of the volunteers to bring news of the action and distribute the dramatic call to arms at right.

FREEMEN OF TEXAS
To Arms!!! To Arms!!!!
"Now 's the day, & now 's the hour."

CAMP OF THE VOLUNTEERS,
Friday Night, 11 o'clock;
October 2, 1835.

Fellow Citizens:—

We have prevailed on our fellow citizen Wm. H. Wharton, Esq. to return and communicate to you the following express, and also to urge as many as can by possibility leave their homes to repair to Gonzales immediately, "armed and equipped for war even to the knife." On the receipt of this intelligence the Volunteers immediately resolved to march to Gonzales to aid their countrymen. We are just now starting which must apologize for the brevity of this communication. We refer you to Mr. Wharton for an explanation of our wishes, opinions and intentions, and also for such political information as has come into our hands. If Texas will now act promptly; she will soon be redeemed from that worse than Egyptian bondage which now cramps her resources and retards her prosperity.

DAVID RANDON,
WM. J. BRYAND,
J. W. FANNIN, Jr.
F. T. WELLS,
GEO. SUTHERLAND
B. T. ARCHER,
W. D. C. HALL,
W. H. JACK,
WM. T. AUSTIN,
P. D. McNEEL.

P. S. An action took place on yesterdy at Gonzales, in which the Mexican Commander and several soldiers were slain—no loss on the American side.

Copy of a letter from John H. Moor, to Messrs. Stepp, Sutherland & Kerr, and to all whom it may concern.

Gonzales, Oct. 1st, 1835.

I inform you that we have about 150 men, and are expecting more troops hourly, and earnestly request that you should spare no pains to send us as much aid as possible. Our situation requires that all of Texas should now aid us. It is the most important crisis that the people of Texas have ever experienced, and our welfare for the future, does depend a great deal on first stroke th... ... is now i...

thrown upon them, has brought the place to the door of starvation. Bread is out of the question with them, and they have no hopes of obtaining meat, except eating their horses or pillaging from the Colonists. The Volunteers are determined never to return until St. Antonio has fallen, and every soldier of the Central Government has be...

William Harris Wharton

... to send them supplies, for Provisions and Ammunition, &c. Columbia and San Felipe ought to, & I have no doubt will do the same. If subscription papers are started, the people will liberally contribute. Let me again implore you to turn out promptly and universally and repair to Gonzales. In this case we will conquer, and that suddenly. Ours is no rebellious or revolutionary or voluntray warfare. It has been forced upon us. Justice, liberty, the consitution, ...

bring himself to cross a river. But as a soldier, Santa Anna was a man of skill, a cool tactician and charismatic leader. In 1829, on the east coast of Mexico, he shattered a Spanish invasion aimed at overthrowing the revolutionary government. The victory won him enormous popularity in Mexico. He took to calling himself the "hero of Tampico," or grander still, the "Napoleon of the West."

Utterly unprincipled, greedy for wealth and fame, he was described by one of his generals as "a man drunk with ambition." He frequently declared, "Man is nothing; power everything!" He also is said to have announced: "Were I made God, I should wish to be something more."

But at the outset the Texas settlers knew nothing of this. When Santa Anna launched a Federalist military campaign to unseat Bustamante, the Texans saw him only as a man fighting for their own ideals and they wished fervently for his success.

Meanwhile, they had Bustamante and the new law of 1830 to contend with. As it turned out, Stephen Austin was able to use his diplomatic skills to soften the effect of the restrictive statute. He became friendly with General Terán, and persuaded him to intercede with his superiors in the Bustamante government. A few troop contingents arrived in Texas and made sporadic efforts to collect customs. But they could not halt the flood of Americans pouring across the Red and Sabine rivers and spreading inland.

All the law of 1830 really accomplished was to put the Texans on notice and undermine Austin's assertions of Mexican good will. A militant faction of set-

Goliad was a vital Mexican supply base before it was captured by the Texans on the seventh day of their revolution. Shown as it looked in 1834,

tlers, long in the minority, began to grow. It found recruits among the rougher, more volatile — and now entirely illegal — newcomers. A trivial but infuriating event soon fanned the sparks of revolt.

In 1831, John Davis Bradburn, a Kentucky-born mercenary colonel in the Mexican Army, arrived to command the garrison at Anahuac, a small American community on Galveston Bay. He was an arrogant and stupid man. Within a few months, for no apparent reason, he abolished the settlement of Liberty and confiscated the colonists' land. When they protested, he declared martial law and arrested several of the more outspoken. Enraged beyond argument, 160 colonists marched on the garrison to rescue their friends. Another group, en route to Anahuac with artillery to reinforce their demands, was intercepted by a Mexican garrison at Velasco, at the mouth of the Brazos River, 80 miles away. There, in a short, sharp fight, five soldiers and 10 colonists were killed before the Mexicans threw down their arms and fled.

The date was June 26, 1832. It was the first bloodshed of what was to become the Texas revolution, and it frightened the Texans. Fearing retribution, they thought it fortunate that Santa Anna was conducting a military campaign against the dictator Bustamante. And when it became clear that Santa Anna would soon succeed, the Texans hastened to assure him of their loyalty to the republic and its constitution. Santa Anna, they were confident, would lend a sympathetic ear to Texas aspirations.

In eager anticipation, the Texans held a convention in San Felipe in October 1832 to prepare formal pro-

the village was dominated by a church and fort, where the insurgents found quantities of powder and lead later used in the siege of San Antonio.

posals requesting more self-government for Texas. For eight years, Texas had been linked with Coahuila as a minor partner in the state of Coahuila y Texas, with minimal representation in the state congress. The tie was a major bone of contention for the Texans, who wished to run their own affairs. Some of the more radical Texans were already advocating absolute if not immediate independence from Mexico. But the majority were loyal to Mexico and prepared to cooperate with any government that would grant Texas a greater degree of autonomy. William Wharton, representing the radical element, stood for president of the convention. Austin, leader of the loyalists, defeated him. But Austin's influence—as evidenced by the very fact of Wharton's challenge—was beginning to wane.

The convention first drafted a petition of support and congratulation for Santa Anna, coupling it with a request for repeal of the anti-immigration law of 1830. The colonists then advanced the majority's most ardent hope: separation from Coahuila, and full Mexican statehood for Texas.

So deeply was Mexico plunged into the civil war that the documents never reached Mexico City. But it scarcely mattered. In January 1833 came the welcome news that Santa Anna had driven Bustamante from the presidency. Exuberant, the Texans called a new convention for April 1 to expand and redefine for Santa Anna their ideas on statehood.

It was during this time of turmoil and hope that Sam Houston first set foot in Texas.

He rode 180 miles south to Nacogdoches from the Red River, passing his nights comfortably in the woods. When he reached Nacogdoches, the largest American village in Texas, he visited with two friends of earlier times: Henry Raguet, late of New Orleans, who ran a general store; and Adolphus Sterne, whom he had known in Nashville and who was now the wealthiest and most influential man in Nacogdoches. After a few days he rode on to San Felipe, hoping to meet Austin. The *empresario* was away. But Houston found a kindred spirit: Jim Bowie, his drinking companion from the *Red Rover*. Bowie had settled in Texas four years before and cut a commanding figure among both Americans and Mexicans. He had married a beautiful Mexican girl, Mariá Ursula de Veramendi,

daughter of the leading family in Coahuila y Texas.

The two men sat down to Christmas dinner in San Felipe. Afterward they went to San Antonio, where Bowie introduced Houston to the Veramendis and other prominent Mexicans. From San Antonio, Houston went north to the Comanche camp, to fulfill his token mission for President Jackson by conducting extensive but inconclusive peace talks with some tribal chiefs. Finally he returned to San Felipe. Austin was at home. The two men—the originator of the Texas dream and the man to whom the power of Texas would ultimately flow—talked privately for several hours.

They could hardly have been more dissimilar. Austin was introspective, diplomatic, idealistic, and pledged to fulfill the obligations of a Mexican citizen; Houston was loquacious, aggressive, flamboyant and uncompromisingly American.

Austin probably suspected Houston of being a militant adventurer, representative of the new breed that was prying loose his hold on Texas. Apparently he even felt a touch of envy tinged with self-pity. "A successful military chieftain is hailed with admiration and applause and monuments perpetuate his fame," he once wrote to his cousin Mary Holley. "But the bloodless pioneer of the wilderness, like the corn and cotton he causes to spring where it never grew before, attracts no notice. No slaughtered thousands or smoking cities attest his devotion to the cause of human happiness, and he is regarded by the mass of the world as a humble instrument to pave the way for others."

In fact, some Texans were already looking to Houston for leadership. Returning to Nacogdoches, he found that the townspeople had nominated him to be their delegate at the forthcoming convention in San Felipe. Houston was honored. At about the same time, he wrote Andrew Jackson a long letter. "I am in possession of some information that may be calculated to forward your views, if you should entertain any, touching the acquisition of Texas by the United States," he began. "That such a measure is desirable to nineteen-twentieths of the population of the Province, I can not doubt. They are now without laws to govern or protect them. Mexico is involved in civil war. The Government is essentially despotic and must be so for years to come. . . . The people of Texas are determined to form a State Government and separate from Coahuila,

COLONEL MILAM

GENERAL CÓS

and unless Mexico is soon restored to order and the Constitution revived and re-enacted, the Province of Texas will remain separate from the Confederacy of Mexico. If Texas is desirable to the United States, it is now in the most favorable attitude perhaps that it can be to obtain it on fair terms."

It was a startling suggestion to make to the President of the United States. If Jackson was as alarmed as the first time he heard such a suggestion in connection with Houston, his reaction is lost to history; there is no record of a Presidential reply. Nevertheless, Houston—after spending a few weeks in Texas, traveling some 500 miles and listening to a sampling of talk—was quite right in concluding that Texas was a most impermanent part of Mexico. Yet this newest of Texans, with his propensity for the dramatic, had overstated the case. The Texans were not yet ready to revolt. They still thought they could work things out with Santa Anna.

Houston settled down quietly in Nacogdoches. He studied Mexican law with his usual intensity and soon had a thriving practice, much of it dealing with land transactions. In a letter to a cousin he wrote, "Jack, Texas is the finest portion of the globe that has ever blessed my vision."

And he was back in the political arena that was the breath of life to him. As the new convention opened in San Felipe on April 1, 1833, it immediately became apparent that this time the radicals were in the majority. Again, both Austin and Wharton stood for president of the convention—but now Wharton won.

The convention under Wharton was not notably more militant than the previous one. There was no call to arms, no declaration of independence. Its main consequence was another petition to Mexico City for statehood. But this time the Texans added a constitution for the new state. Houston helped draft it.

A boldly American document that in many ways echoed the Constitution of the United States, it took no account of the Mexican political structure. It declared that "all power is inherent in the people, and all *free* governments are formed upon their authority." It called for a bicameral legislature, which was anomalous to the Mexican system. Any Mexican reading the proposed constitution would have to conclude that the Texans had lost interest in accommodating to Mexico.

Even the convention was an affront. It was citizen action, and in 1833 that was not the Mexican way.

Before adjourning, the convention chose 39-year-old Stephen Austin to take the petition and constitution to Santa Anna in Mexico City. Austin's health was failing, but there was no one else qualified to go. A decade after his first trip to Mexico City, he set out again—to endure a month of tossing at sea down the east coast of Mexico to Vera Cruz and another seven weeks of grueling overland travel.

In Mexico City, the government was in turmoil. Santa Anna was already destroying the very people who had supported him. In a series of cunning moves, he had begun the ruination of the Federalists. First he would permit their reforms, then nullify them as ineffective; next, he would encourage new reforms, only to cancel them for the same reason. There was just enough truth to his charges, when backed by Santa Anna's enormous prestige, to make the Federalists seem like fools and bunglers. At least they seemed so in Mexico City where the upper classes were never noted for their dedication to democratic reform.

In the midst of all this, the ailing Stephen Austin arrived with the convention documents from San Felipe. He was appalled to learn of Santa Anna's erratic behavior, and deeply discouraged when Mexican officials curtly brushed him aside. On October 2, 1833, after 11 weeks in Mexico City, he sent an undiplomatic letter back to the predominantly Mexican city council in San Antonio. Misjudging the sentiment of its members, Austin declared that Texans should make their own laws and form Texas as a separate state within the Republic of Mexico, whether the national government liked it or not. "The fate of Texas depends upon itself and not upon this government," he said. "The country is lost if its inhabitants do not take its affairs into their own hands."

It was a most indiscreet letter for a man of Austin's experience. Perhaps he wrote it because, as he said in a private letter, "I am so weary that life is hardly worth having." Whatever his reasons, the letter had a disastrous effect on Mexican functionaries in Texas. To them it was a trumpet blast of rebellion and they sent it to the government in Mexico City.

But bureaucracy and the mails being what they were, Austin's letter was slow to circulate. Meanwhile, mat-

Texas volunteers overwhelm Mexican soldiers defending San Antonio in December
1835. After capturing the city, the Texans let their foes return home and even gave
them arms for protection against Indians.

ters improved for Austin. He managed an interview
with Santa Anna, who had no knowledge as yet of
Austin's angry letter, and obtained several concessions.
On separate statehood, Austin got nowhere; but he
did win repeal of the immigration restrictions in the
law of 1830 and that was no small advance.

With this heartening news Austin set out for home.
As he traveled northward, his unfortunate letter was
speeding southward. When the letter finally arrived in
Mexico City, it caused an even greater storm than in
San Antonio. Santa Anna's officials interpreted it as
an American plot to separate Texas from its moth-
erland. They immediately sent a courier to Saltillo, capital of Coahuila y Texas, ordering the authorities to
find Austin and arrest him forthwith. They did not
have far to look. On reaching Saltillo, the unsuspecting

Austin went to the commandant general's office to pay
his respects, as was his polite custom. He was quickly
seized, sent back to Mexico City under guard, and
clapped into prison. For three months, Austin was
kept in solitary confinement. Then he was moved to a
somewhat more comfortable cell, allowed to have
books and write letters. Austin was in anguish. After
all his efforts on behalf of Mexico, he was now seen as
the archrevolutionary. Yet despite the aberration of his
letter, he still fervently sought peace. Fearing that
his imprisonment would precipitate revolution, he
wrote home imploring the Texans, "Keep quiet, dis-
countenance all revolutionary measures or men. Have
no more conventions."

A curious quiet settled over the Texans. They were
obeying Austin's admonition to keep calm and were en-

couraged, too, by the resumption of immigration, which the Mexicans permitted despite their rage at Austin. Also a serious problem absorbed their attention. In 1833, a cholera epidemic swept Texas and many colonists died. From San Antonio Jim Bowie sent his wife, Ursula, and their two babies to safety at her parents' home in Monclova; but cholera struck that area and killed all five, while Bowie escaped entirely. Wild with grief, he all but drowned himself in whiskey.

Houston had returned to Nacogdoches after the convention to resume his law practice and write letters to what he called the "U. States" about the abundant land of Texas. As always he drank heavily. On one such night, finding him talkative, a friend asked what had really happened between him and Eliza Allen. The man reported that Houston's loose expression suddenly froze; he stood up, mounted his horse and rode off into the night.

Late in 1833, Houston filed for divorce from Eliza, claiming only that they were irreconcilably separated. A few weeks after, this lifetime nonbeliever gave his name as Don Samuel Pablo Houston and joined the Catholic Church, as was required of all landowners.

The Texas revolution was still brewing, but relative calm prevailed into 1835. Like Austin, Houston urged patience; the "unrestrained ebullitions of feeling . . . would be likely to plunge Texas into a bloody struggle with Mexico, *before she was prepared for it.*" With the modification of the law of 1830, thousands of new Texans were pouring in. In Saltillo a liberal Federalist legislature increased Texan representation from one to three seats; land was made even easier to acquire, and court reform was ordered.

The lull, of course, could not last. In Mexico City, Santa Anna was moving toward open dictatorship; he installed a puppet congress and rammed through law after law undermining the federal structure established by the Constitution of 1824. Taking aim at Zacatecas, a strongly Federalist state bordering Coahuila, he ordered the local militia disbanded; and when the state government resisted, he sent a column of regular troops to sack the capital. Simultaneously, Santa Anna dispatched an army under his brother-in-law, General Martín Perfecto de Cós, to Saltillo to depose the Federalist governor of Coahuila y Texas and his advisory council. The Governor and his people fled toward Texas, but Cós's troops pursued and captured them.

The Texans found themselves divided into a war party and a peace party that still hoped somehow to get along with Santa Anna. Those who looked to Sam Houston for a signal were disappointed. It was a time, he told his friends, to remain calm; Texas yeomen were not yet ready for a war.

The final showdown began in mid-1835 after the Mexican Army reopened the garrison and customs post at Anahuac. The commander was a petty tyrant and before long he had jailed two merchants for agitating against onerous import taxes. It was a relatively minor affair, but annoying enough so that on June 21, a court day in San Felipe, Texans in numbers gathered to talk about what, if anything, they should do to aid the imprisoned merchants. In the midst of the debate, a Mexican courier suddenly came galloping through the crowded streets. The Texans seized him and read off the three messages he carried. One was from Cós addressed to the *alcalde* of San Felipe, stating that civil government in Coahuila y Texas had been suspended; Cós was to be in complete charge. Another from Cós assured the detested commander at Anahuac that a contingent of troops was on its way to bolster his garrison. The third—and most upsetting—was from another Mexican general to the Anahuac commander: it said that when Santa Anna's army had completed the subjugation of Zacatecas, Santa Anna would personally lead the troops on a punitive sweep across Texas to discipline the upstart Americans.

When word of the dispatches circulated, Texas sentiment swung solidly behind the war party. Public meetings were held in San Felipe and the Texans decided to expel the Anahuac garrison before Cós's troops arrived. William Barret Travis, a flamboyant young lawyer, rallied a force of 25 men and a cannon and set out from San Felipe. The tiny army reached Anahuac on June 29, 1835, and fired a single cannonball. Next morning, the Mexican officer and his 44 troops surrendered and promised to leave Texas.

Travis returned to San Felipe in triumph—to find that people had changed their minds and were condemning his rashness. They wrote an apologetic letter to the commander of Anahuac saying that "it was not by the vote of the majority nor by the will of the inhabitants that those persons were authorized to commit that outrage against the supreme government." Travis wrote his own apology, saying that "there only wants a good understanding between the Government and the people of Texas to set all things right."

But Cós would not be mollified. He demanded that Travis be arrested, and this the Texans would not do. It was one thing to denounce Travis for a fool, quite another to turn him over to a Mexican firing squad. Yet some sort of action was urgently needed. Cós was moving his troops into Texas to enforce his demands, and Texans would have to fight or submit.

At this point, in mid-August, William Wharton issued a call for another convention to be held on October 15, 1835. And now, more than two years after leaving for Mexico City with hopeful petitions in hand, Stephen Austin came home. By a quirk of Mexican politics he had been released under a general amnesty. He arrived in Texas on September 1, and the anxious Texans turned to him for counsel. They found him radically changed. Austin had observed Santa Anna at close range in Mexico City and found him to be a "base, unprincipled bloody monster. . . . War is our only recourse. No halfway measures, but war in full."

Events began to outrun plans. Word came that Cós was nearing Texas with a force of trained regulars. The settlers began to rally. Fall was a convenient time for war because most of the crops were in. All over Texas men oiled their weapons, packed powder and shot and food in their blankets, instructed their wives on caring for the place, and set out to repel Cós.

In what began as an unrelated move and ended as a catalyst in the gathering storm, the Mexican commander at San Antonio, Colonel Domingo de Ugartechea, sent a detachment 70 miles east, to Gonzales, to take from the settlers a small brass cannon given them in 1831 for defense against Indians. Actually, the cannon was virtually useless. But it was important symbolically to keep it from the Mexicans, and the Texans at Gonzales intended to do just that. They sent out word for help.

The Texans who were marching to intercept Cós heard the call and turned toward Gonzales. They gathered in dozens and scores and, together with the men of Gonzales, they mounted the cannon on an oxcart and strung it with a challenging banner: COME AND TAKE IT. The 100 dragoons who had come to take it

met 160 settlers with long rifles at a ford on the Guadalupe River just south of Gonzales on October 2, 1835. The dragoons paused at the unexpected sight and the Texans opened fire.

The Texas revolution had begun.

And it seemed so easy. One Mexican was killed and the others retreated in haste to San Antonio. A bear hunt would have been more exciting. But the Texans were operating under a tragic misconception. What they failed to grasp was that Mexico had sent her worst soldiers to Texas. Often criminals, in effect serving a sentence, they were poorly fed, poorly housed, poorly paid, and poorest of all in military skill and motivation. They had little spine for fighting the independent and individualistic Texans.

In any event, the Texans were in no mood for sober appraisal. By now Cós was in San Antonio with 1,400 troops. But he had left a small detachment at Goliad 95 miles to the southeast to guard some powder and shot and to keep open his supply line to the sea. For the Texans, Goliad presented another irresistible target. At 11 p.m. on October 9, a small company of Texans slipped into Goliad, forced the door of a chapel in which Mexican troops were quartered, fought briefly, and accepted another surrender.

Volunteers were now pouring into Gonzales. Soon there were 500 men. But they were without provisions or command. They elected their officers, obeyed only when they chose, and recognized no commander in chief. Finally, Austin was urged to come to Gonzales. When he arrived, the men elected him as overall commander because he was the one man they all knew and trusted. He did not especially want the job, for he was not a soldier, much less a field commander, and he was exhausted. The prison experience had broken him. He was only 42 but looked much older; his face was lined and he had a persistent cough. In fact, he had little more than a year to live. But the army needed somebody, and Austin was there.

All the while, Houston had been waiting in Nacogdoches, trying lawsuits and winning them, biding his time and watching sentiment build. When word came of fighting at Gonzales, he accepted a draft as troop commander in Nacogdoches and issued a call for volunteers: "The morning of glory is dawning upon us. The work of Liberty has begun." Then he set out for

General Antonio López de Santa Anna guides his prancing horse in this contemporary engraving. Elected Mexico's president in 1833, he became dictator in 1835 and vowed to crush the rebellious Texans.

San Felipe as delegate to the October convention, now called a consultation.

At Gonzales the troops remained in turmoil. The men were all volunteers, not formally enlisted, and they came and went as they pleased; Austin noted at one point that 150 had gone home for warmer clothing. Nevertheless he organized the men into companies as best he could. Then his army, some 300 strong, de- cided to attack San Antonio, and Austin could only go along. Noah Smithwick was one of the volunteers and recorded his impressions of the first Texas army as it began its march to San Antonio on October 13: "Buckskin breeches were the nearest approach to uni- form and there was wide diversity even there, some being new and soft and yellow, while others, from long familiarity with rain and grease and dirt, had become hard and black and shiny. Boots being an unknown quantity, some wore shoes and some moccasins. Here a broad-brimmed sombrero overshadowed the military cap at its side. Here a big American horse loomed up above the nimble Spanish pony, there a half-broke mustang pranced beside a sober, methodical mule. A fantastic military array to a casual observer, but the one great purpose animating every heart clothed us in a uniform more perfect in our eyes than was ever donned by regulars on dress parade."

The ragtag army marched toward the enemy, flying a flag portraying the Gonzales cannon and its slogan: "Come and take it." The cannon itself, hauled by longhorn steers, lost its wheels before the army got halfway to San Antonio and was abandoned.

As the Texans approached San Antonio on October 27, a party of 90 men under Jim Bowie scouted ahead and was attacked the next day by 400 Mexican cavalry. Noah Smithwick was with Bowie and remembered him cautioning, "Keep under cover, boys. . . . We haven't a man to spare." The Mexicans brought up artillery, but abandoned it under devastating Texan fire. The Texans then turned the Mexicans' own weapons against them. Sixty Mexicans were killed; the survivors fled. Only one Texan was lost.

Still another victory. But if the Texans now held the enemy in low esteem, they were not so foolhardy as to attack the 1,400 regulars, under Cós, entrenched in San Antonio. The Texans settled down to a siege.

When Houston reached San Felipe, he found the consultation unable to meet for lack of a quorum, since many of the delegates were under arms, 150 miles away outside San Antonio. Houston joined them there, riding into camp on a little yellow Spanish stallion, his long legs nearly touching the ground. The Texans were in their customary disorder. Austin could not control them, but Houston politely refused when Austin offered him command. The timing, Houston felt, was wrong; he had come to round up delegates.

The consultation was essential to clarify the Texans' position and place a stamp of legitimacy on their actions. But they were unwilling to release the delegates among them. Houston and Austin joined forces in the debate, and at last the Texans agreed to release all delegates who were not staff officers. This stipulation unfortunately deprived the consultation of not only Austin but Wharton and Travis as well. The meeting would simply have to get along without them.

The convention began in San Felipe on November 3, 1835. Anson Jones, who had been two years in Texas and would later serve a term as president of the republic, briefly attended the consultation as an observer and was not impressed. "There appeared to me a plenty of recklessness and selfishness," he noted, "but little dignity or patriotism. I was introduced to Bowie — he was dead drunk; to Houston — his appearance was anything but decent or respectable, and very much like that of a broken-down sot and debauchee."

The primary issue was to decide whether Texas was fighting for independence from Mexico or in defense of the Constitution of 1824. The war party wanted a declaration of independence; the peace party argued for support of the constitution — they would oppose the dictatorship of Santa Anna, but would do so as loyal Mexicans. Surprisingly, Houston took the latter view. In a powerful speech, he argued that to declare independence would be to antagonize the liberal Mexicans who sympathized with the Texans, and add to Santa Anna's strength.

The delegates to the convention declared support for the Mexican constitution and established a provisional state government. Houston was appointed commander of all troops except for those at San Antonio; Austin was authorized to go to the United States to appeal for war funds and volunteers; and command of the army at San Antonio was turned over to an old Indian-fighter, Edward Burleson.

By this time, conditions in the Texan camp outside San Antonio had begun to disintegrate. Food was in short supply, and the men who had turned out with such giddy enthusiasm in late summer were inadequately clad for the cold early December weather. Their resolve crumbled under the waiting and the chill. Some of them began to drift back to the warmth of their homes and families, planning for spring planting. In a council of war the field officers, overruling Burleson, voted to withdraw the volunteers to the safety of either Goliad or Gonzales.

Ben Milam was one volunteer in the Texan camp who viewed the plan with acute displeasure — particularly when a Mexican deserter and three Americans who had escaped from imprisonment in San Antonio

PROCLAMATION

OF

SAM. HOUSTON, COMMANDER-IN-CHIEF

OF THE

ARMY OF TEXAS.

HEAD QUARTERS,
WASHINGTON, TEXAS,
DECEMBER 12, 1835.

CITIZENS OF TEXAS,

Your situation is peculiarly calculated to call forth all your manly energies. Under the republican constitution of Mexico, you were invited to Texas, then a wilderness. You have reclaimed and rendered it a cultivated country. You solemnly swore to support the Constitution and its laws. Your oaths are yet inviolate. In accordance with them, you have fought with the liberals against those who sought to overthrow the Constitution, in 1832, when the present usurper was the champion of liberal principles in Mexico. Your obedience has manifested your integrity. You have witnessed with pain the convulsions of the interior, and a succession of usurpations. You have experienced, in silent grief, the expulsion of your members elect from the State Congress. You have realized the horrors of anarchy, and the dictation of military rule. The promises made to you have not been fulfilled. Your memorials for the redress of grievances have been disregarded; and the agents you have sent to Mexico have been imprisoned for years, without enjoying the rights of trial, agreeably to law. Your constitutional executive has been deposed by the bayonets of a mercenary soldiery, while your Congress has been dissolved by violence, and its members, either fled, or were arrested by the military force of the country. The Federation has been dissolved, the Constitution declared at an end, and centralism has been established. Amidst all these trying vicissitudes, you remained loyal to the duty of citizens, with a hope that liberty would not perish in the republic of Mexico. But while you were fondly cherishing this hope, the Dictator required the surrender of the arms of the civic militia, that he might be enabled to establish on the ruins of the Constitution, a system of policy which would forever enslave the people of Mexico. Zacatecas, unwilling to yield her sovereign rights to the demand which struck at the root of all liberty, refused to disarm her citizens of their private arms. Ill-fated state! her power as well as her wealth aroused the ambition of Santa Ana, and excited his cupidity. Her citizens became the first victims of his cruelty, while her wealth was sacrificed in payment for the butchery of her citizens.

The success of the usurper determined him in exacting from the people in Texas, submission to the central form of government; and to inforce his plan of despotism, he despatched a military force, to invade the colonies, and exact the arms of the inhabitants. The citizens refused the demand, and the invading force was increased. The question then was, shall we resist the oppression and live free, or violate our oaths, and bear a despot's stripes? The citizens of Texas rallied to the defence of their constitutional rights. They have met four to one, and by their chivalry and courage, they have vanquished the enemy, with a gallantry and spirit which is characteristic of the justice of our cause.

The army of the people is now before Bejar, besieging the central army within its walls. Though called together at a moment, the citizens of Texas, improvised as they were in the necessary munitions of war and supplies for an army, have maintained a siege of months. Always patient and untiring in their patriotism and zeal, in the cause of liberty, they have borne every vicissitude of season and every incident of the soldier, with a contempt of peril which reflects immortal honor on the members of the army of the people.

Since our army has been in the field, a consultation of the people, by their representatives, has met, and established a provisional government. This course has grown out of the emergencies of the country: the army has claimed its peculiar care. We were without law, and without a constitutional head. The Provisional Executive and the General Council of Texas are earnestly engaged in the discharge of their respective duties, preparing for every exigency of the country; and I am satisfied, from their zeal, ability, and patriotism, that Texas will have every thing to hope from their exertions in behalf of the principles which we have avowed.

A regular army has been created, and liberal encouragement has been given by the government. To all who will enlist for two years, or during the war, a bounty of twenty-four dollars and eight hundred acres of land will be given. Provision has also been made for raising an auxiliary volunteer corps, to constitute part of the army of Texas, which will be placed under the command, and subject to the orders of the commander-in-chief. The field for promotion will be open. The terms of service will be various. To those who chose to tender their services for or during the war, will be given a bounty of six hundred and forty acres of land: an equal bounty will be given to those who volunteer their services for two years: if for one year, a bounty of three hundred and twenty acres; and to those who may volunteer for a shorter period, no bounty of land will be given, but the same liberal pay, rations, &c., will be allowed them as other members of the army. The rights of citizenship are extended to all who will unite with us in defending the republican principles of the Constitution of 1824.

Citizens of Texas, your rights must be defended. The oppressors must be driven from our soil. Submission to the laws, and union among ourselves will render us invincible; subordination and discipline in our army will guarantee to us victory and renown. Our invader has sworn to exterminate us, or sweep us from the soil of Texas. He is vigilant in his work of oppression, and has ordered to Texas ten thousand men to enforce the unhallowed purposes of his ambition. His letters to his subalterns in Texas have been intercepted, and his plans for our destruction are disclosed. Departing from the chivalric principles of civilized warfare, he has ordered arms to be distributed to a *portion of our population*, for the purpose of creating in the midst of us a *servile war*. The hopes of the usurper were inspired by a belief that the citizens of Texas were disunited and divided in opinion, and that alone has been the cause of the present invasion of our rights. He shall realise the fallacy of his hopes, in the union of her citizens, and their ETERNAL RESISTANCE to his plans against constitutional liberty. We will enjoy our birth-right, or *perish in its defence*.

The services of five thousand volunteers will be accepted. By the first of March next, we must meet the enemy with an army worthy of our cause, and which will reflect honor upon freemen. Our habitations must be defended; the sanctity of our hearths and firesides must be preserved from pollution. Liberal Mexicans will unite with us. Our countrymen in the field have presented an example worthy of imitation. Generous and brave hearts from a land of freedom have joined our standard before Bejar. They have, by their heroism and valor called forth the admiration of their comrades in arms, and have reflected additional honor on the land of their birth.

Let the brave rally to our standard!

SAM. HOUSTON,
Commander-in-chief of the Army.

By order,

GEORGE W. POE,
Acting Adjutant-General.

Printed by Baker and Bordens, San Felipe de Austin.

brought the news that Mexican morale was cracking.

Milam was a Welshman from Kentucky who had been involved in Texan affairs even before Austin. He had done a lot of fighting in his 47 years, and had seen the inside of at least one Mexican prison cell after being accused of conspiring to proclaim a republican form of government in Texas. The idea of walking away from the enemy—and a demoralized one at that—was particularly offensive. Milam expressed his views. He then drew a line in the dust and shouted: "Who will go with old Ben Milam into San Antonio? Who will follow old Ben Milam?" Hundreds of voices roared in response.

On the morning of December 5, 1835, some 300 Texans in two columns drove into San Antonio, with Milam in command of one unit and Francis W. Johnson the other. They fought Cós's troops to the middle of San Antonio and took possession of two sturdily built houses near Military Plaza—the same plaza across which Moses Austin had walked so long ago and met Bastrop and set his Texas plan in motion. One was the De La Garza house; the other was the mansion of the Veramendis, Jim Bowie's late in-laws. From these strongholds the Texans fought their way from house to house, from street to street, from plaza to plaza under heavy artillery fire. The Mexicans' aim was so poor that their cannonades knocked down more Mexican walls than they hurt Texans. After the first assault, Milam and Burleson sent a joint dispatch to the provisional government reporting on the state of the Texan volunteers: "They have so far had a fierce contest, the enemy offering a strong and obstinate resistance. It is difficult to determine what injury has been done him; many killed, certainly, but how many cannot be told. On our side, ten or twelve wounded, two killed."

On the third day of fighting, Ben Milam took a bullet in the head and died instantly. Francis Johnson took over Milam's command as well as his own and the Texans, spurred by the loss of the man who had inspired them, fought on like demons.

Cós began to panic. He was not used to this street fighting, nor to such blazing determination. He entrenched his troops in the Alamo mission but their nerve was gone: 179 men and six officers deserted and fled. The Texans brought up their cannon and mercilessly battered the walls. By the fifth day of fight-

ing, Cós had had enough. He sent out a white flag and a jubilant Burleson marched into San Antonio to accept the Mexican general's surrender of some 1,100 officers and men.

It was a brilliant victory for the Texans: so few against so many; so important a quarry at their mercy.

And then Burleson let them go. He accepted a pledge from Cós that he would never again fight Texans or the Constitution of 1824. Then he provided Cós and his troops with enough weapons and powder to protect themselves against Indians, and sent them marching back across the Rio Grande.

The Texans' courtesy to Santa Anna's commander was a measure of their unwillingness to break all ties with Mexico, an echo of their repeated assurances of loyalty to a constitutional government. And though in the last 42 months they had bloodied Mexican noses some half-dozen times, they still thought that they and the Mexicans could somehow manage to get along.

Indeed, with their overwhelming triumph at San Antonio, they believed that they had won their war. All Texas went wild with celebration. The Mexican Army was whipped, driven off Texan soil, and now all that remained was for Texas to establish statehood within the Mexican republic. The provisional government called for a new convention to meet at Washington-on-the-Brazos on March 1, 1836, to form a more effective state government. Burleson relinquished his command; the Texas irregulars drifted back to their homes.

Sam Houston seemed the only man in Texas who realized that the humiliating defeat of Cós was sure to draw reprisals. He issued a call for troops. The war had just begun, he said: "Our habitations must be defended. Our countrymen in the field have presented an example worthy of imitation. Let the brave rally to the standard." Now, more than ever, it was necessary to recruit and train a disciplined force to "meet the enemy with an army worthy of our cause." And time was short. "The campaign cannot, in my opinion," he declared, "be delayed with Safety to the country much longer than the 20th of February or the first day of March, at farthest."

He might as well have been talking to himself. There was no rallying to the standard. The Texans were sure that relations with Mexico could be easily handled. They were, of course, wrong; the tests were all ahead.

76

3 | The Alamo: victory in death

In the broad perspective of warfare the Alamo could never be counted a major battle. Only 183 Texans defended the rundown old mission against 4,000 besieging Mexican troops under Santa Anna. And the Mexicans' final assault at dawn on March 6, 1836, killed every Texan in barely 90 minutes.

But for sheer fury and bloodshed, for desperate bravery and clawing ha-tred, the Alamo must rank among the most dramatic battles of all time. The Texas commander, Lieutenant Colonel William Travis, fought atop the wall (right) until he was shot off it. Down below him, Davy Crockett flailed away at his attackers until he was overwhelmed. Across the compound, a Texan made an attempt to blow up the Alamo's magazine, but was killed before he could set fire to the powder.

In the end, eight Mexican soldiers were killed for every defender. Santa Anna ordered the bodies of the Texans to be burned. To Americans all over Texas, as the grim news reached them, the lesson was clear: it was a war for victory or death. And they forged a battle cry that would echo around the world: "Remember the Alamo!"

77

Commandancy of the Alamo—
Bejar, Feby. 24th 1836—

To the People of Texas &
all Americans in the ____

Fellow citizens & cor___
I am besieged, by ___
or more of the Mex___
Santa Anna— ___
a continual Bomb___
cannonade for 24 ___
not lost a man ___
has demanded a su___
discretion, otherwise ___
are to be put to ___
the fort is taken— ___
the demand wi___
Not, & our flag ___
proudly from ___
Hall never ___
Then, I call ___
name of Liber___
& every thing de___
character, to ___

with all dispatch— The enemy is
receiving reinforcements daily &
will no doubt increase to three or
four thousand in four or five days.
If this call is neglected, I am determined to sustain myself as long as
possible & die like a soldier
who never forgets what is due to
his own honor & that of his
country—

Victory or Death.

William Barret Travis
Lt. Col. comdt.

P.S. The Lord is on our side—
When the enemy appeared in sight
we had not three bushels of corn—
We have since found in deserted
houses 80 or 90 bushels & got into
the walls 20 or 30 head of Beeves—

Travis

Ninety terrible minutes that forged a nation

"You can plainly see that the Alamo was never built by a military people for a fortress," Green Jameson sadly wrote to Sam Houston in January of 1836. Jameson was a 29-year-old Kentuckian who had left behind a San Felipe law practice to join the victorious Texas volunteers in San Antonio. Jameson may have been miscast as a lawyer anyway; by instinct, he was an excellent military engineer. When the Texans realized that inevitably the Mexicans would make an attempt to recapture the Alamo, Jameson took charge of making it secure. With mounting enthusiasm he set about the task of repairing walls and erecting gun positions.

Jameson was quite right about the Alamo never having been intended as a fortress. It was built in the mid-1700s by Franciscan friars as the Mission of San Antonio de Valero. Located on the little San Antonio River, across from the village of San Antonio de Bexar, it came to be known as the Alamo after a nearby grove of alamo, or cottonwood, trees. The Franciscans used it as a base for their proselytizing campaigns among the Indians until 1793, when it was abandoned in favor of a church in town. Eventually the Mexican garrison in San Antonio converted it into a barracks

Lieut. Colonel William B. Travis

and armory. And it was there that the ill-fated General Cós made his last, futile stand before surrendering to Ben Milam's Texas volunteers.

The mission church had long since collapsed, towers and dome tumbling into the nave, though its stone walls still stood. In addition to the ruined church, there was a two-story stone building known as the Long Barracks and a lengthy one-story structure called the Low Barracks. Except for about 75 feet lying open between the ruined church and the Low Barracks, the whole area was enclosed by stone walls, up to 12 feet high and in places two to three feet thick. The space delineated by the walls formed a compound of nearly three acres in a rough rectangle measuring some 250 by 450 feet.

The walls were strong enough, but they had no parapets from which men could fight. The Mexicans had left more than 20 cannon in the Alamo, but there were no platforms from which guns could fire over the walls. There were no embrasures carefully slitted in the walls so a cannon could sweep the field without exposing the gunners. And there was that gap of 75 feet. Jameson began to correct some of these failings.

He may have been one of the few men just then who was working with a clear-cut plan for the defense of Texas. Ever since Milam's victory, affairs in Texas had been getting more chaotic. The trouble flowed naturally from the confusion in which the Texans had established their provisional government. They were a new people, after all, without tradition or well-defined mutual interests, and they tended to divide whenever

Describing the plight of the besieged Alamo defenders in a dispatch dated February 24, 1836, their commander, William Travis, vowed to fight until "victory or death." Published widely, Travis' account won enormous sympathy for the Texas cause.

there was no immediate threat to force them together.

At the heart of the confusion was the question, still unresolved, of whether the future of Texas lay in self-governing Mexican statehood under the liberal Constitution of 1824—abrogated by the dictatorial Mexican President Santa Anna—or in outright independence. The Consultation of November 1835 at San Felipe had compromised on the issue. First, the delegates elected a legislative council that was ardently for statehood and then, with hardly a thought, they vested executive authority in the hands of Governor Henry Smith, a fiery and uncompromising advocate of independence. It was an impossible conflict of authority. Almost immediately, a fierce political fight arose that left Texas virtually without a government just when it needed firm leadership most. To make matters worse, the one man capable of providing guidance during this critical period was about to leave Texas. Stephen Austin had been named one of the provisional government's representatives to the United States. He left for New Orleans in January 1836 to negotiate loans and enlist American support for the Texas cause.

Many of the men who had taken San Antonio had gone home to their farms and families after the battle. But those who remained under arms, bolstered by new volunteers, were looking for action. There arose a harebrained scheme to invade the Mexican city of Matamoros at the mouth of the Rio Grande. Matamoros contained many Mexican liberals, opposed to the dictatorship of Santa Anna. The plan's originators thought the Matamoros liberals would welcome a Texas expeditionary force; they argued that by capturing the city the Texans would be showing their support of the liberal movement and the Constitution of 1824.

Sam Houston thought the idea insane and refused to lead the expedition. Governor Henry Smith was equally opposed. But the legislative council in San Felipe was all for the idea, believing that it would advance the cause of statehood. Early in January, the council bestowed its blessing on the plan, and chose as commander a very strange man named James Fannin.

Fannin was 32, a tall, gangling Georgian who had arrived in Texas in 1834 and quickly built up a profitable business in land speculation and slave-trading. He had performed well as a volunteer in the fighting around San Antonio, and Houston had offered him a colonelcy in the regular army he was organizing. Fannin boldly requested a brigadier's commission, which he said he could handle "better than any officer." Houston had made him settle for the colonelcy. Now Fannin seized the new opportunity and set out to recruit volunteers for the adventure.

Governor Smith's anger over the Matamoros expedition turned to fury a few days later, when he received a plaintive letter from Colonel James Neill, who was in command at San Antonio. Like Houston, Neill was one of the few Texans who were concerned that the Mexicans might soon be back in force. And since the Alamo was the only fortified position on the logical invasion route from Mexico, he had expected reinforcements. Instead, he found his skimpy garrison being stripped for the Matamoros expedition. Neill reported that 200 men had already left for the rendezvous at Goliad, leaving him only 104 to defend both San Antonio and the Alamo. Furthermore, the departing column had taken the pick of the supplies, most of the food and virtually all of the medicine.

"It will be appalling to you to learn . . . our alarming weakness," wrote Neill. His men were destitute, "many of them having but one blanket and one shirt." And he had no money for pay or provisions: "If there has ever been a dollar here I have no knowledge of it."

Outraged, Smith railed at the legislative council for encouraging the Matamoros venture at the expense of the San Antonio garrison. He called the council members "Judases," "scoundrels," "parricides," and adjourned the body until March 1—when a new convention would meet in the town of Washington-on-the-Brazos to decide once and for all on a permanent Texas government. But the council refused to disband. Loosing its own billingsgate, it called Smith "vulgar and depraved," a man whose "low, blackguardly and vindictive" language disqualified him to be governor, and voted to replace him with the lieutenant governor. With both governor and council claiming authority and neither having it, San Felipe was in the grip of chaos.

The situation was hardly better at Goliad, where hundreds of men were milling around, working themselves up to capture Matamoros. Though Houston was technically commander-in-chief of the Texas army, he had no control over Fannin, who felt responsible only to the legislative council. Nevertheless, Houston went

TEXAS
FOREVER!!

The usurper of the South has failed in his efforts to enslave the freemen of Texas.

The wives and daughters of Texas will be saved from the brutality of Mexican soldiers.

Now is the time to emigrate to the Garden of America.

A free passage, and all found, is offered at New Orleans to all applicants. Every settler receives a location of

EIGHT HUNDRED ACRES OF LAND.

On the 23d of February, a force of 1000 Mexicans came in sight of San Antonio, and on the 25th Gen. St. Anna arrived at that place with 2500 more men, and demanded a surrender of the fort held by 150 Texians, and on the refusal, he attempted to storm the fort, twice, with his whole force, but was repelled with the loss of 500 men, and the Americans lost none. Many of his troops, the liberals of Zacatecas, are brought on to Texas in irons and are urged forward with the promise of the women and plunder of Texas.

The Texian forces were marching to relieve St. Antonio, March the 2d. The Government of Texas is supplied with plenty of arms, ammunition, provisions, &c. &c.

Issued before news of the Alamo's fall but confident of a Texan victory, a New Orleans ad offers free land to attract volunteers.

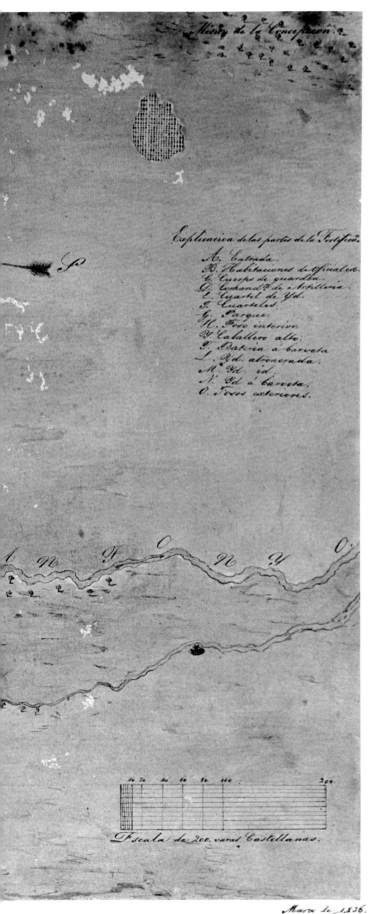

to Goliad, where he strolled about talking to the men. He was magnetic, as usual, and the men listened as he made a vivid speech describing the perils that lay ahead for Texas: the Mexicans were coming and they would be seeking bloody revenge for the humiliating defeat at San Antonio. There would be fighting aplenty without fatal side adventures. He shook enough of the Texans so they decided to pause at Goliad and think it over.

Typically, Houston was almost the only man in Texas with a clear assessment of the immediate situation. In Santa Anna, the Texans faced an enemy coldly determined to crush them so completely that they would never rise again. Two years of military dictatorship had done nothing to improve the general's character. He affected brilliant uniforms and surrounded himself, even on campaign, with pomp and luxury. Separate coaches carried his linen bedsheets and gold ornaments, and courtiers arranged for pretty women wherever he went. Having acquired great power, he thirsted for more; now he took political differences as personal challenges, an attitude that dictated the violence with which he subdued the liberal state government of Zacatecas and the destruction he planned for Texas. But cruelty and love of power and luxury made him no less effective a general. He was a charismatic leader whom his troops admired and feared, and a trained and gifted professional military man.

Santa Anna had virtually emptied Mexico's national treasury to build up his army, spending $7.5 million in 1835 alone. It gave him a disciplined and loyal force far different from the sorry collection of convicts

SANTA ANNA'S MAP OF THE BATTLEFIELD

A map of the San Antonio-Alamo area, prepared by a Mexican army engineer for one of Santa Anna's generals, provided the besiegers with a topographical view of the battlefield, the north-south axis running from left to right. The town of San Antonio de Bexar was bordered by San Pedro Creek to the west and a horseshoe bend in the San Antonio River to the east. About 400 yards of rolling terrain lay between the Alamo (upper left) and a footbridge that crossed the river at the town's east end. The outlying houses of La Villita, which the defenders destroyed to deny shelter to the enemy, were to the south of the Alamo and lined part of its west wall. Due east of La Villita, two rows of trees edged the road leading to Gonzales, 70 miles away.

the Texans had mainly faced up to that time. And now, as the Texans around Goliad debated what to do, Santa Anna was massing 6,000 of these superior troops. Most were gathering at Saltillo, 200 miles south of the Rio Grande. An advance force of 1,500 men under General Joaquin Ramirez y Sesma was already camped on the Rio Grande near Laredo.

Santa Anna's plan was not complicated: he would grind up the Texans by marching 440 miles along the old Spanish road—*El Camino Real*—all the way from the Rio Grande to the Sabine River, which formed the eastern border with the United States. The route would take him through San Antonio, but he expected no serious opposition there—or anywhere else.

To Sam Houston, the Mexican strategy was obvious; there was only that one main route through Texas. He had his own ideas about how to fight the overwhelming Mexican numbers, and those ideas did not include a static defense of stone walls, at the Alamo or elsewhere. Texas should unite all its men and supplies in a flexible army under a single command and meet the Mexicans in the field. The Texans' rifles were much more accurate at greater range than the Mexican muskets. The Texans could operate as ranging cavalry; they knew the terrain. They would be fighting for their own land, and if they remained fluid and harassed the Mexican troops—strike, feint, fall back, divide the enemy, strike again, as their forefathers had done with the British Army 60 years before—they had a fair chance of wearing down Santa Anna's huge forces, stretching his supply lines until they could be cut, stopping him and finally defeating him.

Houston was even more certain that the Alamo was not the place to fight when another message arrived from Neill, written on January 14. In a tone of outrage and dismay, the colonel complained that his men "have been in the field for the last four months, they are almost naked, and this day they were to have received pay for the first month of their enlistment."

The pay had not come and "almost every one of them speaks of going home, and not less than twenty will leave tomorrow, and leave here only about 80 efficient men. We are in a torpid, defenseless situation, we have not horses enough to send out a patrole or spy."

At once, Houston ordered Neill to remove the Alamo's guns, blow down its walls and abandon the place "as it will be impossible to keep up the station with volunteers." Houston sent the orders with his old and trusted friend Jim Bowie and, on January 19, Bowie rode into the Alamo heading a detachment of 30 men who were to assist the evacuation. Houston had great faith in Bowie. "There is no man on whose forecast, prudence and valor I place a higher estimate," he had once said, and it seems clear that Houston expected Bowie to make sure that his orders were carried out.

But the 40-year-old Bowie was not a military man. He was an adventurer—a splendid fighter and instinctive leader. Of military tactics he knew very little. So it was probably natural for him to feel that the Texans had to defend the Alamo, that it was the only obstacle that stood between the Mexicans and an unimpeded drive across Texas. In any event, neither Bowie nor Neill seems to have taken Houston's orders very seriously. Neill replied with a laconic note saying that he lacked the mules, horses or oxen to haul away the cannon left by the Mexicans in December. And despite Neill's gloomy assessments, Bowie found the garrison in a mood to fight. In fact, the men had passed a formal resolution: "We consider it highly essential that the existing army remain at Bexar." Green Jameson, who was hard at work building fortifications, thought that if properly supplied the Texans at the Alamo would "do duty and fight better than fresh men, they have all been tried and have confidence in themselves."

Bowie's arrival gave everyone heart. He quickly renewed his warm ties with the Mexicans in San Antonio—warmer, perhaps, because of the terrible loss of his family—and obtained from them food, supplies and forage, which had not been offered before. One of Bowie's men, James Bonham, organized a rally on January 26, at which the men passed a resolution demanding more supplies from the government, emphasizing that "we cannot be driven from the post of honor." The first signature on the resolution was Bonham's. The second was that of Jim Bowie.

A few days later, Bowie spelled out his convictions in a prophetic letter to Governor Smith: "The salvation of Texas depends in great measure in keeping Bexar out of the hands of the enemy. It serves as the frontier picquet guard, and if it were in the possession of Santa Anna, there is no stronghold from which to repel him in his march toward the Sabine. . . . Colonel Neill and myself have come to the solemn resolution that we will rather die in these ditches than give it up to the enemy." He then added a chilling postscript: "I have information just now from a friend whom I believe, that the forces at the Rio Grande are 2 thousand complete; he states further that 5 thousand more are a little back and marching on. Perhaps the 2 thousand will wait for a junction with the 5 thousand. . . . My informant says that they intend to make a descent on this place in particular, and there is no doubt of it."

Bowie's informant, one of several Mexicans in San Antonio who risked their lives to spy for the Texans, was basically correct, both as to numbers and intentions. In fact, Santa Anna was already moving north.

On January 25, Santa Anna had held a grand review at Saltillo. It was a dazzling spectacle, with massed bands blaring and dozens of red, white and green Mexican tricolors flapping in the breeze. Senior officers trotted by on horseback, attired in scarlet and blue uniforms, while behind them trudged the infantry in their white cotton uniforms and tall hats. Then came the cavalrymen, their ribboned lances held high and metal breastplates gleaming in the sun.

Santa Anna took their salutes. He was a handsome man on his fine horse, and he moved with a restless energy that reflected his strength and assurance. Supremely confident, he considered the campaign already over, its execution but a formality. He had even authorized a special medal for his soon-to-be-victorious soldiers.

On February 1, Santa Anna led his army out of Saltillo toward the Rio Grande. There were two infantry brigades, a brigade of cavalry, artillery units and a tough battalion of fighting engineers — the *Zapadores,* or sappers. A smaller force of infantry and cavalry, under General José Urrea, separated from the main army and headed for Matamoros. Santa Anna's spies had told him about the Texans' expedition, and he planned a warm welcome for them at Matamoros. Meanwhile, Santa Anna prepared to join Sesma's men on the Rio Grande and launch his drive into the heart of Texas.

Even as this formidable force began closing in on them, the Texans remained uncertain as to what they should do. Neill and Bowie were calling for a stand at the Alamo and pleading for help. But Fannin, still dreaming of capturing Matamoros, refused to budge his troops scattered around Goliad. Actually, at this point not many people in the splintered Texas government took the Mexican threat very seriously. Governor Smith did, but his powers were limited by the dispute with the legislative council. Sam Houston of course did, but Houston was a commander without an army, completely frustrated in his defensive strategy. In a disgusted letter to Governor Smith on January 30, he said that it was impossible for him to function as commander-in-chief and asked to be relieved. Instead, Smith placed him on leave until March 1, and Houston made himself useful in the only way left: he went off to use his prestige with the Cherokee Indians to make certain that they would not attack the Texas rear while Santa Anna threatened its front.

At about that time, the man whose name would be most indelibly linked with the Alamo, William Barret Travis, rode into the fort at the head of 25 men. Travis was 26 years old, a tall, sinewy, raw-boned man with reddish hair and a ruddy face. An unadulterated romantic, he believed that he was marked for a "splendid future" or an early death. Travis was born in South Carolina and grew up in Alabama, where he married, had a child and read the law. Like so many who came to Texas suddenly, he had problems at home. He suspected that his wife had taken a lover; there was talk around Texas that he had killed the man he thought involved, but no one seemed to have the facts. ⊙

Davy Crockett's adventures in life and legend

By far the most famous defender of the Alamo, better known even than Jim Bowie, was a graying, 49-year-old folk hero from Tennessee: Davy Crockett. In a wilderness where men survived by their marksmanship, Crockett was renowned for his ability to shoot the wick off a candle at 300 feet. He was a great hunter who once bagged 47 bears in a single month, and a fearsome fighter who was tested in frontier battles throughout the War of 1812.

No less was Crockett a spell-binding backwoods orator and humorist, who loved spinning such tall tales as the one about the time he idly pointed his rifle at a tree and a raccoon yelled out, "Don't shoot, Davy, I'll come down." So popular did Crockett become in Tennessee that he was elected to Congress in 1827, 1829 and 1833. At one point, there was even talk of Crockett for Vice President on the Whig ticket. But his political career ended bitterly in 1835 when he was defeated for re-election by a Democratic candidate supported by President Jackson. Crockett reportedly told his erstwhile constituents that he was going to Texas and they could go to hell.

Yet if Crockett was gone, he was hardly forgotten. That same year an en-terprising Nashville publisher printed the first issue of what was called "Davy Crockett's Almanack." Along with the usual almanac information, it featured a number of illustrated fantasies, ostensibly by Davy, that expanded wildly on his many exploits.

The periodical was a huge success, in no small part due to Crockett's martyrdom at the Alamo. Over the next 20 years, five different publishers put out 55 issues of the almanac, filled with wonderfully impossible accounts of Davy scrapping with panthers and bears, sinking pirate ships, and outwitting everyone from Indians to redcoats.

In this almanac cartoon, a knife-slashing, rifle-shooting Davy Crockett rides his pet bear, Death Hug, down a 90-foot waterfall to escape from an army of Spaniards.

In a Crockett vs. bear encounter, his dog holds a leg, his wife rams a rail down its throat, a neighbor swings an ax at its head —and Davy readies a final knife thrust.

Believing pirates akin to Yankee swindlers and unworthy to be "kilt like Christians" — meaning, with a gun — Davy blows them up by shooting lightning from his eyes.

Defending New Orleans against the besieging British, Crockett charges into battle on an appropriate land-and-sea mount: an alligator carrying a cannon and ammunition.

Many of the almanac cartoons celebrated Crockett's heroic deeds at the Alamo. Here Davy fells Mexican soldier after Mexican soldier with lethal sweeps of his rifle butt.

With two blades in his chest and a bayonet in his back, Davy Crockett finally succumbs. The accompanying article mourned him as a man who "never war known to refuse his whiskey to a stranger."

Despite an intense fusillade of fire, Davy gives an enemy the old one-two, kicking him and lopping off his head at the same time. In all, according to the almanac, Crockett leveled some 200 Mexicans.

Travis had arrived in Texas in April 1831, applied for land and opened a law office in San Felipe. He mastered enough Spanish to facilitate his practice and soon he was successful and enjoying himself. A diary he kept during this period shows that he divided his spare time between pursuing women and reading romantic novels. He pored over the pages of Sir Walter Scott, and it is easy to assume that he saw himself as a flamboyant Scott hero.

Though young, Travis had a sense for command. It was he who had marched on the Mexican garrison at Anahuac the previous summer and accepted its surrender. When the revolution began, Travis persuaded Governor Smith to appoint him a lieutenant colonel of cavalry. And when one of Neill's angry letters arrived, the Governor asked Travis to recruit volunteers and march to San Antonio. He accepted with reluctance, arguing that "I am unwilling to risk my reputation with such little means, so few men, and them so badly equipped." Yet, in barely a week after his arrival, he had changed his attitude and had become caught up in the garrison's total commitment to defend the Alamo. On February 12, he wrote the Governor: "We consider death preferable to disgrace, which would be the result of giving up a Post which has been so dearly won, and thus opening the door for the Invaders to enter the sacred Territory of the colonies. I am determined to defend it to the last, and should Bejar fall, your friend will be buried beneath its ruins."

But if all doubts had been washed from Travis' mind, he found himself enmeshed in the petty bickerings that seemed to accompany any undertaking in Texas. Neill had been forced to go on leave because of illness in his family. He departed on February 11, leaving Travis temporarily in command. It was not a popular choice for most of the men of the garrison, who preferred the legendary Bowie. "I feel myself delicately and awkwardly situated," acknowledged Travis, and agreed to an election that overwhelmingly chose Bowie to be Alamo commander, with the rank of colonel.

Bowie was a sick man. Though he had seemed strong enough when he first arrived, his condition deteriorated rapidly. He probably was suffering from tuberculosis, and he may even have been in the early stages of typhoid-pneumonia. His resistance to alcohol was gone. His men drank with him and soon he was leading drunken parades through the streets of San Antonio, shouting and jostling people. Travis angrily wrote that Bowie was "interfering with private property, releasing prisoners . . . & turning everything topsy turvy." He added that he was "unwilling to be responsible for the drunken irregularities of any man."

Perhaps Bowie perceived the danger of the situation, for on the 14th he and Travis agreed on a joint command of the Alamo, with Bowie as head of the volunteers and Travis of the regulars. All decisions were to be made and signed by both men.

By now, Santa Anna and his vanguard were only 150 miles away, encamped on the Rio Grande at Presidio de Rio Grande. There he had joined Sesma's 1,500 troops, who had come upriver from Laredo, and was resting briefly until the remainder of the army arrived. While waiting, Santa Anna completed his plans for retribution. All leaders of the Texas revolt would be executed; all rebellious settlers would be expelled; their lands would be redistributed to selected French, English, German and Spanish immigrants.

Finally, on February 16, Santa Anna was ready. His 5,400 men and 21 cannon—accompanied by 1,800 pack mules, 33 four-wheeled wagons and 200 two-wheeled carts—began crossing the Rio Grande. On the other side they formed a long, dusty train that, one observer wrote, "more nearly resembled great convoys of freight than an army on the march."

Only a man as vain and as eager for revenge as Santa Anna would have ventured onto the barren plains below San Antonio in midwinter. There was little water and only a stubble of winter grass, inadequate to feed livestock. The nights were brutally cold; 50 yoke of oxen froze to death the first night after crossing the Rio Grande. Soon there was a trail of abandoned equipment and dead animals and men strung out behind. But the army continued to move and Santa Anna mercilessly whipped it forward.

It made no difference to Santa Anna that the Texans surely knew of his coming. But he would have been more than a little surprised at the curious calm that pervaded the Alamo. Like most of the Texans in the Alamo, Travis was sure that Santa Anna would wait for the new crop of spring grass before attempting to cross the plains from the Rio Grande to San Antonio. By that reasoning, the Mexicans would not arrive

The ordeal of a Mexican aristocrat who fought for Texas

Cheerfully will I encounter formidable dangers to assure my country's independence. I would joyfully perish on the field of battle shouting the war cry, God and Liberty, Victory or Death, of those heroes.

The time was February of 1837, just after the Texas war of independence, and the heroes were the Alamo dead, who were being belatedly buried with honors. But the officer who gave the funeral oration was not an American. He was a Texas-born Mexican named Juan Nepomucena Seguin, and his own life was one of courage amid grave danger and of high honor coupled with tragedy.

Scion of an old San Antonio family that first settled there in 1722, Juan Seguin came naturally by his affinity for the bold American colonists. His father, Erasmo, as *alcalde,* or mayor, of San Antonio in 1821, was one of the officials who greeted Stephen Austin on his first journey to Texas. During the years preceding the Texas revolution, the elder Seguin used his influence with Mexican authorities on behalf of the Americans.

A liberal like his father, Juan Seguin entered politics and in 1834, at the age of 28, was appointed political chief of the San Antonio district. He soon came to champion the Texans' demand for more self-government and grew to be an outspoken critic of the dictatorial policies of Mexico's President Santa Anna. Indeed, in September 1835, when General Cós marched against the rebellious Texans, Juan Seguin recruited a force of Mexican ranchers and led them against their countrymen. So distinguished was Seguin's conduct in the resulting victory at San Antonio that he won a commission as a captain of cavalry in the regular Texas army.

But for fate, Seguin would have perished in defense of the Alamo. He

Juan Seguin in 1838 as a Texas colonel

was among the 25 brave men who on February 3, 1836, rode in with Lieutenant Colonel William Travis to reinforce the pitifully small garrison. But on the night of February 25, when the Alamo had been surrounded by thousands of Mexican troops personally commanded by Santa Anna, Travis drafted an urgent plea for aid addressed to the Texas commander at Gonzales, 70 miles away. Because Seguin spoke Spanish and knew the terrain intimately, he was chosen to carry the message through enemy lines. He was on his way back, on March 6, when the Alamo finally fell to Santa Anna's overwhelming numbers, and the defenders' bodies were unceremoniously put to the torch.

As the Mexican Army pressed on, and the Texans — soldiers and settlers both — grimly retreated eastward, it was Juan Seguin who brought up the rear, following orders from Sam Houston not to leave any family behind. Seguin fought fiercely in the Battle of San Jacinto that won Texas its independence. "On this great and glorious day my company was conspic-

uous for efficiency and gallantry," he proudly recalled in his memoirs.

The Texans promoted him to lieutenant colonel and posted him to set up a military government in San Antonio until civilian rule could be reestablished. And it was there that he gave an honored burial to the ashes of the Alamo dead.

A life of service to Texas seemed in store for Seguin. He was elected to the Senate of the new republic in 1838, and twice won election as mayor of San Antonio. Then, quickly, it all turned to dust. The city was swarming with newcomers — "adventurers," as Seguin described it, "who were beginning to work dark intrigues against the native families. My countrymen ran to me for protection." Seguin's encounters with the volatile American newcomers sometimes ended in the use of force. Rumors circulated that he was a traitor in league with the Mexicans, who were then planning to invade and retake Texas. Eventually the campaign to discredit him reached a crescendo; Seguin fled for his life — and in 1842 sorrowfully crossed into Mexico "to seek a refuge amongst my enemies."

But Seguin found no peace. Typically, Santa Anna presented him with a cruel choice: either rot in jail or join a Mexican expeditionary force in a probing attack on Texas, and by "spilling my blood, vindicate myself." Seguin chose the latter, and went on to fight without injury in the campaign that saw Mexican troops retake and briefly hold San Antonio before returning to Mexico.

Seguin's service earned him the right to live in Mexico. But he never ceased to yearn for Texas, and in 1848, he was permitted to return home to the land whose cause he had "embraced . . . at the report of the first cannon which foretold her liberty."

until March 15, at the earliest—fully a month away.

Not even a report received on February 20 could shake Travis' conviction. On that day, a Mexican spy raced into San Antonio to say that he personally had witnessed the Mexicans crossing the river in force. Travis called his officers together for a council of war; it lasted for hours and in the end they decided to ignore the report as too implausible to be believed. When Travis finally got to sleep that night, the forward elements of the invading army were encamped on the Rio Hondo, less than 50 miles away.

Despite the Texans' incredulity, they were not totally unprepared. Green Jameson had done his work well with the limited resources at hand. The 75-foot gap between the ruined church and the Low Barracks was now closed by a high palisade of upright timbers backed by an earthen embankment from which riflemen could fire. Weak spots in the stone wall were reinforced with sloped banks of earth, firmly shored with timbers. Parapets of earth and timber lined the inside of the walls, permitting rifle fire in all directions.

In mounting the guns Jameson worked closely with a 26-year-old blacksmith named Almeron Dickerson, who commanded the Alamo's batteries. Dickerson was a muscular Tennessean who had settled in nearby Gonzales. After the capture of the Alamo, he had brought his young wife and baby daughter to San Antonio.

Dickerson had at least 18 cannon ready for service in the Alamo. They ranged from four-pounders to one huge gun that hurled an 18-pound ball. For this weapon Jameson's men built a large barbette, or sloped mound, in the southwest corner; situated there, the cannon commanded all of San Antonio. Four of the four-pounders were spaced along the parapet backing the newly built palisade between the church and the Low Barracks, while the larger eight-pounders were placed on platforms along the walls and within the plaza.

Jameson and Dickerson also utilized an ingenious artillery position that had originally been fashioned by the Mexicans within the roofless church. They had used debris to build a ramp running from the front of the church to the former altar site. There a scaffold of heavy timbers formed a gun platform, about 15 feet above the ground and sturdy enough to support three 12-pounders. Finally, a small gun was placed on top of the Long Barracks, where it could defend the eastern

approaches. Ultimately it would do terrible damage.

Ammunition was limited, so Sam Blair, a 29-year-old Tennessean and the Alamo's ordnance chief, chopped up horseshoes to provide deadly grapeshot. The second floor of the Long Barracks was converted into a hospital by Dr. Amos Pollard, the Alamo's chief surgeon. Pollard was 33, had practiced in New York before drifting south, first to New Orleans and then to Texas. By scrounging around San Antonio, he had somehow replaced virtually all of the medical supplies carried off by the Matamoros volunteers.

The other men of the Alamo garrison in the diversity of their ages and backgrounds formed a microcosm of Texas itself. They ranged from teenagers like William Malone, an 18-year-old Georgian who ran away to Texas because he was afraid to face his father after getting drunk, to Robert Moore, a 55-year-old private from Virginia, the oldest member of the garrison.

There was Marcus Sewell, 31, a shoemaker in England before emigrating to Gonzales; and Henry Warnell, 24, a onetime jockey from Arkansas who, after the death of his wife, left his infant son with friends and moved to Texas. Micajah Autry, 43, had drifted from North Carolina to Tennessee to Texas unsuccessfully trying to make a living as a teacher, writer, lawyer and storekeeper. Autry enlisted, in part, because of the generous grant of land promised to volunteers. Now he wrote to his wife from the Alamo: "I am determined to provide for you a home or perish."

David Cummings, 27, left Lewiston, Pennsylvania, in 1835 to deliver to Sam Houston a box of rifles provided by his father, a prosperous bargeman and a friend of Houston's. His errand done, he stayed on to fight. John Forsyth, 39, a native of New York, had been trained as a physician but had never practiced. He left home shortly after his wife's death in 1828, and was one of the volunteers recruited by Travis. John Flanders, 36, left the family factory in Massachusetts after a quarrel with his father and went to New Orleans, where he became caught up in the Texas adventure.

And finally there was the most famous enlisted man in the Alamo, Davy Crockett. He arrived unexpectedly on February 8, at the head of a dozen sharpshooters he called his "Tennessee Mounted Volunteers"—mostly men who had fallen in with him on the long ride from Nacogdoches to San Antonio. Crockett was nearly 50 and a storied figure on the frontier (pages 87-89). His arrival, with his country fiddle and the long rifle he called "Betsy," touched off a joyous celebration. Travis offered him a command, but Crockett turned it down with a stirring speech: "I have come to aid you all that I can in your noble cause . . . and all the honor that I desire is that of defending as a high private . . . the liberties of our common country."

Why did such a variety of men flow to Texas and end in the Alamo, where it was obvious that serious fighting lay ahead? There were two dominant motives, which a letter from a young Kentucky lawyer named Daniel Cloud summed up nicely.

Cloud was 22. The legal fees were skimpy at home and he had set out with another lawyer, Peter James Bailey, 24, to seek a livelier practice. At each place they visited they were confounded "by the coldness of the climate [and] the smallness of the docket." They turned southward and at Nacogdoches they joined Crockett's troop. "Ever since Texas has unfurled the banner of Freedom, and commenced a Warfare of liberty or death, our hearts have been enlisted in her behalf. . . . If we succeed, the Country is ours, it is immense in extent and fertile in its soil, and will amply reward all our toil. If we fail, death in the cause of Liberty and humanity is not a cause for shuddering."

Cloud probably spoke for most of his fellows at the Alamo: they were imbued with a genuine feeling for liberty inextricably linked with the conviction that, if they succeeded, their fortunes would be assured in the new country of Texas.

This pragmatic patriotism, coupled with the strategic estimate that this was the place to fight—the "post of honor"—led the men of the Alamo to expect full support from Texas. They knew that Fannin's men were still at Goliad—only 95 miles away—since the Matamoros expedition had never started. But Travis had received no reply from a message sent to Goliad on February 16, the first in what would become a series of increasingly urgent pleas for reinforcements. In fact, Fannin, the man who assured Houston that he could handle command "better than any officer," had decided to hole up in the Goliad mission, renamed Fort Defiance, to await a possible Mexican attack.

Now time was running out for the men at the Alamo. In late afternoon on Sunday, February 21, Santa Anna and his advance guard camped on the Rio Medina, only 25 miles from San Antonio. So close were the Mexicans to the Texans that Santa Anna considered a swift attack that very evening. Hearing a report that the Texans planned to attend a fiesta in San Antonio, he immediately ordered a column of dragoons to cross the river and race into San Antonio to take the dancing Texans by surprise. When a cloudburst caused the river to rise abruptly, the raid was called off.

By the next night, the Mexican advance units were in position to see San Antonio from the hills south of the town. At dawn on February 23, many of the panic-stricken inhabitants of San Antonio were hastily packing their belongings into carts and fleeing the town. Incredibly, Travis refused to believe that a Mexican army was at hand in strength. He posted a lookout in the belfry of the San Antonio church. When the man caught the flash of sunlight on shiny cavalry lances, Travis sent two trusted civilians to investigate: a doctor named John Sutherland and a merchant named John W. Smith. They reached a hill about a mile and a half from town and from its crest stared down at an awesome sight: a long line of Mexican cavalry assembled in battle formation as an officer galloped up and down with drawn sword.

The two men started back down the hill at such a pace that Sutherland's unshod horse slipped and fell, landing on the doctor's legs. He remounted in great pain and they galloped on. When the lookout saw them coming, he began ringing the church bell.

The Texans who had been living in San Antonio swarmed toward refuge in the Alamo, taking their families and Mexican friends with them. A Mexican woman, watching them hurry across the bridge, cried: "Poor fellows, you will all be killed." The ailing Bowie personally escorted the two sisters of his late wife and their children into the fortress. Almeron Dickerson left his cannons long enough to gallop to the house where his family was staying. His wife Susannah, a blond 18-year-old, was waiting for him with their 15-month-old baby Angelina. "Give me the baby!" Dickerson shouted. "Jump on behind and ask me no questions." In a moment, the entire family was galloping toward the Alamo.

When the gates were finally closed and barred, there were 150 fighting men in the Alamo, quartered in the

An improvised fortress too large to defend

The fortifications drawn to scale in this view of the Alamo as it appeared on the eve of the siege were the inspiration of Green Jameson, a 29-year-old Texas lawyer turned military engineer.

The most critical structures were the wood and earth platforms that partially protected sharpshooters and artillerymen along the 12-foot-high walls. On the southeast side, Jameson built a palisade of heavy logs to seal off a 75-foot gap between the church and the Low Barracks; he also constructed a semi-circular gun position, or "lunette," to guard the south gate. In the southwest corner, he put an 18-pound cannon to command the approach from San Antonio, and spotted remaining guns, ranging from four- to 12-pounders, at other strategic sites. A pair of eight-pounders in the plaza were last-ditch weapons in case the Mexicans broke through.

Makeshift as it was, the Alamo proved a mighty bastion. But its very size contributed to its doom; it sprawled across nearly three acres, giving 183 men a perimeter of about a quarter-mile to defend. It was a task, as one Alamo scholar commented, for which "a thousand men would have barely sufficed."

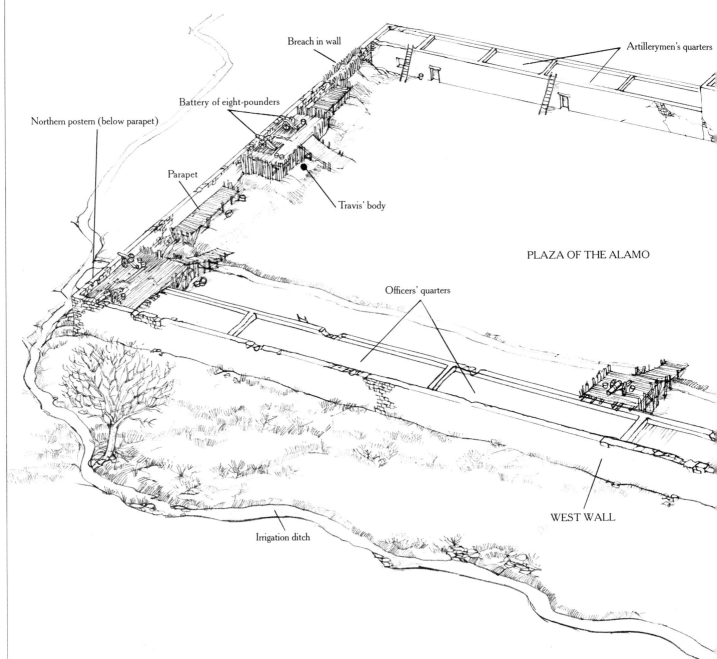

Breach in wall

Battery of eight-pounders

Northern postern (below parapet)

Parapet

Travis' body

Artillerymen's quarters

PLAZA OF THE ALAMO

Officers' quarters

WEST WALL

Irrigation ditch

94

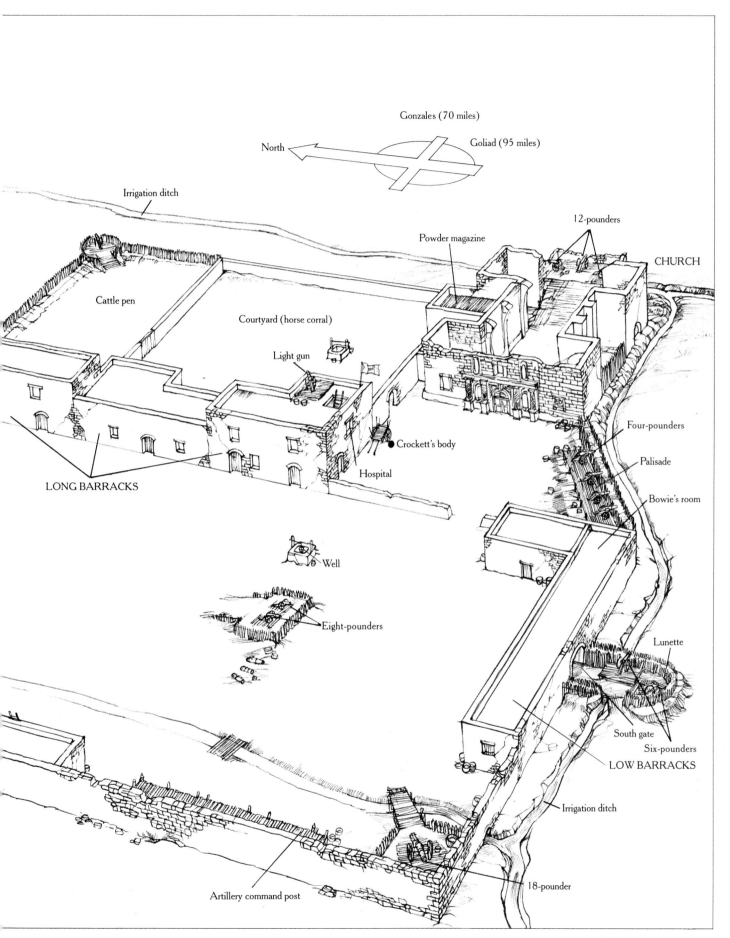

Gonzales (70 miles)

Goliad (95 miles)

North

Irrigation ditch

12-pounders

Powder magazine

CHURCH

Cattle pen

Courtyard (horse corral)

Light gun

Four-pounders

Palisade

Crockett's body

Bowie's room

Hospital

LONG BARRACKS

Well

Eight-pounders

Lunette

South gate

Six-pounders

LOW BARRACKS

Irrigation ditch

18-pounder

Artillery command post

Isaac Millsaps wrote this letter from the Alamo to his blind wife on March 3, while the defenders still expected help. When the Texans retreated east after the Alamo, Mrs. Millsaps and her seven children were left behind in Gonzales until Houston discovered the blunder and rescued them.

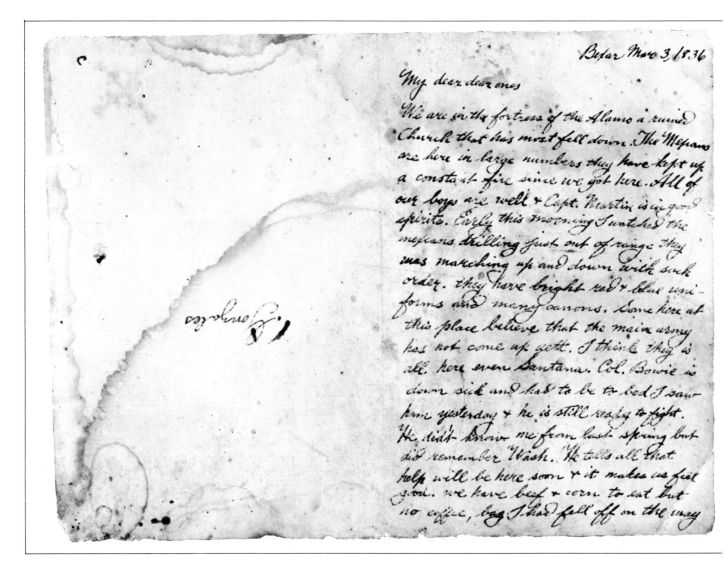

two barracks and smaller structures along the east and west walls. There were also about 25 noncombatants crowded into the old church, mostly women and children and including several black slaves brought in as servants by Travis and other officers. Travis listened to the report from Smith and Sutherland. There was still no word of help from Fannin at Goliad. The only other town close enough to send reinforcements was Gonzales, about 70 miles east of San Antonio. Travis scratched a message to the *alcalde* of Gonzales: "The enemy in large force is in sight. We want men and provisions. Send them to us. We have 150 men and are determined to defend the Alamo to the last. Give us assistance." In a postscript Travis urged that the message

be relayed at once to the government at San Felipe.

Sutherland and Smith rode out of the Alamo shortly after 3 p.m. Travis then dispatched a second messenger to Fannin demanding help from the troops at Goliad. Looking back from a small ford south of the Alamo, the couriers could see Santa Anna's cavalry beginning to ride into the main plaza of San Antonio.

Travis began to deploy his men for battle. Davy Crockett now said: "And here I am, Colonel, assign me to some place and I and my Tennessee boys will defend it all right." Travis posted Crockett and his men at the newly built palisade between the church and the Low Barracks, where he felt the fortress was most vulner-

96

here so it was all spilt. I have not
see Travis but 2 times since here he
told us all this morning that Fanning
was going to be here early with many
men and there would be a good fight.
He stays on the wall some but mostly
to his room. I hope help comes soon
cause we cant fight them all. Some
says he is going to talk some tonight
+ group us better for defence. If
we fail here get to the river with
the children all Texas will be
before the enemy we get so little
news here we know nothing.
There is no discontent in our
boys some are tired from loss
of sleep and rest. The mexicans
are shooting every few minutes
but most of the shots fall inside, +
do no harm. I dont know what
else to say they is calling for all
letters, kiss the dear children for
me and believe as I do that all
will be well + God protects
us all.

Isaac

If any men come through there
tell them to hurry with powder
for it is short I hope you
get this + know — I love you all

able. All of the men in the garrison were soon assigned positions, and got to work putting the final touches on Green Jameson's fortifications or foraging for badly needed supplies. Protected by the Alamo's guns, they quickly searched abandoned farm huts and fields just beyond the walls and hurried back with about 80 bushels of dried corn and nearly 30 steers and cows.

In the now-silent town of San Antonio, a flag was raised from the church belfry. It was not the familiar tricolor of Mexico, but a great red banner that coiled and snapped in the breeze. Every Texan recognized it as the ancient signal of no quarter for the enemy; Santa Anna would take no prisoners. Within the Alamo, Travis gave a command and the 18-pounder hurled an iron ball in answer. There was no answering fire, but soon a bugle call was heard that some interpreted as a request to parley. Bowie seized the opportunity to scribble a message to the Mexicans: it asked if they would agree to a surrender in which the Texans would be disarmed and allowed to return to their homes — virtually the same terms imposed on Cós and his men at the Alamo in December. Jameson agreed to carry the message under a white flag. He returned with a reply from an officer of Santa Anna's staff: the only terms were unconditional surrender.

Bowie's unilateral action infuriated Travis, who had belatedly sent out his own emissary to parley with the Mexicans — with the same result. His anger could have flared into a serious dispute over command, but illness was catching up with Bowie. The fever was rising within him. By morning he could not stand; he fell on his cot and full authority was in the hands of Travis.

The first pieces of Mexican artillery had come up during the night, and by daybreak on the 24th were dug in on the riverbank, 400 yards from the Alamo. The first rounds were fired from two nine-pounders that battered the walls and a five-inch howitzer that hurled shots into the Alamo. The Texans' great 18-pounder was dismounted, but no defender was hit.

During a lull in the bombardment, Travis took up his pen and wrote a message that eventually would travel around the world. It was sent to Gonzales but spread to New Orleans, to New York and Boston, and to Europe. The message, certified by the subsequent battle itself, fixed in the world's eye an image of gallantry and of the Texans not simply as rebels but as a new people inextricably linked with Americans.

Travis' document, which flowed over two pages of small note paper in his fluid, impatient hand, was addressed "To the People of Texas & all Americans in the world—" and said: "Fellow citizens & compatriots —I am besieged, by a thousand or more of the Mexicans under Santa Anna—I have sustained a continual Bombardment & cannonade for 24 hours & have not lost a man—The enemy has demanded a surrender at discretion, otherwise, the garrison are to be put to the sword, if the fort is taken—I have answered the demand with a cannon shot, & our flag still waves proudly from the walls—*I shall never surrender or retreat.* Then, I call on you in the name of Liberty, of patriotism & everything dear to the American character, to come to our aid, with all dispatch—The enemy is receiving reinforcements daily & will no doubt increase to three or four thousand in four or five days. If this call is neglected, I am determined to sustain myself as long as possible & die like a soldier who never forgets what is due to his own honor & that of his country—*Victory or Death."*

The last words were underlined three times. At dusk on the 24th the Alamo gates opened and Captain Albert Martin slipped out with the message that would alert the world.

But Texas itself was too disorganized to respond. Travis' second courier reached Fannin at Goliad on

the 25th after a hard two-day ride. The news that the Mexicans were actually in San Antonio finally stirred Fannin to action. He readied 320 men to march to the Alamo. But fate and his own fickle character were to conspire against Fannin's relief expedition. Setting out on the 26th, the men had gone only a few hundred yards when a supply wagon broke down. The column stopped while the wagon was being repaired and Fannin decided to wait until the next morning to start anew. Then somehow the wagon's oxen got loose during the night and it took most of the next day to recapture them. By late afternoon of February 27 — some

24 hours after the expedition had started out — it was ready to move again. But now Fannin was having second thoughts about the wisdom of leading his men to the Alamo. He called an impromptu council of war with his officers and they agreed that it would be best to return to Fort Defiance in Goliad.

Only the men of Gonzales responded to Travis' appeal for help, delivered by Sutherland and Smith on the 24th. They had recently formed a 25-man militia company under George Kimbell, a 26-year-old hatter who had come from New York to open a small shop in Gonzales. With courier Smith guiding them, they left on February 27 and, on the night of the 29th, picked their way slowly and carefully through the darkness and into the Mexican lines. At 3 a.m. on March 1, they rode up to the Alamo. They were fired on from the walls but, when one militiaman loosed a loud oath, the firing stopped, the gates flew open and the reinforcements rode in.

But Travis knew he needed many more men to defend the Alamo. There was a note of desperation in yet another message he had scrawled to Gonzales on the night of February 25. "It will be impossible for us to keep them out much longer. If they overpower us, we fall a sacrifice at the shrine of our country, and we hope posterity and our country will do our memory justice. Give me help, oh my Country!"

The courier chosen to deliver the message was Captain Juan Seguin, a prominent San Antonio Mexican who had cast his lot with the Texans (page 91). Seguin rode out that evening on Jim Bowie's fast horse, bluffed his way past a Mexican patrol and raced to Gonzales with Travis' futile plea.

The Alamo had been through a nerve-wracking week under sporadic daily bombardment. Miraculously, no Texan had yet been killed. At one point, the Mexicans had made a heavy probing attack and the Texans had beaten them back with rifle fire from the walls and cannon loaded with grape, leaving scores of dead Mexicans in the fields outside. But Santa Anna's army was growing as more units arrived. His troops surrounded the Alamo. There were batteries on several sides and each night, under the cover of darkness, the Mexican gunners dragged them closer and dug new earthworks to protect them. Santa Anna's patrols reconnoitered the Alamo's walls cautiously, since any area within 200 yards of the Alamo was deadly ground before the long rifles of the defenders.

A Mexican officer, Captain Rafael Soldana, later described a man firing from the palisade who could have been Davy Crockett. He was "a tall man, with flowing hair" who "wore a buckskin suit and a cap all of a pattern entirely different from those worn by his comrades. This man would rest his long gun and fire, and we all learned to keep at a good distance when he was seen to make ready to shoot. He rarely missed his mark, and when he fired he always rose to his feet and calmly reloaded his gun, seemingly indifferent to the

shots fired at him by our men. He had a strong, resonant voice and often railed at us. This man I later learned was known as 'Kwockey.'" However, the sharpshooters could not prevent the Mexican cannon from moving closer, and the walls of the Alamo took an ever-heavier pounding.

Inside, the Texans worked hard, shoring up the broken fortifications, resetting guns knocked from their mounts, digging trenches in the plaza and standing watch on the walls. Bowie's influence was still strong. Sometimes, when he was coherent, he had his cot carried among the men so he could encourage them. The Texans cooked and ate at their stations, and when the cannonading paused they talked or slept. Now and then, to keep the garrison's spirits up, Davy Crockett produced his fiddle and staged musical duets with John McGregor, a 34-year-old Scot from Nacogdoches, who played the bagpipes. According to one of the women bystanders, the contest was to see who could play loudest and longest—no one argued about best. And always the men speculated on the Texas troops they still felt sure would come marching to their aid. That is why they were so delighted by the arrival of the Gonzales contingent after six straight days of siege.

From their walls, the Texans could see more and more Mexican troops in San Antonio, and each morning the siege batteries were closer and the pounding against the walls more dangerous. The engineers hurried about inside, repairing weak places. On March 3, Travis decided to send out a last letter to be carried by John W. Smith. He described his situation: "At least two hundred shells have fallen inside of our works without having injured a single man; indeed, we have been so fortunate as not to lose a man from any cause, and we have killed many of the enemy. The spirits of my men are still high." Travis' hopes were still alive: "I look to the colonies alone for aid; unless it arrives soon, I shall have to fight the enemy on his own terms. I will, however, do the best I can and I feel confident that the determined valor and desperate courage heretofore exhibited by my men will not fail them." He was as sure as ever that this was the place to stand. He asked for supplies. "If these things are promptly sent and large reinforcements . . . this neighborhood will be the great and decisive ground. The power of Santa Anna is to be met here or in the colonies; we

Mexican infantrymen launch their final assault on the Alamo in this 1885 reconstruction by a Texas artist. Troops pour into the courtyard through the northern postern *(left)*, while a second force gets ready to breach the southern palisade under fire from Texans on top of the church.

had better meet them here than to suffer a war of devastation to rage in our settlements." Even if his men were "sacrificed to the vengeance of a Gothic enemy," he thought that "the victory will cost the enemy so dear, that it will be worse for him than defeat."

But Travis was not expecting to die. He gave Smith verbal instructions that the reinforcements were to bring plenty of ammunition and 10 days' rations. The Alamo's 18-pounder would be fired at dawn each day as a signal that the defenders had not surrendered.

Other men were busily scrawling notes to their friends and families, and Travis also took time to jot some personal messages. One was addressed to the man who had been caring for Travis' son Charles since the divorce. Another went to a woman in San Felipe who may have been his sweetheart. And still another went to a friend: "Let the convention go on and make a declaration of independence . . . and the world will understand what we are fighting for."

All of the notes were given to the trusty Smith. Shortly after midnight, while some of the men distracted the Mexicans by firing on them from the north wall, Smith slipped out through the south wall on a fleet horse and headed for Gonzales and San Felipe.

On Friday morning, March 4, the Mexicans' cannon were emplaced only 250 yards away and stone chips flew like hail across the plaza. All day long the bombardment continued and when it was resumed on the morning of the 5th, the Mexican gunners were firing from 200 yards — tantalizingly close to the effective range of the Texans' rifles. The walls were beginning to crumble faster than the weary defenders could shore them up and in the distance Mexican soldiers could be seen making scaling ladders.

A sense of doom began to penetrate the beleaguered fort. Davy Crockett spoke the feelings of many of the men when he said, "I think we had better march out and die in the open air. I don't like to be hemmed up."

At about 5 o'clock that afternoon Travis took advantage of a brief respite to summon his men. In the two days since sending out his last message, his attitude had changed. With no sign of reinforcements — and no hope that a relief column could break through the Mexican lines if help did come — Travis at last realized that he and his men were alone at the Alamo. He told them that and listed the options: surrender, try

A doomed Davy Crockett swings an empty rifle at on-rushing enemy soldiers in Robert Onderdonk's *Fall of the Alamo*. Though Onderdonk has Crockett defending the south wall gate *(right)*, Alamo survivor Susannah Dickerson saw his body nearer the chapel *(left)* after the battle.

to escape, or fight to the end. His own choice was to fight in order to delay the Mexican advance. But anyone who wanted to leave was free to try. Only one man came forward to accept the offer. He was Louis Rose, a soldier of fortune and veteran of the Napoleonic wars, who had ridden into the Alamo with Bowie. A survivor by instinct, he went over the walls in the dark and made his way safely through the Mexican lines. Every other man stayed.

At 10 o'clock on Saturday night, March 5, the Mexican guns fell silent. Exhaustion gripped the Texans. They had been on the walls with hardly a pause since the bombardment had begun 11 days before, eating and resting when they could. Now they slept, wrapped in blankets against the night's chill. Travis walked around the post and finally lay down on his cot in his clothes, his sword and his shotgun beside him.

Across the river in San Antonio, Santa Anna was drinking coffee and reviewing the plans for the final attack. His infantrymen would be divided into four columns—about 800 men each, it has been estimated. Two would attack the northeast and northwest corners; another would strike the east wall and the fourth would take the vulnerable palisade on the south. The cavalry, perhaps 300 strong, would be held to the east to pick off the Texans if they tried to break out. Santa Anna would direct the battle, with the fierce *Zapadores*—the fighting engineers—included in the 400-man reserve. In all, he would use about 4,000 men.

That afternoon, couriers had taken his orders to the unit commanders. His men were fed and advised to sleep. About midnight, their officers began awakening them. By 1 a.m. on Sunday, March 6, they were moving. They took muskets and 10 rounds of ammunition each, and some carried scaling ladders, picks and spikes. In position by 4 a.m., they lay on the chill ground, quiet and waiting. The moon was obscured by clouds.

It was still dark just after 5 a.m., the eastern sky taking on a faint glow, when the troops got ready. Their excitement grew and finally one man yelled, "Viva Santa Anna!" Hundreds echoed his cry as Santa Anna signaled to his bugler to sound the attack. The darkness was filled with the rumble of thousands of thudding feet as the Mexicans rushed toward the Alamo.

Captain John Baugh, Travis' adjutant and second in command, was on the walls. He shouted the alarm and

ran to Travis' room crying, "Colonel Travis! The Mexicans are coming!" Travis leaped up from sleep, seized his sword and a double-barreled shotgun and ran to the north wall. Out of the gloom came the running Mexican soldiers. The Texas riflemen opened fire from the walls and the gunners atop the church thrust loads of grape down the barrels and sent them howling at the running men below. A Mexican colonel leading one of the northern columns, Francisco Duque, was cut down in the first blast. The men behind him trampled his body as they ran on.

Travis jumped onto the north parapet. He slung his jacket on a peg by a cannon and cheered his men to their posts, his sword overhead, hoarse-voiced: "Hurrah, m'boys! Hurrah!" With the Texans' cannon firing over their heads and into the oncoming Mexicans, the riflemen drew careful beads on easy targets, fired, reloaded, fired again. Some of the men had stacked three or four loaded rifles at their stations, and got off all of them before reloading.

The attack did not go well. The column striking from the east was pinned by the murderous shot from the cannon on the church, and Crockett's men and the small guns on the palisade blew back the column assigned to take the south wall. On the north side, a few Mexicans reached the walls, safe from the Texas cannon which could not depress to reach them. But the bulk of both northern columns stopped and milled.

Travis was on the walls, shouting and exhorting the Texans. He fired both barrels into the mass of men below. Then a Mexican bullet struck him in the forehead. He dropped the shotgun over the wall and reeled back, tumbling down the embankment to the bottom, where he sat up stunned and staring. He was dying.

The Mexican officers whipped their men forward with the flats of their sabers. They came on again and, for the second time, the withering sheets of grape and rifle fire turned them. On the third thrust the column coming to the northwest corner drifted to the east. The eastern column, held down by fire, drifted to the north, and both merged with the northeast column. Now all three columns—a single mass of men, the front rows falling like grass before the scythe—came surging to the walls of the Alamo.

Their ladders were gone, dropped and trampled to kindling, and most of the spikes and picks had been lost in the carnage. The men huddled helplessly under the walls for some 15 minutes, out of range of the cannon but taking rifle fire from the walls directly overhead. But this was as costly to the Texans as to the Mexicans, for a man had to perch on the wall to shoot down and at that range the Mexican muskets were as effective as the Texas rifles. Surging along the walls, stung by the fire from above, the Mexican troops reached a redoubt that Jameson had built of earth and timber in front of a crumbled section of wall. Despite the bite of the bullets a general named Juan Amador began to climb the redoubt and his frenzied men climbed with him.

The Mexican Army band was playing the *Degüello* — the "fire and death call" that signaled total annihilation. And now Santa Anna committed his reserve. The *Zapadores* ran into the battle. The troops still behind those already at the walls were firing as rapidly as possible and the shots that were too low smashed into the men ahead who were struggling against the wall. Raked by both Mexican and Texan fire, they were frantic. General Amador reached the top of the redoubt, his men beside him, and tumbled over onto the parapet. The Mexicans were inside the Alamo.

At the same time, the attackers hurled themselves at the northwest corner and poured over faster than the Texans could work the guns. The first ones in cleared the parapets of the Texans, who were falling back, and opened the northern postern from the inside. Now, the Mexicans came through like a tide, bayonets gleaming. "I can tell you the whole scene was one of extreme terror," a Mexican soldier later wrote his brother. "After some three quarters of an hour of the most horrible fire, there followed the most awful attack with hand arms."

The Texans met the enemy in the open plaza. After a few minutes of vicious hand-to-hand fighting, Captain Baugh shouted the command to retreat to the Long Barracks. Swiftly, every Texan within earshot ran for the barracks, leaving the plaza to the Mexicans. It was the moment that the gunners who were handling the light gun on top of the barracks had been waiting for. They turned the gun around, lowered the barrel and sent charge after charge of grapeshot shrieking into the swarming Mexican soldiers below. Other Texan gunners whose positions had not been overrun turned their cannon around to rake the plaza with their loads of chopped horseshoes. The Mexican dead lay in stacks.

But when these guns were turned inside the Alamo, the Mexicans to the south were free to scale the walls. They topped the wall in the southwest corner, ran across the few yards and up the barbette that held the 18-pound gun, and bayoneted the gunners. Crockett's men, attempting to fight their way to the Long Barracks, turned to face the new threat and the Mexicans seized the palisade, effectively surrounding them in front of the church. The Texans fought hard, loading and firing, and finally fighting with knives and clubbed rifles as the Mexicans overwhelmed them.

A Mexican sergeant, Felix Nuñez, later described one who might have been Crockett — or any of his men: "He was a tall American of rather dark complexion and had on a long buckskin coat and a round cap without any bill, made out of fox skin with the long tail hanging down his back. This man apparently had a charmed life. Of the many soldiers who took deliberate aim at him and fired, not one ever hit him. On the contrary, he never missed a shot. He killed at least eight of our men, besides wounding several others. This being observed by a lieutenant who had come in over the wall, he sprang at him and dealt him a deadly blow with his sword, just above the right eye, which felled him to the ground, and in an instant he was pierced by not less than 20 bayonets."

Inside the Long Barracks, the Texans made their last stand. Each doorway facing the courtyard was guarded by a semicircular parapet of dirt held in place by stretched cowskins. The Texans fired from these parapets and from loopholes in the walls. But within minutes the Mexicans had manned the cannon along the walls, aimed them at the barracks and blown down the parapets one by one. A musket volley drove the Texans from the doorways and the Mexicans bounded through with fixed bayonets. Methodically, the Mexicans moved through the barracks with bayonets until the building was theirs and the Texans were dead.

In his room in the nearby Low Barracks, Jim Bowie lay helpless on his cot. Mexican soldiers burst through the door and, in the words of his horrified sister-in-law, "tossed Bowie's body on their bayonets until his blood covered their clothes and dyed them red."

The last defenders were in the church. Susannah Dickerson was in the sacristy, clutching Angelina in

Susannah Dickerson, the young widow of
an Alamo defender, was spared by Santa
Anna so she could carry the news of the
slaughter and warn other Texans of the fate
awaiting them if they fought the Mexicans.

her arms and listening to the crash of guns and the cries of the wounded. The 18-pounder had been turned and now its great balls pounded the church walls at point-blank range. Moments before, she had seen her husband for the last time. Almeron Dickerson had left his guns for a moment. He ran into the room, crying, "Great God, Sue, the Mexicans are inside our walls!" He embraced her. "If they spare you, save my child!" he cried, and ran out, back to the guns still firing in the scaffold above. She held the child and listened; the church walls shivered each time a ball struck.

The Mexican infantrymen battered down the main door of the church and poured inside. Robert Evans, who had been passing powder, took a torch and crawled toward the magazine. The soldiers shot him. The door of Susannah Dickerson's room flew open and Jacob Walker, 31, a gunner from Nacogdoches, ran in. He went to a corner and seemed to be trying to hide, she said later; but four soldiers came in, shot him and lifted his body on their bayonets.

It was quiet outside. The sun was up; it was 6:30 a.m., just 90 minutes after the bugler signaled the attack. A Mexican officer appeared in the doorway. "Is there a Mrs. Dickerson here?" he asked. He had been sent by Santa Anna, who had promised to spare Mrs. Dickerson's life at the pleading of one of her Mexican friends in San Antonio. When she hesitated, the officer snapped, "If you value your life, speak up." She stepped forward, carrying Angelina. The soldiers who had killed Walker started to seize her but the officer said sharply, "Let her alone. The general has need of her." As she followed him across the yard someone fired and the bullet hit her right calf and she fell, bleeding heavily. The officer ordered his men to carry her and Angelina. In her pain, shock and fear, the young woman remembered very little of the scene. But she did recognize "Colonel Crockett lying dead and mutilated between the church and the two-story barracks; I even remember seeing his peculiar cap by his side." A Mexican surgeon later dressed her wound.

Santa Anna was outside, surveying the carnage. Travis' slave, who was known only as Joe, was asked to identify the bodies of Bowie and Travis.

"The enemy loss was all," a Mexican officer wrote later, "that is to say 183. Among this number there were five who hid themselves, and when the action was over, General Castrillon found them and brought them into the presence of Santa Anna who for a moment angrily reprimanded the said general, then turning his back, at which act, the soldiers already formed in a line, charged the prisoners and killed them."

That was the end. All of the Texas defenders were dead save a handful of women and children, the slave Joe, and a San Antonian who managed to persuade the Mexicans that he had been held a prisoner in the Alamo. Francisco Ruiz, *alcalde* of San Antonio, described what happened next. "Santa Anna sent a company of dragoons with me to bring wood and dry branches from the neighboring forests. About 3 o'clock in the afternoon of March 6, we laid the wood and dry branches upon which a pile of dead bodies was placed, more wood was piled on them, then another pile of bodies was brought, and in this manner they were all arranged in layers. About 5 o'clock it was lighted."

Santa Anna wanted the Texans to know. He summoned Mrs. Dickerson, and gave her careful instructions, making certain that she comprehended fully what had happened. She was to go to the Texans and tell them, and she was to give them Santa Anna's word: this would be his treatment of all those who opposed him. She understood. He gave her a horse and an escort — an American Negro who had been his servant — and with Angelina in her arms she set out for Gonzales to carry to Texas the story of the Alamo.

In Santa Anna's view it "was but a small affair." To be sure, his losses were huge — possibly 1,500 killed by the Texans' fire, more than a third of the estimated attacking force. No one ever really knew because he quickly ordered the Mexican bodies buried. When space in the cemetery proved insufficient, dozens of bodies were dumped in the river. But in military terms the Alamo fight seemed insignificant; it barely slowed his army's march across Texas. It did, however, have a powerful psychological impact on Texas, on America, on the world. The story of the defenders' brave stand swept across oceans and was often compared with the gallantry of the ancient Greeks at Thermopylae. In Texas it was now understood that there were no alternatives, that Texans must win their freedom or die in the attempt. The sacrifice and the slaughter at the Alamo did something else: it set off a deep, lasting rage in Texans that cried out for revenge.

Led by Houston *(center)*, Texans close fiercely with Mexicans in this 1892 reconstruction of San Jacinto by L. M. D. Guillaume.

4 | San Jacinto: a vengeful slaughter

Each of Texas' two greatest military actions took place in but a blink of time's eye. The sacrifice at the Alamo, which began at 5 a.m., was over and done with before the sun was fairly above the horizon. Six weeks later, on a coastal plain 225 miles to the east, the Texans reversed their fortunes and won independence from Mexico in a fire fight that lasted scarcely 18 minutes.

What happened at San Jacinto, on April 21, 1836, should not really be called a battle; "blood-letting" is the more accurate description. Owing to Sam Houston's tactical genius and their own terrible rage, 800 ragtag Texans caught 1,250 unsuspecting Mexicans under General Santa Anna nodding on a drowsy mid-afternoon and proceeded to slaughter them like so many sheep. In all, 600 or more Mexicans were killed and all who survived were captured. The Texas losses: nine men dead, 26 wounded.

The killing ground was a broad field into which the Texans charged from hidden positions behind trees opposite the Mexican camp. Astride a prancing stallion and brandishing a saber, Sam Houston personally directed the battle. As the waves of slashing, shooting Texans swept down on them, all of Santa Anna's soldiers broke and ran for the shelter of a tree line. Death followed them there; the revenge-bent Texans, oblivious of their officers, continued to inflict casualties after all organized resistance had ceased. As one Texan later told his colonel: "If Jesus Christ were to come down from Heaven and order me to quit shooting Santanistas, I wouldn't do it, Sir!"

The long retreat to victory

February 29, 1836, was a sullenly warm day for the season. But that night the wind sprang up from the north and brought down a thunderous storm of cold rain upon the village of Washington-on-the-Brazos, 35 miles upriver from San Felipe. By morning the temperature had fallen to 33° and the delegates to the Texas Constitutional Convention shivered in their spartan quarters. There were 59 of them, come to form a new government of Texas. The time for debate was past. The long-held hope of becoming a semiautonomous state within the Mexican federation was shattered. Texans felt that Santa Anna's tyranny had left them with one course: to declare their independence as a free and sovereign nation.

Washington-on-the-Brazos was a dismal place for a momentous meeting. Virginia lawyer William Fairfax Gray, in Texas on business, observed the convention and recorded his impressions in his diary. The one street, he noted, was ankle-deep in mud, and the chilling rain left the delegates dispirited. But Sam Houston's arrival electrified the convention—"created more sensation," said Gray, "than that of any other man. He is much broken in appearance but has still a fine person and courtly manners." Houston would be 43 on March 2. Weeks of travel, constant crises and an attack of malaria had worn him down. Yet, with Stephen Austin in the United States seeking funds and volunteers, Houston was the one man to whom Texans knew they could turn in the coming conflict. On Tuesday, March 1, the convention met in a building

so new that its boards oozed sap: "an unfinished house," as Gray described it, "without doors or window glass. Cotton cloth was stretched across the windows, which partially excluded the cold wind." That day and the next were spent in drafting a declaration of independence. As the delegates worked, 150 miles away in San Antonio Santa Anna was tightening his noose around the Alamo. On the evening of March 2, a dispatch from William Barret Travis at the Alamo, reporting a skirmish with 300 Mexican troops, caused some concern at the convention. However, wrote Gray, "Colonel James Fannin is reported to be on the march from Goliad with 350 men for the aid of Travis. It is believed the Alamo is safe."

The delegates reconvened in the makeshift convention hall at 9 a.m. on March 3. The finished copy of the Declaration of Independence was read by George C. Childress of Tennessee, its chief author: "When a government has ceased to protect the lives, liberty, and property of the people, and when that government has become a military dictatorship, it becomes the right of the people to abolish such a government and create another to secure their future welfare and happiness. The Mexican nation has allowed General Santa Anna to overturn the constitution of this country. He now offers us the cruel choice of either abandoning our homes or submitting to his tyranny."

The choice was no choice. The declaration was unanimously approved and signed by all members present. A committee set to work immediately to draft a constitution, a labor that was to occupy them for nearly two weeks. When it was completed, it would provide for an interim government to serve until the Republic of Texas was born, after which there would be a popularly elected president and vice president, a congress composed of a senate and a house of representatives, and a supreme court—very much a United

---

Mexico's General Santa Anna was roundly defeated by the Texans at the Battle of San Jacinto, and was later discovered hiding, dressed in peasants' clothing. The photograph, based on a damaged 1850 daguerreotype, has been retouched for this volume.

States style of government. But for a time it seemed as if no one would remain in Washington long enough to frame so much as the constitution's first article.

On Sunday, March 6, wrote William Gray, "a dispatch was received from Travis, dated Alamo, March 3, 1836. The members of the Convention and the citizens all crowded into the Convention room to hear it read." Wrote Travis: "We have contended for ten days against an enemy whose numbers are variously estimated from fifteen hundred to six thousand men. I hope your honorable body will hasten on reinforcements, ammunitions and provisions to our aid so soon as possible. . . . God and Texas—Victory or Death."

Travis and his men were already dead when the delegates heard the dispatch, and the wood that would be ignited to cremate their bodies was being gathered by Mexican troops. But the men in Washington-on-the-Brazos did not know that, and the message stirred the convention into great excitement and a burning desire to speed to Travis' rescue. One delegate moved that the convention "do immediately adjourn, arm and march to the relief of the Alamo." "A great many persons," Gray noted in his diary, "are preparing to start to the scenes of fighting."

But the idea was preposterous, as Houston with his political and military experience well knew. Establishing a legitimate government was an overriding priority; part of the disaster Texas now faced grew from its disorganization. He spoke to the delegates, his sonorous, compelling voice holding them in silence. It was, he said, of the utmost importance that they stay in Washington-on-the-Brazos and busy themselves with forming the government. Meanwhile, as commander-in-chief of the army, he would go instantly to Gonzales and rally a force to stand against the advancing Mexicans. If mortal power could avail, he pledged, he would relieve the brave men in the Alamo.

With that, Major General Sam Houston strode from the hall, three-inch rowels fashioned as daisies jingling on his spurs, a long feather in his hat. Mounting his horse, he galloped out of town accompanied by his personal aide, Colonel George W. Hockley, and an escort of three volunteers. Some miles along the road west he called a halt, dismounted and—so the legend goes—pressed an ear to the ground. It was a trick he had learned from the Indians; if there was still firing at

the Alamo, 150 miles away, he would probably detect the vibrations. After long moments he raised his head and gravely told his companions that he feared the cannon at the Alamo had fallen silent. Full of apprehension, they rode on to Gonzales.

Arriving at 4 in the afternoon on March 11, Houston found 374 men gathered in four groups, led by Alexander Somervell, James C. Neill, Sidney Sherman and Edward Burleson, the old Indian-fighter who had accepted Cós's surrender at San Antonio the previous December. Colonel James Fannin, he learned, was still at Fort Defiance in Goliad, 65 miles to the south, although he had been ordered to rendezvous with Houston on the west bank of Cibolo Creek and march from there to Travis' rescue. Just after dark two Mexicans arrived in Gonzales with the terrible news that the Alamo had fallen. Houston immediately dispatched a courier to Fannin countermanding his previous order and instructing him to blow up Fort Defiance and fall back "as soon as practicable" to the town of Victoria on the Guadalupe River. He then sent three scouts—led by Erastus "Deaf" Smith—to San Antonio to confirm Travis' fate.

On March 13 the three scouts found Mrs. Susannah Dickerson, the Alamo survivor who had been released by Santa Anna to warn the Texans of the consequences of further resistance. She was discovered on the road 50 miles east of San Antonio, and at twilight she was brought into Gonzales. To Houston and an assembled crowd she reported the frightful details of the massacre at the Alamo. The women of Gonzales, about 30 of whom had lost their husbands in the siege, clustered close around her and drew out every awful particular. "I remember most distinctly the shrieks of despair with which the soldiers' wives received news of the death of their husbands," wrote a young soldier who observed the scene.

There was still more disconcerting news. Santa Anna, said Susannah Dickerson, had vowed to drive all Americans out of Texas. A detachment of 700 Mexican troops under General Joaquin Ramírez y Sesma was even then marching from San Antonio toward Gonzales. The vanguard could not be more than a few days away.

Gonzales was in immediate danger. Houston decided to evacuate the town with all haste. His tiny army, formed only the day before, could not possibly defend it. Giving orders to strike camp, Houston assigned three of the army's four baggage wagons to transport civilians and deliberately sank his two small cannons in the Guadalupe River. The desperate measure was necessary because the earth was so muddy from the heavy spring rains that artillery would only have bogged down the retreat.

At 11 o'clock on the starless night of March 13, 1836, the troops headed east from Gonzales. Lights flickered in all the houses as the people packed up their goods with frantic speed to keep up with the army. From a doorway a man cried, "In the name of God, gentlemen, I hope you are not going to leave the families behind." "Oh, yes," answered a dry voice from the ranks, "we are all looking out for number one." In fact, they were not; Houston had detached a rear guard to bring along every last soul in Gonzales.

At this point, Houston was forced to retreat into the colonies. The Gonzales area was thinly settled and his men poorly supplied. But if he were to fall back some 50 miles and cross the Colorado River, he would be near the most populous part of Texas; supplies and reinforcements could be gotten from the farms and ranches there. Furthermore, the river would form a temporary barrier against the heavily equipped Mexican troops. His rear guard could shepherd not only the refugees from Gonzales but the few settlers who were scattered between Gonzales and the Colorado.

Weeks earlier he had ordered the Alamo evacuated and destroyed; and Texas was made to pay for the disobedience of those orders. Now, as he put it in a letter to a friend, "I will if possible prevent all future murders of our men in forts."

Thus, Sam Houston embarked on the campaign that would win Texas its freedom and its empire (map, page 118). In six weeks of retreat and skirmish that reached an awesome climax at the Battle of San Jacinto, he was to settle the issue once and for all.

The rain fell unrelentingly and Houston drove his troops at an exhausting pace along the muddy roads. His temper—always volatile—was not easy, and time and again he unleashed blistering curses.

Grain was in short supply and the commander knew that grazing on the muddy prairie would be too sparse to support many horses. As a result, only Houston, a small cavalry detachment and the men gathering up the civilians were mounted. Trooper J. H. Kuykendall remembered that Houston "did not want many mounted men, and many of those who repaired to the army on horseback, rather than be dismounted, returned to their homes." For those who did stay and gave up their horses, it was a real sacrifice. "Considering that our people were as much attached and accustomed to mounted service as the Cossack or Comanche," said Kuykendall, "the voluntary relinquishment of the horse was a strong manifestation of patriotism."

The Texans experienced precious few light moments during their long march, but they did cherish one incident. Noah Smithwick, the young blacksmith-pioneer, was with a group of scouts in Bastrop to the north of Houston's column when they awoke one morning to find that a full Mexican division of 700 men under General Antonio Gaona had encamped on the other side of the Colorado River. The Texas scouts moved out so hurriedly, Smithwick reported, that they almost forgot the guard they had posted at a nearby river crossing: Uncle Jimmy Curtis. At 64, Curtis may have been the oldest soldier of the revolution; certainly he was one of the feistiest. He had lost a son-in-law named Washington Cottle at the Alamo, and in the fighting to come he had his own battle cry: "Remember Wash Cottle!"

Now Smithwick—as he related the incident—"galloped back and found Uncle Jimmy sitting leaning against a tree, with a bottle of whiskey beside him, as happy and unconscious of danger as a turtle on a log. 'Hello, Uncle Jimmy,' I cried, 'mount and ride for your life. The Mexicans are on the other side and our men are all gone.' 'The hell they are! Light and take a drink.' 'There's no time for drinking. Come—mount and let's be off. The Mexicans may swim the river and be after us any moment.' 'Let's drink to their confusion,' he persisted, and thinking it was the quickest way to start him I drank with him and we struck out. 'Well, we can say one thing; we were the last men to leave,' said he, not in the least disturbed."

As a result of the incessant spring rains, the Colorado River was at flood when the Texas army—now bolstered by new recruits to some 600—reached Burnham's Crossing on March 17, with the frightened ref-

The rude birthplace of a new nation

As Santa Anna was marshaling his forces for his last assault on the Alamo, 59 Texans met at Washington-on-the-Brazos to sign the document creating the Republic of Texas.

The drafting of the declaration of independence, unanimously approved on March 2, 1836, was largely the work of George C. Childress, a former Tennessee lawyer. He started by listing the Texans' grievances against the Mexican government that was imposing its will upon them "at the point of the bayonet." He ended with the words: "We do hereby resolve and declare that our political connection with the Mexican nation has forever ended; and that the people of Texas do now constitute a free and independent republic."

If it is the fate of nations to be born in humble surroundings, Texas had an auspicious start: the site was bleaker than most. One observer described Washington-on-the-Brazos as a "disgusting place. It is laid out in the woods, about a dozen wretched cabins or shanties constitute the city; not one decent house in it, and only one well-defined street, which consists of an opening cut out of the woods. The stumps still standing. A rare place to hold a national convention in."

The delegates adjourned on March 17, after writing a U.S.-style constitution and electing a president. But Santa Anna was closing in and the Texans, in the words of one of those present, were "hourly exposed to attack and capture, and perhaps death." Three days after it was established, the new government packed up and fled eastward 100 miles to Harrisburg.

The building in which George Childress (*inset above*) drafted Texas' declaration of independence was an unfinished structure lacking doors and windows, and was scarcely less rude in 1893 when this picture was taken. The horseman at far right is aiming a rifle, but at what remains a mystery.

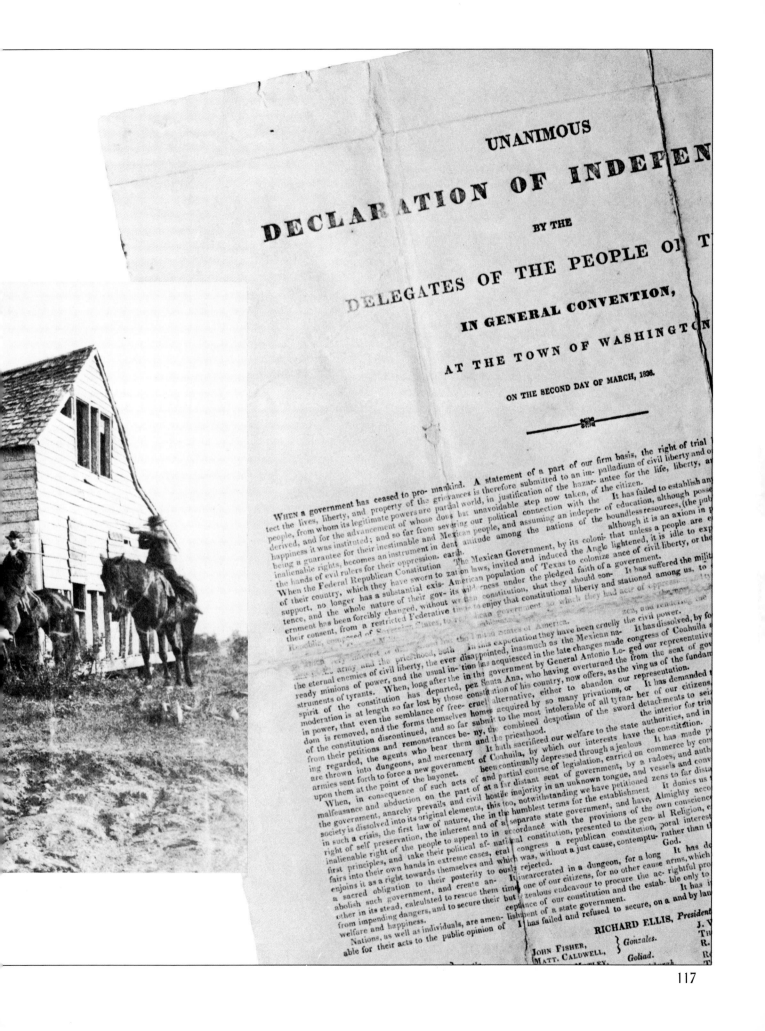

ugees straggling behind it. Houston sent the civilians across the river ahead of his main force; and then, on the 19th, took his troops across. They pitched camp on the east bank at Beason's Ford. There they were joined by several more groups of volunteers, bringing the army to about 700 men.

On the 21st, Houston got his first sight of the enemy: the 700-man division under General Joaquín Ramírez y Sesma that had swept through Gonzales and set out in pursuit of Houston's army. Now, having caught up while Houston rested his troops at the Colorado, the Mexicans appeared on the west bank of the river, only two miles above the Texan position. The two armies faced each other across the swollen river. For five days they poised there, preparing to fight, each attempting to assess the other's strength. Unbeknownst to the Texans, Sesma received reinforcements, bringing his strength to at least 1,200 men.

Meanwhile, events were moving forward at the convention. The delegates had finished the new republic's constitution at midnight on March 16 and elected David Burnet provisional President. Burnet was 47, a grim, humorless man who carried a pistol in one pocket of his tight black coat and a Bible in the other. A New Jerseyite by birth, he had roamed the world before arriving in Texas in 1826 to start his own colony. Like Stephen Austin, he strongly disapproved of liquor and profanity; and like Austin he heartily disliked the hard-drinking, hard-swearing Sam Houston. For his part, Houston had nicknamed the stern little man "Wetumpka," which Houston told everyone was Cherokee for "hog thief"—without explaining what Burnet had done to deserve that personal estimate.

Just then the new President of Texas was an extremely nervous man. Hardly had he assumed office when a report reached the town on March 17 that a Mexican force was at Bastrop, only 60 miles away. The news created panic. President Burnet and his provisional government immediately fled 70 miles eastward to Harrisburg, on Buffalo Bayou.

Houston, playing his waiting game with Sesma's division across the Colorado, received word of the government's flight in a letter dispatched to him from Harrisburg by Thomas Rusk, whom the convention had named Secretary of War. Another dispatch, this one from President Burnet, ordered him to abandon his

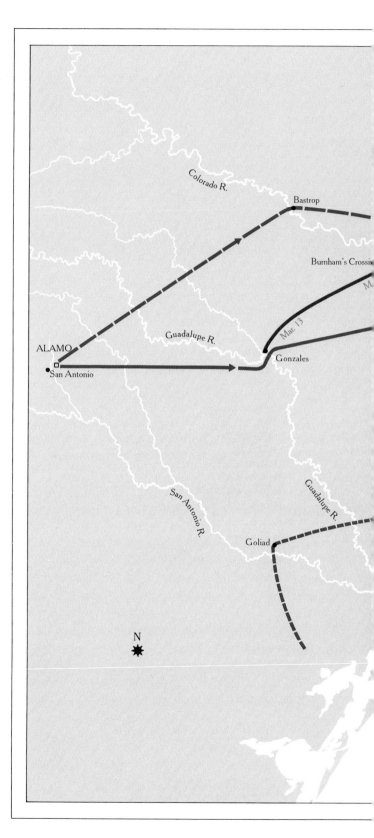

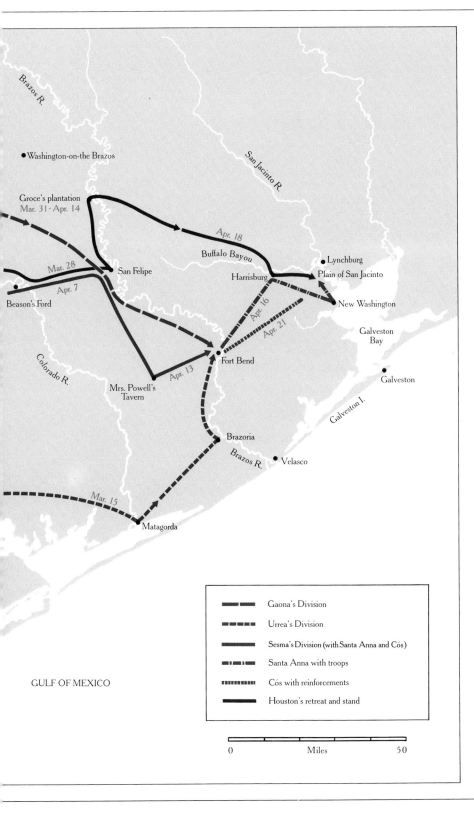

Brazos R.

Washington-on-the-Brazos

San Jacinto R.

Groce's plantation
Mar. 31 - Apr. 14

Apr. 18

Buffalo Bayou

Lynchburg

Mar. 28

San Felipe

Harrisburg

Plain of San Jacinto

Apr. 7

Apr. 16

New Washington

Beason's Ford

Apr. 21

Galveston
Bay

Colorado R.

Fort Bend

Galveston

Mrs. Powell's
Tavern

Apr. 13

Galveston I.

Brazoria

Brazos R.

Velasco

Mar. 15

Matagorda

Gaona's Division

Urrea's Division

Sesma's Division (with Santa Anna and Cós)

Santa Anna with troops

Cós with reinforcements

Houston's retreat and stand

GULF OF MEXICO

0   Miles   50

Pathways to disaster
for the Mexican invaders

After the Alamo, Santa Anna devised a three-pronged strategy designed to overwhelm what remained of the Texas forces. General José Francisco Urrea would drive up from the south with 1,400 men; General Antonio Gaona would sweep across the north with a column of 700 men; and Santa Anna and General Joaquin Ramírez y Sesma would lead 1,200 men through the center of Texas.

General José Urrea's southern pincer swiftly destroyed a contingent of 400 Texans under the leadership of Colonel James Fannin at Goliad. But Sam Houston made a successful retreat from Gonzales, crossing the Colorado River to San Felipe and finally arriving at Groce's plantation on the Brazos River with a force that eventually increased to 800 men.

At this point, Santa Anna might have waited for his three heavily armed columns to concentrate at Fort Bend before taking on Houston's forces. But as he brought his army across the country, he learned from prisoners that the Texas government had fled to Harrisburg on Buffalo Bayou. Perceiving a chance for a master stroke, Santa Anna impatiently set out ahead with only 750 men in an attempt to capture the Texas leaders.

As it turned out, the attempt was futile. Worse yet, when Sam Houston marched south to intercept him and do battle at San Jacinto, Santa Anna had lost his great numerical superiority. And though he received last-minute reinforcements, bringing his strength up to 1,250 men, they were no match for Houston's 800 enraged Texans.

119

On March 2, 1836, his 43rd birthday and the day the independence of Texas was declared, Houston issued this proclamation from Washington-on-the-Brazos, urging Texans to aid their beleaguered troops.

ARMY ORDERS.

———— ✳ ————

CONVENTION HALL, WASHINGTON, MARCH 2, 1836.

War is raging on the frontiers. Bejar is besieged by two thousand of the enemy, under the command of general Siezma. Reinforcements are on their march, to unite with the besieging army. By the last report, our force in Bejar was only one hundred and fifty men strong. The citizens of Texas must rally to the aid of our army, or it will perish. Let the citizens of the East march to the combat. The enemy must be driven from our soil, or desolation will accompany their march upon us. *Independence is declared*, it must be maintained. Immediate action, united with valor, alone can achieve the great work. The services of all are forthwith required in the field.

SAM. HOUSTON,

Commander-in-Chief of the Army.

P. S. It is rumored that the enemy are on their march to Gonzales, and that they have entered the colonies. The fate of Bejar is unknown. The country must and shall be defended. The patriots of Texas are *appealed to, in behalf of their bleeding country.* **S. H.**

plans and proceed to Harrisburg to protect the government personnel.

Houston was bleakly digesting all this when scouts brought him devastating news. James Fannin's force —mostly well-armed young recruits from the United States—had been surrounded and was being battered by a vastly superior body of Mexicans. The vacillating Fannin had delayed his retreat from Goliad until March 19. When he was only six miles out of Goliad, on an open plain hung with fog, two Mexican divisions under General José Urrea had caught up with him. The odds were overwhelming: Urrea had 1,400 men compared with Fannin's 400.

Sam Houston, poised to fight on the Colorado River, was shaken. "Hockley," he said to his aide, with a grim nod toward his own small, untrained army, "there is the last hope of Texas. We shall never see Fannin nor his men."

The news of Fannin's terrible predicament altered Houston's plans. Now his force was the only one left to defend Texas. One battle lost would lose the war. On the other hand, even a victory on the Colorado —storming across the river and defeating Sesma's men on the western bank—would accomplish little; there would still be Santa Anna and the main body of the Mexican army to contend with.

Houston's men were sure that the Colorado was the place to make their stand; any further retreat, they felt, would expose the heart of the most populous portion of Texas. All settlements east of the Colorado would be endangered, and the lives of hundreds of women and children would be at stake.

On March 26 Houston pored over his maps, cutting big chews of tobacco with a clasp knife. Word flashed around camp that they were about to attack. Men eagerly readied their weapons. And then, at midafternoon, came a stunning order from Houston. They were to break camp, gather their gear and be ready to retreat at sunset. As they fell into line the Texans were close to mutiny. Staff officers rode along the column shouting, "Close up! Close up!"

The men moved out, cursing and complaining. A rumor raced through the ranks that Houston intended to flee all the way to the Louisiana border in order to involve United States troops. Disgruntled or not, the Texans marched 30 miles without a break in driving rain and bivouacked late the second day near San Felipe on the Brazos River.

There were more marching orders at dawn on March 28, and the men again formed ranks reluctantly. Two captains, Moseley Baker and Wiley Martin, refused to retreat. Houston paused wearily and scribbled special orders; both were good officers and he could not afford to alienate them altogether. Baker's 120 men were to take up defensive positions along the river at San Felipe, and Martin's 100 would go about 30 miles downstream to the crossing at Fort Bend.

The rest of the army sloshed on, still not knowing where it was going. The rain came down in cascades; men staggered under it and slid off the trail. Houston moved among his soldiers in an old black dress coat —threadbare, rain-soaked. Some scoundrel had stolen his ground blanket, he complained, and he was sleeping —when he slept—on his saddle blanket. Finally he told his troops where he was leading them.

"My friends," he said, "I am told that evil-disposed persons have reported that I am going to march you to the Redlands"—the Louisiana border. "This is false. I am going to march you into the Brazos bottom near Groce's, where you can whip the enemy ten to one and where we can get an abundant supply of corn."

He drove the troops for three more desperate days through rain that rarely broke. They covered a bare 18 miles, but on March 31 they made camp on the west bank of the Brazos River, opposite Groce's plantation. And it was there that the Texans received the news of what had befallen the hapless Fannin.

Fannin had pulled his men together and formed a square of wagons and equipment. From that fragile fortress they fought gallantly for two days, killing 250 Mexicans while losing seven men killed and 60 wounded—including Fannin himself. On March 20, they had surrendered to General Urrea on the promise that they would be treated with honor and sent on parole to the United States; it was the only way, they thought, to save the wounded. For eight days Fannin and his men were held captive in Goliad and humanely treated. Then the orders arrived from Santa Anna: the prisoners were a hindrance and an expense, and were to be shot immediately.

Early on Palm Sunday, March 27, Mexican troops marched the prisoners out of Goliad, telling them that

Colonel James Fannin, the Texas commander at Goliad, was wounded before his capture. When he and 40 other injured men could not walk in the death march, the Mexicans executed them separately.

they were to be freed on parole and sent to New Orleans. One of the few who survived the day described what happened next:

"Mexican soldiers were drawn up in two lines, so we were closely guarded on both sides. There were four hundred volunteers and at least seven hundred Mexicans. The Mexican soldiers were unbearably silent; our men were grave; the atmosphere was hot and close. I noticed for the first time their parade uniforms and lack of baggage."

Suddenly, near the San Antonio River, about half a mile from the fort, the Mexicans turned and formed one line to face them.

"A command to halt given in Spanish struck our ears like the voice of doom. The Mexican officer shouted at us to kneel. A man who spoke Spanish cried out, and a fearful crash interrupted him, then all was quiet; thick clouds of smoke rolled slowly toward the river. The blood of my lieutenant spurted on my clothes. I saw no more; quickly making up my mind, I sprang up and took advantage of the thick smoke which hid me

to make for the river. A heavy blow on the head from a sword made me reel; the small form of a Mexican lieutenant emerged from the smoke. In a moment I was on him. He did not put up any fight, but fled. I jumped into the waters. . . ."

All told, perhaps 60 of the Texans had managed to survive. About 30 — doctors, artisans and some of the wounded — were spared; about 30 more fled into the river marshes. Fannin was not among them. Unable to walk in the death march because of his wound, he and some 40 other injured men were executed separately in Goliad.

The news of Santa Anna's gothic slaughter only heightened the terror engulfing Texas. The civilian exodus from the settlements became a frantic scramble. Soldiers deserted to help families flee. "I now left the army," one wrote later, "and with the families set out on the retreat." Afterward, a little shamed, the Texans called it the "Runaway Scrape."

Noah Smithwick, riding east with Uncle Jimmy Curtis, saw panic signs everywhere. "Houses were standing open, the beds unmade, the breakfast things still on the tables, pans of milk moulding in the dairies. There were cribs full of corn, smokehouses full of bacon, yards full of chickens that ran after us for food, nests of eggs in every fence corner, young corn and garden truck rejoicing in the rain . . . all abandoned."

Across from Groce's plantation, Houston struggled to turn his rabble into something resembling an army. The number of men fluctuated daily as the result of desertions and the arrival of new recruits, but probably averaged about 800. He had formed one regiment at Gonzales under Colonel Edward Burleson; now he organized a second, to include a 60-horse cavalry unit, giving command to Colonel Sidney Sherman, who months before had sold his business in Kentucky and used the money to equip a company of 52 volunteers whom he brought with him to Texas.

Two weeks passed while Houston trained his army and worked to build discipline. He kept patrols moving constantly through the woods, maintained a strict sentry watch, and drilled and redrilled his men. Rifles were repaired, knives were sharpened. Food was mostly boiled beef, slaughtered from Groce's pastures, and corn from Groce's cribs. Each mess of 10 men had a portable corn grinder and a pack horse for carrying pro-

Four Texas veterans meet in 1880. John Duval *(seated left)* survived Goliad. The older woman is identified as Grandma Winn, aged 95.

An illustrious quartet of comrades in arms

SIDNEY SHERMAN. A Kentucky manufacturer of cotton bagging, Sherman sold his plant, raised a volunteer company for Texas and led it into battle as a lieutenant colonel at San Jacinto. He later built Texas' first railroad, from Harrisburg to the Brazos River.

ROBERT M. WILLIAMSON. Called Three-Legged-Willie because of a wooden limb attached to a leg bent backward by childhood illness, Williamson was a Georgia lawyer who fought in Texas as a cavalryman and went on to become a State Supreme Court justice.

visions when the time came to move. Coffee was eternally in short supply; only chewing tobacco was plentiful, since Houston had somehow obtained a huge store. As for uniforms, years later one of the men observed, "Rags were our uniform, Sire! Nine out of ten of them was in rags. And it was a fighting uniform!"

Artillery donated by the citizens of Cincinnati arrived at Groce's: two mounted six-pounders which the men named the Twin Sisters. Colonel James C. Neill, the officer who had turned the Alamo over to Travis, took command of the cannon. A mounted scouting troop was set up under Captain Henry Wax Karnes, with Deaf Smith as its most notable figure.

Smith's defective hearing, which was caused by a childhood disease, had sharpened his other senses

acutely. His eyesight was particularly keen, and his intuitiveness was such that the intrepid old reconnoiterer could detect people and animals long before most other scouts could. Married to a young Mexican girl, he spoke faultless Spanish and was so thoroughly versed in Mexican customs and manners that his very appearance was Mexican—all of which made him invaluable to the Texans. He was one of the half-dozen men on whom Sam Houston relied the most, and his loyalty was unswerving.

Houston still was forced to sleep on his saddle blanket and he often wore moccasins, since his only pair of boots was giving out. In his saddlebag he carried ears of raw corn on which he gnawed, and copies of *Gulliver's Travels* and *Caesar's War Commentaries.*

JOHN M. ALLEN. A Kentucky native and soldier of fortune, Allen joined the Texas revolutionary army in 1835 as an infantry captain and was an acting major at San Jacinto. In 1839 he was elected the first mayor of Galveston, a position he held for seven years.

MIRABEAU BUONAPARTE LAMAR. A Georgia painter, poet and publisher, Lamar volunteered for the Texas army after the Alamo and was a cavalry colonel at San Jacinto. Later he proved a magnetic politician and in 1838 succeeded Houston as president of Texas.

Long after the men were asleep he stayed awake, reading and studying maps. He carried no liquor; he could be abstemious when necessary. But he did keep a vial of ammoniacal spirits into which he had introduced the shavings of deer horns — his nostrum for warding off colds; he sniffed it so regularly that it became a nervous gesture and caused people to believe, falsely, that he took opium.

He needed his wits, not only against Santa Anna, whose columns were moving across Texas, but to counter the incipient mutiny in his own camp. The belief persisted that Houston intended to retreat clear across the Sabine River into the United States, avoiding any battle with the enemy. That they simply were not yet ready for war was something neither officers nor men could comprehend. Increasingly, they doubted Houston's courage. And it was not Houston's way to explain himself.

The feeling grew that he should be ousted from command. A man who would later play a major role in the history of Texas, Mirabeau Buonaparte Lamar — a poet and onetime Georgia newspaper publisher — appeared in camp with a plan to rally men to himself and march off to glory against the Mexicans. Houston had some graves dug and announced that anyone who attempted to "beat for volunteers" would be shot forthwith. Lamar prudently decided to serve in Houston's cavalry. Shortly afterward a number of volunteers nominated Colonel Sidney Sherman as the best man to command them. Houston responded with posted notices threat-

An ensign bearing a sword-swinging Goddess of Liberty was the only flag carried by the Texans at San Jacinto. It was crafted by Kentucky women for Sidney Sherman, a Texas army colonel born in Kentucky.

ening court-martial and execution for such mutineers.

Undoubtedly Houston's uncommunicative attitude increased the widespread discontent. He refused to confer with his officers or even hint at his strategy. His only hope, as he saw it, was to draw Santa Anna deeper and deeper into Texas, until the Mexican lines of supply and communications were overextended, and then strike when circumstances were most opportune. Discussion of such a formless plan was pointless. Writing to Thomas Rusk, the Secretary of War who was

then with the government in Harrisburg, Houston said: "I consulted none. I held no council of war. If I err, the blame is mine."

Houston's difficult position as a commander making unpopular decisions was further complicated by the attitude of President Burnet. "Sir," he angrily wrote to Houston, "the enemy are laughing you to scorn. You must fight them. You must retreat no farther. The country expects you to fight." To Secretary of War Rusk, who delivered the message personally, Houston complained that Burnet's own government had been the first to run and had run the farthest. Rusk had the authority to depose Houston if he thought it necessary. Instead, he remained to fight at Sam Houston's side and became his strongest supporter.

To Santa Anna, the end now seemed in sight. He was deploying his forces and closing in on the Texans. He had left San Antonio on March 31, joined Sesma's division — which he had ordered to wait for him on the Colorado — then crossed ahead of it and marched on to San Felipe, where he arrived on April 7. The town was in ashes. Moseley Baker's men had put it to the torch to keep it from enemy hands, and had retreated across the Brazos River, taking every boat with them. Santa Anna's men built rafts to follow across, but Baker's riflemen opened fire and kept them from crossing for four days.

Impatient, Santa Anna did not await the outcome of the fight. He paused to send orders to two of his commanders — General José Urrea with 1,150 troops in the south and General Antonio Gaona with 700 in the north — to march to Fort Bend and concentrate their forces there. He then took 750 of Sesma's reinforced troops and a cavalry detachment, and himself swung south toward the crossing at Fort Bend. His scouts had already reported it deserted — Wiley Martin having decided that he could not defend it.

On the night of April 10, Santa Anna rested at a tavern that its owner, Mrs. Elizabeth Powell, had refused to abandon, and forced her to feed him and his officers. By this time Santa Anna knew through his scouting patrols that Houston was across from Groce's plantation, upriver from San Felipe — but he also knew that the Texas government was at Harrisburg, only 30 miles beyond the crossing at Fort Bend. With luck, he felt, he might be able to capture the government and then turn north to crush Houston's army. Santa Anna sent word to General Sesma, who had advanced to San Felipe, to bring up his column immediately. In the morning, he resumed his march on Fort Bend.

No sooner was Santa Anna out of sight than Mrs. Powell's son, Joseph, set out for Houston's camp with news of the Mexican advance. Joseph Powell understood Spanish and had listened well to the Mexican officers discussing their strategy. On April 12 he reported to Houston that Santa Anna was passing through Fort Bend with only 750 men and would try to seize the government at Harrisburg.

It was the opportunity Houston had been praying for — a chance to fight Santa Anna on something approaching equal terms. On the 13th, at nightfall, he led his troops across the Brazos to Groce's on the east bank. Next day they moved three miles and camped in the pasture of a settler named Donoho, who complained to Houston that the men were cutting his timber for firewood. Dryly, Houston reprimanded them: why take Donoho's timber when they could more easily burn the carefully split rails that made his fence?

Next morning, the Texans marched southeast intending to intercept the Mexican general at Harrisburg. By now, Captain Moseley Baker had disengaged from the Mexicans at San Felipe and rejoined the army. Captain Wiley Martin and his men also showed up, but the headstrong officer still refused to serve under Houston. So the general had Martin's company take charge of the refugees who were fleeing eastward before the Mexican troops.

That day, Santa Anna reached Harrisburg and found, to his intense chagrin, that the government had fled. The town was empty but for three printers who had stayed to put out one last edition of *The Telegraph and Texas Register,* which they planned to carry with them and distribute in towns to the east. Under questioning the printers told Santa Anna that Burnet and the other officials had escaped just the morning before aboard the steamer *Cayuga.* It was heading down Buffalo Bayou to the San Jacinto River, and thence to Galveston Bay and the town of New Washington. The news pleased Santa Anna. The route of the steamer was circuitous but New Washington was only 20 miles away by land. Swiftly he dispatched a company of dragoons to the town in hopes of capturing Burnet.

The printers had another tempting bit of information. They had heard that Houston would try to defend Lynch's Ferry, which crossed the San Jacinto about 15 miles east of Harrisburg, thus blocking Santa Anna's advance through the rest of Texas. Santa Anna made his plans. He would go southeast to New Washington, deal with Burnet, and then double back to Lynch's Ferry to destroy Houston's forces. On the

16th he burned Harrisburg to the ground and set out after his dragoons.

Houston and his troops had now marched to a point about 45 miles from Harrisburg and the road forked just a few miles ahead: one route led to Louisiana and nonconfrontation, the other toward Harrisburg and battle. Which would Houston take, Moseley Baker angrily demanded to know? Houston ignored him. The men marched sullenly on, threatening to rebel if led toward Louisiana. Houston halted them a mile short of the fork—and all night long the men complained and wondered. Next morning Houston abruptly ordered his army down the road to Harrisburg. He simply gave the direction, without explanation. The men hurried on still muttering, but with rising spirits. At last they were going to fight.

Meanwhile, about 60 miles away, as the Mexican dragoons approached New Washington, they were spotted by one of Houston's scouts, a young man named Mike McCormick. Spurring his horse, McCormick galloped into New Washington and arrived only minutes ahead of the Mexicans. Seeing a schooner in the harbor, he headed for the wharf side. Burnet was on the dock; at McCormick's shouted alarm, he quickly stepped into a rowboat and yelled for his companions to follow him. Burnet, his wife and several members of the Texas cabinet were only a few yards offshore in Galveston Bay when Santa Anna's dragoons clattered up. The Mexicans started to shoot but their commander, Colonel Juan Almonte, quickly ordered a halt: there was a woman in the line of fire. Through one man's chivalry, the Texas government survived. Burnet and his officials rowed out to the schooner that took them on to Galveston.

For Santa Anna, who arrived in New Washington with his 750 troops on April 18, the government's escape was an annoying but minor disappointment. If Burnet had eluded his grasp, Houston would not. Santa Anna sent messages to his generals at Fort Bend to bring up reinforcements, and then made plans to trap Houston at Lynch's Ferry, only 10 miles away. He was so confident that he repaired to rest for two days at nearby Morgan's plantation, finding pleasure in opium and a handsome slave girl named Emily.

But like the defenders of the Alamo, Santa Anna had sorely underestimated the speed with which a determined enemy could move. Now it was the Mexicans' turn for a rude surprise. After taking the fork to Harrisburg on the 16th, Sam Houston had marched his army 60 miles in two and a half days, and reached Buffalo Bayou, exhausted, just before noon of the 18th. Across the bayou, Harrisburg lay in ashes; Santa Anna had obviously moved on. Houston pored over his maps, trying to determine Santa Anna's move. Luck and Deaf Smith gave him the answer.

The veteran scout swam his horse across the bayou and seized a Mexican courier carrying a saddlebag of dispatches for Santa Anna. The bag had the name "William Barret Travis" stamped into the leather. The infuriated Texans would have killed the captured courier on the spot, but Houston restrained them. Only the messages were important—very important indeed. They were from Fort Bend, where Santa Anna's main forces were encamped. They indicated that Santa Anna was at New Washington with about 750 men, and therefore vulnerable. But one dispatch informed Santa Anna that 500 reinforcements were coming on with all possible speed to join him at Lynch's Ferry.

Once again, the time for victory or death was drawing near. On the 19th of April Houston ordered his men into parade formation. He mounted Saracen, a big white stallion he had picked up at Groce's plantation, and made a stirring speech. They would fight now, he said; and then, his big voice rising, he cried, "Victory is certain! Trust in God and fear not! The victims of the Alamo and the names of those who were murdered at Goliad cry out for vengeance. Remember the Alamo! Remember Goliad!" And the ragged, dirty, tired men roared back, "Remember the Alamo! Remember Goliad!"

While the men broke camp Houston wrote a friend: "This morning we are in preparation to meet Santa Anna. It is the only chance of saving Texas. We go to conquer. It is wisdom growing out of necessity to meet the enemy now; every consideration enforces it. No previous occasion would justify it."

They crossed Buffalo Bayou on rough rafts (Houston ripping his pants on a nail). On the Harrisburg side of the bayou they remained in the woods until dark. Then they traversed the wooden bridge over Vince's Bayou and marched until 2 a.m., slept for an hour on wet grass, then continued their march. Just

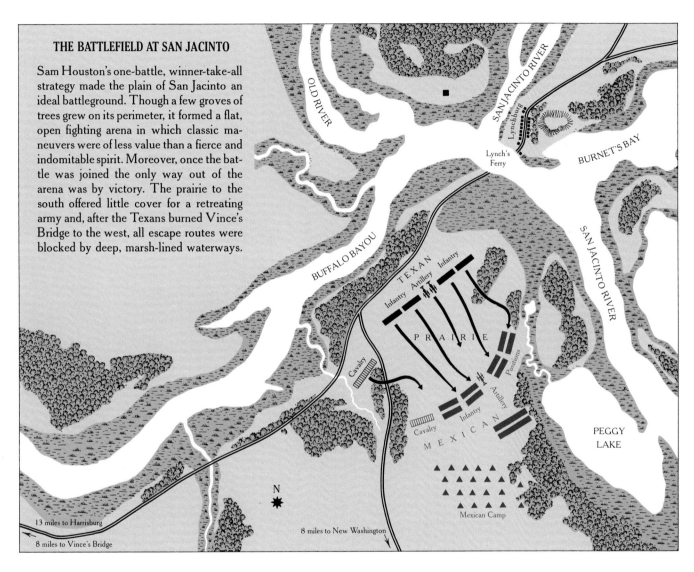

THE BATTLEFIELD AT SAN JACINTO

Sam Houston's one-battle, winner-take-all strategy made the plain of San Jacinto an ideal battleground. Though a few groves of trees grew on its perimeter, it formed a flat, open fighting arena in which classic maneuvers were of less value than a fierce and indomitable spirit. Moreover, once the battle was joined the only way out of the arena was by victory. The prairie to the south offered little cover for a retreating army and, after the Texans burned Vince's Bridge to the west, all escape routes were blocked by deep, marsh-lined waterways.

OLD RIVER

SAN JACINTO RIVER

Lynchburg

Lynch's Ferry

BURNET'S BAY

BUFFALO BAYOU

SAN JACINTO RIVER

T E X A N

Infantry   Artillery   Infantry

Infantry

P R A I R I E

Cavalry

Positions

Artillery

Cavalry   Infantry

M E X I C A N

PEGGY LAKE

N

Mexican Camp

13 miles to Harrisburg

8 miles to Vince's Bridge

8 miles to New Washington

after dawn on the 20th, they approached Lynchburg on the San Jacinto River and, without crossing, took control of Lynch's Ferry. Houston then sent some of his men on patrol and withdrew the bulk of his army to a protecting wood.

Early that same morning, Santa Anna burned New Washington and finally set out for Lynch's Ferry, fully expecting to trap Houston there. The Texans could see the smoke of New Washington as they awaited the Mexicans across the plain of San Jacinto.

What would become the battlefield lay before them, a mile of grass as high as a man's knees. Behind the Texans were the woods skirting Buffalo Bayou, a tangle of live oak hung with ghostly strands of Spanish

moss. To the Texans' left was the San Jacinto River and Lynch's Ferry. The woods and marsh ran along the San Jacinto for a mile, where the river bent back to the right to form a small basin called Peggy Lake. This, too, was skirted by marsh and woods, running at nearly right angles to the river and thus enclosing the mile-long field.

When the surprised Mexicans sighted Houston's patrols, they hurriedly took position in the woods on the far side of the field. The Texans remained within their tree line, well protected, their two six-pound Twin Sisters cannons out about 10 yards on the plain. They waited. Mexican artillerymen brought forward a six-pounder and began to fire. The Texans, in return, fired

Attacking Texans crash the Mexican barricades in this detailed panorama of the battle of San Jacinto. Sam Houston leads the charge, waving his hat as he leaps from his wounded horse *(left of center),* while Santa Anna, in a white sombrero *(center, right),* gallops past a tent in full flight.

131

Erastus "Deaf" Smith, though hard of hearing, functioned ably as Houston's chief scout against the Mexicans. It was he who brought Mrs. Almeron Dickerson to Houston with news of the Alamo massacre.

one of the Twin Sisters for the first time, because powder had been too precious to use for practice; the lucky shot bowled over several Mexican dragoons. Santa Anna suddenly appeared in person, riding among his gunners. He had recovered from his initial shock at discovering the Texans already on the scene. Still supremely confident, he remained with the artillerymen for a while and then retired.

Clearly, Santa Anna would try to draw the Texans into the open, but Houston did not intend to fight on the enemy's terms. His men stayed under cover and the Mexicans withdrew to the woods on the opposite side of the plain. From there they kept up a brisk musket fire that fell short of the Texans' lines.

The men were grumbling again. They had fully expected a fight that day and once more Houston had

ducked it. They went to sleep that night itching for battle and hoping to fight at first light. But, at dawn, Sam Houston did not awaken. He had left orders not to be disturbed and slept peacefully until 8 in the morning, his first sound sleep in many days. There was going to be no early battle.

But Santa Anna had apparently thought so — or at least felt it necessary to fortify his position. All night, while the Texans slept, the Mexicans labored to erect barricades of pack saddles and supplies. For most of the night Santa Anna personally supervised the work. At about 9 a.m. his reinforcements arrived from Fort Bend: 500 men under his brother-in-law, General Martín Perfecto de Cós. The new arrivals raised Santa Anna's force to about 1,250 men. But they were as tired as the rest, having marched all night. When the Texans seemed in no mood to fight, the Mexican camp relaxed and the men rested.

Deaf Smith had seen Cós's men coming from the direction of Vince's Bridge and awakened Houston to report their appearance. It was not unexpected, and not really bad news; far better that they should come now than reinforce Santa Anna in the midst of battle. Houston was feeling good that morning. He later said he had seen an eagle overhead, as he often did at propitious moments.

He had breakfast while John Wharton and Moseley Baker complained of his inaction and harangued the men. "Boys, there is no other word today but fight, fight!" Wharton cried. Houston ignored him. But as one of his men, James W. Winters, later recalled, "Some time before noon Houston passed around among the men gathered at the campfires and asked us if we wanted to fight. We replied with a shout that we were most anxious to do so. Then Houston replied, 'Very well, get your dinners and I will lead you into the fight, and if you whip them every one of you shall be a captain.'"

On Houston's orders, Deaf Smith galloped back to burn Vince's Bridge, or if necessary, chop it down. Cós's men had come over it just as had the Texans earlier, and no more forces would be permitted to use it — either coming or going. As Houston said afterward, "It cut off all means of escape for either army. There was no alternative but victory or death." As Deaf Smith departed, Houston told him: "Unless you hasten you will find the prairie changed from green to red on your return!"

About noon, Houston called his officers together and posed a single question: "Shall we attack the enemy in position, or receive their attack in ours?" To his amusement, the assembled men fell into a cacophony of confusion, but generally they expressed the belief that attacking over an open field was too risky. He laughed and dismissed them. Several hours passed. And then at 3:30 Houston ordered the attack—over the open field of San Jacinto.

The Texans were ready—rested, fed, their weapons primed, every nerve on edge. A soldier recalled: "Around 20 or 30 campfires stood as many groups of men, all unwashed and unshaved, their long hair and beards matted, their clothes in tatters and plastered with mud. A more savage looking band could scarcely have been assembled." The sun was high and warm, the breeze was light; it was a good day.

Captain Juan Seguin, the Mexican liberal who was committed to the Texan cause (page 91), remembered Colonel Thomas Rusk asking him, " 'Do you feel like fighting?' I answered that I was always ready and willing to fight, upon which the Colonel rose, saying, 'Well, let us go!' The Colonel proceeded along the line, speaking to the Captains, and our force was

soon under arms. General Houston and Colonel Rusk delivered short addresses, and we formed into line of battle in front of the enemy."

The attacking wave of foot soldiers was two men deep, the men in each row separated by a couple of yards or perhaps a little more. The line stretched some 900 yards along the front of the woods. The enemy soldiers were a mile away across the tall grass, behind breastworks, water-blocked, their only escape to the southwest. Texas cavalry, led by Mirabeau Lamar, moved into position on the right wing to prevent that escape. To the cavalry's left was the artillery with the musicians: three fifes and a drum; and four companies of infantry. Burleson's First Regiment was positioned to the left of the artillery; and on the extreme left-hand side of the field was Sherman's Second Regiment (map, page 129).

The Mexican camp was silent. From high in the trees Texan lookouts reported no patrol activity and no sentries in sight. In fact, most of the exhausted Mexican troops were asleep, their arms stacked. Santa Anna was lying under the shade of a tree, in deep—possibly opium-aided—sleep. Cós, after settling his men into camp, was also taking his ease.

Now, on the Texan side of the plain, there were no more speeches. General Houston on Saracen rode the

Mud-spattered and downcast, Santa Anna is brought before the wounded Sam Houston after San Jacinto. As Deaf Smith and other Texans look on, in this 1886 recreation by William Huddle, Houston offers the defeated general a seat on an ammunition box before accepting his surrender.

The rewards of victory for the Texans who fought at San Jacinto were donation certificates issued by the Secretary of War entitling each recipient to 640 acres, equal to one square mile, of unclaimed Texas land.

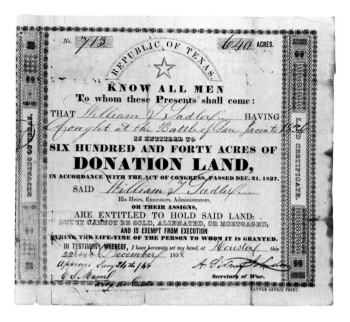

length of the line and paused before the First Regiment, about 30 yards ahead of Burleson and his men. "Trail arms! Forward!" he called in a firm, clear voice, and turned his horse toward the enemy. It was 4:30 p.m., April 21, 1836.

The ground was soft after the heavy rains and the cannon wheels cut deep furrows into the loam. The gunners cursed softly and heaved against their draglines. Save for their grunting oaths and Houston's voice, held low—"Hold your fire, men, hold your fire!"—there was almost no sound. "We marched upon the enemy with the stillness of death," John S. Menifee wrote later. "No fife, no drum, no voice was heard." Colonel Sherman and his regiment stayed back under cover of the trees, in their far-left position, to reinforce the attack when the moment came.

Lamar's cavalry was sent to engage the enemy's left flank, while the Texan cannons—the Twin Sisters —moved forward. When they were 200 yards from the Mexican barricade, Houston signaled with a sweep of his battered campaign hat. The gunners wheeled and fired, shattering the quiet. The drum rolled and the fifers broke into their favorite song, a slightly salacious popular ballad, "Will You Come to the Bower?" The angers and frustrations that had been building during the long retreat across their country and the cautious stalk across the field fired up the men, and the cries,

"Remember the Alamo! Remember Goliad!" went echoing down their lines until every Texan was running and shrieking, "Remember the Alamo!"

A bugle finally sounded in the Mexican camp and the soldiers leaped up in groggy confusion to find the howling, raging Texans almost upon them.

The command went along the Texans' line: "Halt! Fire! And then charge!" But many of the Texans felt they were too far away to fire effectively and they ran forward, rifles ready, screaming their battle cry. Houston, the soldier, knew that if the Mexicans were waiting, they would cut his men down like wheat unless they were themselves pressed with rifle fire. But the Texans were not soldiers. "Halt! Halt!" Houston roared. "Now is the critical time! Fire away! God damn you, fire! Aren't you going to fire at all?" Ben McCulloch snatched back the flare he was touching to one of the Twin Sisters when he saw Houston's white horse prance in front of its muzzle.

Moments later, when the men were 60 yards from the barricades, Deaf Smith suddenly galloped down the length of their line. "Vince's Bridge is down!" he yelled. "Fight for your lives! Vince's Bridge is down!" Houston wanted his men to know that they had no choice, that they must win now or die. The Texans started to shoot. "All discipline was at an end," Private Alphonso Steele wrote. "We fired as rapidly as we could. As soon as we had fired, each man reloaded and he who got his gun ready first moved on without waiting for orders."

The line was now 1,500 yards long and coming at a run, and the fifers were energetically tootling the inappropriate strains of:

Will you come to the bow'r I have shaded for you?
Our bed shall be roses all spangled with dew.
There under the bow'r on roses you'll lie
A blush on your cheek but a smile in your eye!

Forty yards from the Mexican barricades five musket balls struck Saracen in the chest and he sank silently to the ground. Houston stepped off as his horse collapsed beneath him. On the right Lamar's cavalry had collided with the Mexican cavalry and unhorsed many of the hastily awakened dragoons. Riderless horses caromed frantically through the Texas line; a soldier caught one and Houston swung into its saddle. In another moment a copper ball struck Houston just above the ankle, shattering both bones in his right leg, and his second horse fell. Someone gave him another and he mounted and galloped into the barricade, a flimsy five feet of pack saddles and packing cases from which Mexican soldiers already were fleeing. The Texans came up over the barricade yelling, rifles and long fighting knives in their hands.

At the far left, Sherman's men were still out of sight behind the edge of the woods. Now they struck swiftly and without warning. The Mexicans were in utter confusion as the second prong of Houston's attack ripped into their barricades. Most of them never had a chance to unstack their weapons. They fled in panic through the trees and onto the plain. The Texans followed, shooting, clubbing or knifing each man they caught.

"The most awful slaughter I ever saw was when the Texans pursued the retreating Mexicans, killing on all sides, even the wounded," said Sergeant Moses Austin Bryan, Stephen Austin's nephew. "I had a double-barrel shotgun and had shot only four times when we crossed the breastworks. After that I shot no more at the poor devils who were running."

Houston, his boot filling with blood from his leg wound, galloped among the trees, slashing at running men with his saber. A Mexican general named Manuel Fernandez Castrillon jumped on an ammunition box and tried to rally his battalion, but his troops were wild with fear. He stood there, arms folded, glaring at the Texans. Walter Lane remembered: "He drew himself up, faced us and cried out in Spanish, 'I've been in 40 battles and never showed my back. I'm too old to do it now.' Colonel Rusk hallooed to the men: 'Don't shoot him!' And Rusk knocked up some of the Texans' guns but others ran around and riddled the Mexican general with balls. I was sorry for him. He was a Castillian gentleman, General Castrillon."

Deaf Smith's horse was exhausted after the break-neck ride back from Vince's Bridge. It stumbled and Smith flew over its head. He landed at the feet of a Mexican lieutenant who slashed at him with a saber. Smith tried to shoot the man, but his pistol misfired. John Nash, another scout, rode his horse into the officer and bowled him over, and Smith seized the Mexican's saber and killed him with it. Then he caught a riderless Mexican horse, sprang into the saddle and

killed a Mexican colonel with a single saber blow so violent it snapped the blade at the hilt. John Robbins was jolted from his horse and fell into hand-to-hand combat with a powerfully built Mexican officer. A nearby Mexican infantryman with a lance could have killed Robbins; instead he leaped on Robbins' horse and galloped off while Robbins thrust his Bowie knife into the officer's throat.

The sound of the attack had roused Santa Anna from his slumber. He later insisted that he tried to organize a defense even though his troops were giving way all around him. But an aide who hated him said, "I saw his Excellency running about in the utmost excitement, wringing his hands and unable to give an

Holding aloft a Lone Star flag, more than 100 veterans of the revolution reunite at Belton in 1883, nearly 50 years after Texas had won its

independence. Members of the Old Three Hundred were admitted to the Texas Veteran Association, whether they had actually fought or not.

order." In any event, though overrun, Santa Anna knew he had some 2,500 fresh troops at Fort Bend on the Brazos, about 45 miles away. He seized a big black stallion and rode off, with a number of his officers following close behind. Texas Captain Robert Calder thought this development came quite early: "Santa Anna and a good portion of his staff broke from the field at the first discharge, escaping around our right wing. I saw their heads as they rode from the camp." Several Texans attempted to pursue Santa Anna, but lost him in the woods.

The battle, according to Houston's account, lasted scarcely 18 minutes. He measured it from the moment the Texans opened fire to when they were in possession of the enemy camp. But if the fighting was over, the killing continued. Texans armed themselves with Mexican bayonets and went about stabbing wounded Mexicans they found lying on the ground. Sergeant Moses Bryan, who had had enough of killing and had put his shotgun away, came upon "a young Mexican boy (a drummer, I suppose) lying on his face. One of the volunteers brought to Texas by Colonel Sherman pricked the boy with his bayonet. The boy grasped the man around the legs and cried out in Spanish, '¡Ave María puríssima! ¡per Dios, salva me vida! (Hail Mary most pure! For God, save my life!).' I begged the man to spare him, both of his legs being broken already. The man looked at me and put his hand on his pistol, so I passed on. Just as I did so, he blew out the boy's brains."

The Mexican camp was hemmed in at the rear by the marshy Peggy Lake and a tidewater bayou. The bayou was not very wide, but too deep to wade across swiftly. A surviving Mexican officer recalled that "the men, on reaching it, would helplessly crowd together and were shot down by the enemy, who was close enough not to miss his aim. It was there that the greatest carnage took place." Texas Private James W. Winters related later that "the Mexicans and horses killed made a bridge across the bayou. The Mexican infantry would jump in occasionally and dive to get away from our shots."

A Mexican officer climbed on this bridge of bodies and faced the Texans, sword defiantly in hand. He was shot down. Private William Foster Young remembered, "I sat there on my horse and shot them until my ammunition gave out. Then I turned the butt end of my musket and started knocking them in the head."

Arriving at the body-choked bayou, Colonel John Wharton ordered the Texans to stop the killing. Sergeant Moses Bryan was there too: "One of Sherman's men, Joe Dickson, said, 'Colonel Wharton, if Jesus Christ were to come down from heaven and order me to quit shooting Santanistas, I wouldn't do it, sir!' Colonel Wharton put his hand on his sword. Joe Dickson stepped back and cocked his rifle. Wharton, very discreetly (I always thought) turned his horse and left."

The Texans were like madmen, totally out of control, blood-crazy, and they were never more vulnerable than at that moment. Houston was in dread of the arrival of Mexican reinforcements. At one point, half-blinded with pain, he saw a group of several hundred prisoners whom Rusk had herded together. Thinking them to be Mexican reinforcements, he cried out, "All is lost! My God, all is lost!" Later Houston said that at that moment a hundred disciplined Mexican troops could have wiped out the berserk Texans. Somehow, he managed to call off enough men to form a guard for prisoners in the center of the Mexican camp.

By twilight the guns were silent and the carnage done. Houston returned to his camp across the plain and the doctors found his wound serious indeed. But he permitted only the barest of ministrations. Lying on a blanket with his head against a tree, sipping water from a gourd, he took reports from his officers. Incredibly, the Texans had only two dead and 23 wounded, of whom six would eventually die; Mexican casualties in the slaughter were about 600 killed and some 650 taken prisoner.

Yet the war was not over. Santa Anna had escaped and would undoubtedly try to reach his fresh troops. Houston, in pain, spent the night of April 21 worrying. If only the Mexican dictator could be found, he would be the Texans' security against further attack. "You will find the Hero of Tampico, if you find him at all," Houston predicted, "retreating on all fours in high grass. And he will be dressed as badly, at least, as a common soldier. Examine every man you find very closely." Detachments of Texans went off to search.

Santa Anna had quickly left his companions behind, for a lone rider could more easily elude pursuit. As night fell on the strange and flooded countryside, he lost his bearings and wandered about for hours seeking the road to Fort Bend and his waiting troops. Eventually he abandoned the black stallion and spent the remainder of the night hiding in tall grass by a bayou. At morning light he crawled around the edge of the bayou to a deserted house, where he changed into some discarded clothing. Then, his sense of direction completely gone, he wandered back along the bayou—and walked into a Texan search party.

They identified him immediately as a Mexican officer; in his vanity he still wore his elegant linen shirt with jeweled studs beneath the newly acquired blue cotton jacket. But they did not recognize him as Santa Anna until they brought him into the prisoners' compound and the prisoners cried out, "El Presidente!" Colonel Hockley took him at once to Houston.

"I was lying on my left side, in a kind of daze," said Houston later, "when I felt some person clasp my right hand. I looked up as Santa Anna stood before me. He announced his name and rank."

Texan soldiers crowded around threateningly. Santa Anna began to tremble and asked for his medicine box. Houston sent an aide to bring it from the captured Mexican camp; Santa Anna opened it eagerly and replenished his spirits with a bit of opium. Houston motioned him to a seat on a nearby ammunition box.

"That man may consider himself born to no common destiny who has conquered the Napoleon of the West," said Santa Anna grandiloquently. "And now it remains for him to be generous to the vanquished."

"You should have remembered that at the Alamo," Houston replied.

When Santa Anna offered the excuse that "the usages of war" justified what he had done at the Alamo because the defenders had refused to surrender, Houston grew angry. "You have not the same excuse for the massacre of Colonel Fannin's command," he roared. "They had capitulated on terms offered by your general. And yet after the capitulation they were all perfidiously massacred."

Santa Anna, obviously concluding that Houston would exact a like revenge, began to shake with fear. But Houston needed him alive and was already formulating plans around his captive. "My motive in sparing the life of Santa Anna," he later explained, "was to relieve the country of all hostile enemies without further bloodshed, and secure his acknowledgement of our independence, which I considered of vastly more importance than the mere gratification of revenge."

Houston impressed upon the Mexican dictator that, if he wished to live, he must order all his remaining forces out of the country forthwith. Santa Anna prepared the necessary dispatch, ending with the note: "I have agreed with General Houston upon an armistice, which may put an end to the war forever."

Deaf Smith and Edward Burleson carried the message to Santa Anna's men at Fort Bend. On its receipt, 4,000 troops packed up and marched out of Texas, leaving their president a prisoner in Texan hands. To make certain that Mexico did not soon mount another assault, the Texans kept Santa Anna captive until November, and then released him.

For a year Santa Anna remained in the seclusion of his hacienda in Vera Cruz. Then, taking advantage of an unsettled political situation, he returned to Mexico City, where it did not take him long to re-establish his despotic rule. In the years to come, he never really recognized Texas independence, remaining implacably hostile. As a matter of fact, sporadic fighting continued for the better part of a decade. But to all intents and purposes the war of revolution was over; Texas had won its cherished liberty.

Meanwhile, Houston remained encamped at San Jacinto through the remainder of April, attending to the disposition of the spoils of war and writing his report to the government. The prisoners were moved to Galveston and then on to Anahuac and Liberty before being released in April 1837. Houston's wound grew worse. By May 5, his shattered leg was so seriously infected that doctors advised him he would not live without the sort of advanced medical treatment available in New Orleans. Houston wearily turned his command over to Thomas Rusk. Two days later he sailed for New Orleans. A cheering crowd awaited him there and a welcoming band struck up a march. He lurched off the boat on crutches and fainted on the dock. The crowd fell silent, the music stopped and a schoolgirl named Margaret Lea burst into tears.

A little more than a month later, still weak but with his wound finally healing, Sam Houston returned to Texas to run for president of the new republic.

A bold adventure that ended in tragedy

For years after San Jacinto the Republic of Texas remained under pressure from Mexico, which refused to recognize its independence. To assert its sovereignty south to the Rio Grande, Texas sent raiding parties against Mexican river towns. Some of these raids became fierce battles; none was more tragic for the Texans than the brave venture called the Mier Expedition.

In November 1842, a force of 700 Texans under General Alexander Somervell managed to capture the Mexican towns of Laredo and Guerrero. But by December, Somervell, recognizing that he was outnumbered and overextended, ordered his men to pull back from the Rio Grande and return to their base at San Antonio. Almost half his troops, flushed with their successes and minimally disciplined, refused his order. They chose William S. Fisher, a colonel who also wanted more action, to command them and planned an attack on the city of Mier, 15 miles down the Rio Grande from Guerrero.

The expeditionary force moved out on December 20. Four small riverboats captured near Guerrero carried 40 of the men downstream. A detachment of Texas Rangers, who had also been with Somervell, scouted along the river's west—or Mexican—bank and Fisher, with the main body, proceeded down the east bank. After two days the expedition was opposite Mier. The Rangers reported that a large force of Mexicans was assembling a few miles away and advised against crossing. But Fisher ignored their warnings and ferried all his men, except for a camp guard detail, across into Mexico. In disgust, the Rangers quit the expedition, leav-

Burning Mexican boats, a party of Texans moves down the Rio Grande toward Mier. The drawing, like those on the following pages, was made by Charles McLaughlin, a British-born member of the expedition.

After overpowering guards in the courtyard of the hacienda at Salado, the captured Texans fight their way past Mexican troops outside.

ing Fisher to do his own scouting.

Finding no troops inside Mier, Fisher extracted a promise of provisions from the mayor and withdrew across the Rio Grande. A day passed and, when no delivery was made, Fisher reentered Mier on Christmas afternoon. This time 3,000 soldiers were there. The Texans, with weapons more deadly than the enemy's, killed some 600 Mexicans while losing only 12 men in fighting that lasted into the next day.

But then they ran out of supplies — and luck. With their ammunition gone they could not continue the fight. Eventually they were forced to surrender. Fisher and other officers were taken to prison in Mexico City.

Most of his men were ordered into a column for a long march to the same destination. Halted at a Salado hacienda, they suddenly seized their guards' guns and fled. However, without food or water in the parched mountains, 176 of the Texans — all but 17 — were recaptured within a week. In retribution,

As Mexican soldiers look down from a parapet, Texas prisoners draw beans to decide which 17 of them will die for trying to escape.

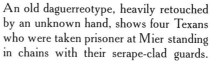
An old daguerreotype, heavily retouched by an unknown hand, shows four Texans who were taken prisoner at Mier standing in chains with their serape-clad guards.

One captured Texan who was spared any part in the Salado tragedy was John C. C. Hill. Only 13 when he fought at Mier, he so impressed Santa Anna that the commander sent him to school instead of prison; he became a mining engineer in Mexico.

Santa Anna ordered every 10th man executed. The prisoners drew lots from a jar containing 176 beans: 159 white, and 17 black — for death.

The 159 Texans who drew white beans stood by helplessly while their 17 doomed comrades were herded into an enclosure, tied together and shot in the back by Mexican soldiers. Nor was the killing ended then. Among the holders of a white bean was Captain Ewen Cameron, a dashing Scot who had led the Salado escape. Santa Anna was enraged when he heard that Cameron was spared. On April 25, 1843, as the prisoners neared Mexico City, the party was met by a courier with an order from Santa Anna for Cameron's execution. The next morning he was taken before a firing squad. He refused to confess to a priest, opened his hunting shirt and, presenting his bared chest to the row of muzzles, cried "Fire!"

The other 158 were clapped into dungeons. And there most of them remained until their release under a general amnesty on September 16, 1844, almost two years after they had embarked on their star-crossed expedition.

Ewen Cameron, leader of the Salado breakout, is

executed by a Mexican firing squad. Disdaining a blindfold, he cried, "For the liberty of Texas, Ewen Cameron can look death in the face!"

5 | Harvesting the fruits of liberty

Land was the only visible asset of the infant Republic of Texas. But it was a treasure greater than gold—endlessly abundant, thickly carpeted in grass and trees, and fertile beyond dreams. The rugged early days of planting corn with a sharpened stick were ended; now, as sturdy steel plows turned over the soil, the Texans began to enjoy the fruits of their labor.

The harvests were well nigh incredible. A typical East Texas farm could be expected to harvest up to 80 bushels of corn or 2,000 pounds of cotton per acre. And soon, Texas farmers were spinning tall tales of 12-foot cotton plants that renewed themselves each season, and soil so rich that "if you put ten-penny nails in the ground you will have a crop of iron bolts."

Even when utilizing only a small portion of his land, a Texan could routinely expect to produce far more than he could possibly use. The surpluses were bartered not only for necessities but also for such manufactured niceties as store-bought clothing, furniture and comfortable carriages. By the time these farm scenes were painted, between 1851 and about 1864, signs of the good life were everywhere. Snug farmhouses had replaced crude log cabins —through whose cracks a visitor once maintained he could toss a cat "at random"—and stump-filled clearings had been changed into luxuriant gardens.

Dressed in their Sunday finery, a Texas farmer and his family go visiting by ox-drawn carriage in this painting by artist Richard Petri.

A farm family enjoys the garden adjoining its vine-covered cabin in this rural scene by artist Louis Hoppe. Visitors to such homes often were surprised by unexpected signs of affluence: feather beds, pianos and, in one instance, a bookcase filled half with classics and half with sweet potatoes.

In a cowpen filled with assorted livestock and poultry, the sister and sister-in-law of artist Richard Petri milk the cows on the family farm near Fredericksburg, Texas. In the background, farmer-artist Hermann Lungkwitz—Petri's brother-in-law—rides out to tend the farm's free-roaming cattle.

"A free-fighting, money-hunting country"

After the stunning victory at San Jacinto, the Texans who had fled before the Mexican armies hurried back to their homes. Dr. Pleasant W. Rose returned to his farm near the Brazos River, arriving early on a Sunday morning. His daughter Dilue later recalled, "The first thing that father did after breakfast was to go to the cornfield. He had planted corn the first of March and it needed plowing. He didn't wait to put the house in order, but began to plow at once." The doctor tackled this chore in high spirits and, his daughter noted, "He said Texas was going to be a great nation."

This combination of ebullient optimism and good, practical labor was to dominate the 25-year period the Texans now entered. Their country had emerged from the war of independence deep in debt and with scarcely an asset save for its vast land and determined people; they faced hard times through their 10 years as a nation, struggling on the frontier, fending off constant attacks by hostile Indians and sporadic invasions by bellicose Mexican generals. Yet the Texans were suddenly free to create their own institutions, to accept every challenge and make the most of every opportunity. Now they could form their own government — suited to American, not Mexican, tastes and traditions. Now, with an end to all immigration barriers, a rising tide of settlers could roll south to the Rio Grande, and north and west across the endless plains, homesteading where they chose. They would plant vigorous towns, develop their cotton industry into one of the world's largest, and lay the foundations of a cattle empire that would

become greater still. And in 1846 the embattled nation would triumphantly join the United States as its biggest state, then grow prodigiously in strength during the 15 years thereafter.

These feats and more the Texans accomplished with their feisty, risk-loving, me-first Texas style. For liberated Texas was nothing if not a land of rampant individualists. An old settler called it a "free-fighting, stock-raising, money-hunting country," and a newcomer found it "full of enterprising and persevering people. The timid and the lazy generally return to the States."

The first order of business was to replace the makeshift war-time government with one of solid permanence. In the first election, held on September 5, 1836, Texas males 21 years of age and older were eligible to vote. A large percentage of them—perhaps 50 per cent, or about 6,000—went to the polls and ratified the constitution drafted by the convention the previous March; it called into being a republic much like the United States, with a president, a two-house congress and a supreme court. To no one's surprise Sam Houston was elected president by a landslide; the hero of San Jacinto received 5,119 votes to 743 for former provisional governor Henry Smith and only 587 for Stephen Austin. The first Congress created 22 counties and invested each with the power to elect its own administrators and three-judge court. With each town electing its own mayor and council, the Texans finally possessed the kind of home rule that Mexico had denied them.

So far, so good. But the task of financing this far-flung government was beyond the means of a cash-poor people, many of whom could not pay taxes and had to get by chiefly on barter. Duties levied on imported goods brought in some hard cash, but not nearly enough to support even the Texas army, which was soon disbanded in favor of a much less expensive militia sys-

Prosperous settlers, John and Mary Alexander farmed some 200 acres of land and raised horses near Austin in 1857 when they sat with the sixth of their 11 children for this early daguerreotype portrait.

tem. Congressmen, mindful of Texas' rich and immense public domain, hoped eventually to finance the government by emulating the United States, which had recently balanced its national budget by selling some of its public lands to homesteaders at $1.25 an acre. But before the shaky young nation could compete for land sales with the strong United States, it had to prime the pump of immigration by offering new settlers a better value in land.

The bargain Texas offered was unbeatable: a huge grant of free land for all newcomers. At first, each family was given, at absolutely no charge, 1,280 acres (two square miles) from Texas' public domain: each unmarried man received 640 acres. Over the years, the amount of free land was gradually reduced and, after 1844, new settlers — regardless of marital status — received 320 acres, which was still twice the size of the average homestead in the American West.

Thanks largely to the free land policy, the population jumped from about 35,000 in 1836 to more than 140,000 in 1847, a year after Texas joined the United States; and in the wake of these gains came a torrential influx during the next 13 years, when the population soared to 604,000. As early as 1838, the *Telegraph and Texas Register,* published in the new town of Houston, reported, "A gentleman who lately arrived from Bastrop County states that immense numbers of emigrants are constantly arriving in that section." About the same time the *Matagorda Bulletin* trumpeted, "The Colorado River, up to the base of the mountains, is alive with the opening of new plantations, and towns and villages seem to be springing up spontaneously along its banks."

Nine out of 10 newcomers were Americans, most of them hailing from the southern states. In their motley ranks were ambitious speculators, slave-owning planters and doughty merchants; for them, Texas was all the more enticing because their sound American dollars would go further there than in the United States. The enterprisers were joined by smiths, millers and other much-needed craftsmen, lured to remote communities by the promise of free town lots in addition to their normal land grants. Also, as in prerevolutionary days, there was an influx of lawless adventurers and luckless debtors who fled America one jump ahead of the sheriff and typically left behind the defiant message "G.T.T." — "Gone to Texas." But, again as in the past, the newcomers were preponderantly frontier farmers — the restless, obdurate, independent men who periodically moved on as neighbors encroached on their isolated homesteads.

Loading all their worldly goods on a wagon or two, land-hungry emigrants from the United States trundled west over so-called roads that were quagmires in the spring and thick with choking dust the rest of the year. It was a hard trip. Newspapers of the day quoted one lad found bawling beside his family's wagon. Asked his trouble, the boy shouted: "Fire and damnation, stranger! Don't you see mammy there shaking with the ager! Daddy's gone a-fishing! Jim's got every cent of our money there, playing poker! Sal's so corned she don't know that stick of wood from seven dollars and a half! Every one of the horses is loose! There's no meal in the waggon! The skillet's broke! The baby's in a bad fix, and it's half a mile to the creek. I don't care a damn if I never see Texas!!!"

Only a few American immigrants came by boat; sea travel was too expensive for ordinary folks bent on saving all of their meager resources for the best possible start in Texas. But relatively well-heeled immigrants from Europe ordinarily came by ship from New York, disembarking at the new port of Galveston. The largest number were Germans — substantial, well-educated people who were seeking greater personal freedom and better business opportunities than their homeland afforded them. Many arrived in groups organized by a German emigration society, and they made tracks for established German colonies centered in New Braunfels and Fredericksburg. Smaller numbers of immigrants came from France, Belgium, England, Ireland, Sweden, Norway and Mexico.

Like the Germans, most American immigrants arrived in Texas with a general idea of where they wanted to settle; they were guided by letters from friends and relatives who had preceded them. On reaching the preselected area, or while traveling toward it, each man went before a board of county commissioners, which had replaced the *empresarios.* From the board the immigrant received a certificate that authorized him to select his appropriate quota of acreage anywhere in the public domain. Many newcomers spent a good deal of time exploring the area in search of the best property;

they found it as hard to choose among the countless good farm sites, an old settler remarked, "as children in a toy shop." But once the immigrant had decided on a piece of land, he had only to get it surveyed and send a description of its boundaries, along with his land certificate, to the oft-moved Texas capital, where the General Land Office would issue title.

The whole procedure was remarkably easy—so easy, in fact, that it started a lively business in the transferable land certificates. Some newcomers immediately sold their certificates to speculators, pocketed the cash and settled down as squatters on the public domain or on someone's unoccupied land. Many an immigrant, unable to work all of the large grant due him, would file for only a portion of it; he thereupon received, along with his title, a remainder certificate, which could be used to claim more land at a later date, but which he often gladly sold to a speculator instead. By 1860, Texas had distributed land certificates that represented nearly 70 million free acres, and about 15 per cent of these certificates passed through the hands of at least one speculator before any settler actually used them to claim and occupy a specific property. Still more of the

land—just how much is not known—passed into the hands of individuals and speculators as a consequence of the Republic's desperate money policy. Lacking gold or silver to guarantee its currency, the Texas government issued paper scrip that was backed by public lands; the bills, of various denominations, could be redeemed at any time at the rate of an acre for each 50 cents of face value.

Under these circumstances, the speculator's business was chancy at best. A few well-heeled operators bought handfuls of land certificates and used them all to claim a single huge tract of promising land, which they promoted vigorously in an effort to make a killing. Sometimes they were successful, sometimes not. Other Texans speculated in land on a smaller scale; they were less likely to succeed.

A typical example of the small speculator was Christopher Columbus Goodman, who came from New York to fight for Texas' independence. In 1836, when the Republic rewarded its veterans with a land bonus that was based on their length of service, Goodman received a munificent grant of 3,182 acres—nearly five square miles—for his nine months' duty. Goodman

A settler lassoes a wild mustang while his companion pursues another one across the plains. In the 1830s the small wiry horses, descended from the Spaniards' Arab stock, cost about $4 each when broken to saddle.

soon fell sick and was forced to sell all his land for only $65, though he had been offered $300 for it earlier. Undismayed by this reverse, Goodman worked as a surveyor to acquire a new stake of virgin land, which he improved and then sold. He repeated this process several times, making small profits and suffering normal losses. As late as 1855, when good unimproved farming land could still be had for $1 an acre, Goodman was still speculating; he wrote his brother in New York: "The farm I had when I wrote to you before, I sold. Also I sold the house I built at the town of Navarro. I improved another farm and sold it, another and sold." For all of his diligent wheeling and dealing, Goodman at the time had accumulated nothing more than a typical frontier farm in Leon County. Its 160 acres lay on a flowering prairie seven miles from the nearest store and 30 miles from the nearest real town, Centerville.

Petty land deals such as Goodman's played an important part in Texas' growth. Every time a man sold or traded the improved land he lived on, he had to move elsewhere. In any given year, uncounted hundreds of established Texans joined the flood of newcomers spreading into the unsettled areas. Former pioneers, having fallen behind the swiftly advancing frontier, were constantly rejoining it.

The frontier moved in an unplanned but logical pattern. From the early settlements along the lower reaches of Texas' principal rivers, daring farmers pushed rapidly upstream, away from the Gulf Coast, westward and northwestward, into the dangerous plains where fierce Comanche warriors hunted buffalo on horseback. Behind the frontier, towns and villages increased in size and number, and changed in character too. Starting out as simple depots, whose chief role was to supply the frontier farmers with American manufactures and to send out their cotton, several towns quickly grew to be commercial centers and took on the vigor and variety of city life.

While the frontiersmen made Texas, the land was shaping them. Advancing by leaps and bounds through the wilderness, they left formidable distances between communities, and the large size of their land holdings left considerable distances between neighbors. Amid the wide open spaces, it took so long to get anywhere and back that they were riveted to the land between planting and harvesting. The growing season virtually stopped social activity, business trips and civic functions such as court sessions.

These were the conditions that forged the Texas character. Isolation intensified the Texan's self-reliance — and his appreciation of neighbors. Braving solitude as well as the constant threat of attack from Indians, the Texan became self-willed, impatient with laws and conventions, and dead set against any restraints on his freedom and enterprise.

During their 10 years as a nation, the Texans had to make do without most of the public services promised in their constitution; their government, broke and understaffed, simply could not deliver. Then, during their first 15 years as a state, they saw public services improve dramatically; in 1850, Texas sold to the United States its claim to enormous tracts of land in what would become New Mexico. The proceeds—a settlement of $10 million—provided a secure foundation for the new state. Meanwhile, in spite of their government's difficulties, the citizens of Texas from the beginning made steady and substantial economic progress.

As Stephen Austin's colonists realized in the early 1820s, Texas was in every way ideal for cotton culture. The bottomlands along its rivers were incredibly rich and yielded enormous crops, running as high as 2,000 pounds of cotton per acre. Moreover, the riverside cotton lands afforded easy access to cheap transportation. Flatboats and steamboats collected the cotton harvest in 500-pound bales and carried their cargoes downstream to new ports — chiefly Galveston — that sprang up along the Gulf of Mexico. Here the bales were transferred to seagoing vessels bound for cloth-manufacturing centers in the eastern United States and Europe.

Cotton culture boomed in Texas in spite of floods, droughts, a financial panic in 1837 and a severe depression in the early 1840s. The cotton crop, estimated at 10,000 bales in 1834, jumped to 58,000 bales in 1849. In the 1850s, when the population trebled and the number of farmers doubled, Texas became one of the world's major cotton producers; its cotton production increased tenfold, reaching 431,000 bales in 1859. Of course this phenomenal success increased the demand for — and therefore the value of — prime riv-

erside land suitable for the cultivation of cotton. In one three-year period in the 1830s, cotton lands rose in price as much as 400 per cent, and in the next decade a large, well-developed plantation sold for as high as $8.50 an acre.

The average plantation was relatively small and was worked intensively by four or five slaves, whose purchase price averaged $600 in 1846. Though cotton prices fluctuated, it ordinarily cost the owner of a plantation about five cents to raise one pound of cotton, which he sold for eight to 10 cents a pound. After all his expenses were paid, the planter ended up with a comfortable annual income of $3,500 or more. However the big profits that were made from cotton went not to the growers but to the commission merchants who bought their crops and arranged to ship the cotton bales to market.

One pioneer in this lucrative field was Williams, McKinney & Company. Samuel May Williams came from Rhode Island in 1824 to work as Stephen Austin's secretary, and Thomas McKinney was a Kentuckian who reportedly could hit a squirrel squarely in the head with a rifle bullet while both were running at full tilt. Williams was speculating extensively in land in 1834 when he entered into a partnership with McKinney, who was a general merchant, and they opened a large warehouse in the new settlement of Quintana at the mouth of the Brazos River. From there, the partners soon transferred their base of operations to Galveston Island.

Williams knew that his former boss, Austin, had dreamed years before of setting up a port on Galveston Island to handle Texas' promising cotton crops. The dream became a reality at the end of the revolution, when the Republic appointed Gail Borden, a New Yorker who later founded the Borden milk company, to establish a customs house there. The lion's share of Texas cotton cleared Galveston, with its exports soaring from 26,000 bales in 1850 to 84,000 bales just four years later.

Williams and McKinney capitalized on Galveston's success in many ways. In 1837, they joined with other enterprisers to form the Galveston City Company and built wharves to handle the swelling volume of sea and river traffic. From the planters under contract to them, they collected a commission for transferring cotton car-

The noble "Society for the Protection of German Immigrants"

With his plumed hat, broadsword and riding crop, Prince Carl of Solms-Braunfels cut a curious figure on the raw frontier of the Republic. Yet he was a true pioneer and founder of the most enduringly successful German colony in Texas.

Prince Carl was one of 25 German noblemen who, in 1844, formed a company called the Society for the Protection of German Immigrants in Texas. The society's plan was to channel German immigration to Texas into a cohesive German colony. In one stroke, the noblemen thought, they could provide homes for deserving German workers, open markets for German products, and develop trade between Germany and Texas. Each society member contributed toward a working capital of $80,000.

The society planned to charge each family $240. In return it would grant 320 acres, transportation to the colony, a house, farm tools, and sustenance until the first harvest. The site of the colony was already set, or so it seemed. One Henry Fisher, holder of a colonization contract with Texas, had arrived in Germany looking for buyers while the nobles were setting up their society. In June 1844, they paid Fisher $9,000 for a 4-million-acre grant between the Colorado and Llano rivers that he had described as ideal for their purposes.

But when Prince Carl arrived in Texas to pave the way for the first contingent of settlers, he found that Fisher had misrepresented the grant. Instead of being near the coast, it was some 250 miles inland—much too isolated for convenient trade, or even easy colonization.

The initial group of 439 immigrants reached Texas by December. Embarrassed but undaunted, Prince Carl left the arrivals at Matagorda Bay and went off to find a tract be-

Prince Carl of Solms-Braunfels

tween the coast and the grant that could serve as a halfway station to the colony. As he left, the generous but impractical Prince left orders for the immigrants to be given fresh meat three times daily, and unlimited credit against the society's funds. By March 1845, when he finally bought a 9,000-acre site 29 miles northeast of San Antonio for $1,111, the society's capital was nearly depleted.

The 439 immigrants arrived at the site before the end of April. Prince Carl named it New Braunfels after his German estate, and distributed land to the colonists, who set to work building cabins and a stockaded fort. The financial situation, however, continued to deteriorate. The soil was rich, but the immigrants believed it too late in the year to plant crops.

Nor did they feel any need to raise food, for they expected the society to feed them for at least another year.

On June 4, Prince Carl, regarding his mission as advance agent accomplished, returned to Germany. He had asked the society to replace him with a highly capable man, and John O. Meusebach, who had come shortly before, was just such a person.

Meusebach was appalled to find that the society's capital was now exhausted. With 4,000 or so settlers slated to arrive that winter, Meusebach estimated his costs at a staggering $140,000 by year's end.

In response to Meusebach's urgent pleading, the society in Germany sent $60,000. Over the next two years, though still strapped for cash, Meusebach settled not only his 4,000 new arrivals but another 3,000 as well. Pushing out from New Braunfels, he founded Fredericksburg, 80 miles to the northwest in 1845, and Castell, on the original Fisher grant 50 miles farther north, in 1847.

The society never recovered from Prince Carl's largesse, and declared bankruptcy in 1847. But Meusebach stayed to live out his life as a farmer and legislator. And while there were no further such attempts to found German communities in Texas, he and Prince Carl had provided the impetus for a flood of immigration that by the mid-1850s brought 35,000 Germans to Texas, making them second only to Anglo-Americans in numbers. Wrote one settler to Germany in 1850, "Dear brothers, sisters and friends, leave Germany and come here where you can live happily, well and contentedly. If you work only half as much as in Germany, you can live without troubles. We ourselves vote for our magistrates, everyone is equal and the poorest amounts to as much as the rich one."

goes from riverboats to the seagoing export vessels. They extended credit at interest to their clients; Texans distrusted banks and refused to support any, so the commission merchants acted as bankers in disguise. They also earned middleman's fees for shipping to upriver storekeepers the imports off-loaded in Galveston: hardware, clothing, tobacco, boots, soap, wine, plows, brick, medicines, mill-finished lumber. And the commission merchants invested their profits from all these sources in all sorts of ventures — hotels, sawmills, steamboats and still more land speculation.

Williams and McKinney might have dominated the commissions business — except for the biggest entrepreneur of the period. He was Robert Mills, a Kentuckian who in 1830 set up in business as a general merchant in the town of Brazoria. Besides dealing in everything throughout the Brazos and Colorado valleys, Mills sent merchandise to Mexico on burro trains and brought back his profits in silver bars, which he stacked like cordwood in his counting house.

Upon moving to Galveston in the late 1840s, Mills entered the commissions field and grew so big so fast that only a few strong rivals — Williams and McKinney in particular — were able to survive in his shadow. Mills plowed some of his immense profits gained from the cotton trade back into cotton growing; by 1860, he owned four cotton and sugar plantations with a total of 3,300 acres under cultivation, not to mention 200,000 unimproved acres. Mills was also the largest slaveowner in Texas, possessing as many as 800 chattels, and at the height of his fame was known as the "Duke of Brazoria."

While Texas cotton was booming, Texas cattle was beginning to become an industry. Unlike premium-priced cotton acreage, grazing land remained plentiful and relatively cheap. As late as 1856, an affluent newcomer named Charles C. Cox paid only $2 an acre for nearly 1,500 acres of good pasturage above the new town of Corpus Christi. Then he bought 650 head of cattle for $3,900 and was instantly in business as a medium-sized stock raiser. After assembling his land and animals, the cattleman had only minimal expenses. As an American visitor remarked during the 1830s, "No country in the world can be compared to this in the ease and facility of raising stock. All the herdsman has to do is to look after them, so they may not stray,

and some portion of the year, yard them to prevent their growing wild."

The basic stock for Texas' commercial herds was longhorn cattle, which Mexican ranchers had introduced long before the first American settlers arrived. In the early days the animals, left to roam and multiply in the wilderness, belonged to any Texan who roped and branded them. To improve the longhorns, several cattlemen imported expensive blooded bulls and bred them to choice native cows. One serious breeder was a steamboat operator named Richard King, who entered the cattle business on a large scale in 1852, buying 75,000 acres in Nueces County. From this holding would grow the largest cattle empire of all time, the King Ranch, which eventually covered more than 1.25 million acres in four counties.

The first of the great Texas cattle barons emerged in the 1840s. He was James Taylor White, an illiterate farmer who arrived from Louisiana around 1828 with three cows and two ponies. White settled near Anahuac in Chambers County, and about three years later he had amassed a herd of some 3,000 cattle. In the next 10 years, White hit the big time. An American visitor reported in 1842 that White "now owns about 40,000 acres of land, upwards of 90 negroes, about 30,000 head of cattle, has $60,000 in specie deposited in New Orleans, marked and branded 3,700 calves last spring, and sold last fall in New Orleans 1,100 steers weighing about 1,000 pounds each."

For all of White's success, the relatively small size of his cattle drive to New Orleans underscored the transportation problems that held back cattle raising throughout the period. Unlike bales of cotton, live animals could not be conveniently shipped downriver or on long sea voyages. Texas railroads offered little help; a total of 10 companies laid only 311 miles of track by 1860, and most of it ran along the Gulf Coast toward New Orleans, whose market was small and unconnected by railroad to the populous Eastern states. Texas cattlemen would have no reason to drive their herds north until the late 1860s, when the railroads pushed westward into Kansas; from there, Texas beef could be quickly processed and distributed throughout the United States.

But before that, Texas stockmen were virtually boxed into Texas; for the most part, their beef was con-

sumed locally and only the hides were exported. On this score, the Texans had no complaints. They bought the best steaks for as little as four cents a pound, and they made the beef barbecue a Texas institution.

As cattle and cotton production rose, the quality of life improved everywhere in Texas, even along the frontier. Some of the changes were small and barely perceptible. As late as 1860, the typical house built on the frontier looked very much like the hand-hewn log cabin that an Austin colonist lived in during the 1820s. But now certain amenities had become standard features, such as partitions for the bedrooms and planks that were used to weatherproof the inner walls. Other improvements could hardly be overlooked by anyone who remembered the shortage of supplies during the 1820s. Shiploads of necessities and even luxuries were arriving constantly in Galveston; and riverboats

were hauling the goods upstream on a regular basis.

The small farmer, who raised a few acres of cotton and perhaps a dozen cattle in order to complement his subsistence crop of corn, still had little money to show for his labors. But every industrious farmer was able to make a decent living; and he could always trade his produce for anything that he wanted, from a new plow to fine fabric for the family's Sunday best. The prices of imported goods remained high, but no Texan had to deny himself those two prized items, coffee and tobacco. Everyone drank coffee—lots of it—and practically everyone used tobacco in some form. Francis Sheridan, an English visitor who claimed he saw a Texan teaching a two-year-old child how to chew tobacco, wrote in his diary around 1840: "High & low, rich & poor, young & old, chew, chew, chew & spit, spit, spit, all the blessed day & most of the night." ◉

163

Bitter chronicles of Comanche atrocities

The Texans tangled with many Indian tribes as they pushed their empire west and north. None engaged them in more bitter, cruel fighting than the Comanches. These prairie hunters, who had swept down in the early 18th Century from their old homeland along the upper Yellowstone to the South Plains and who had harassed the Spanish and Mexican settlers before the Anglo-Americans moved in, were a warrior people. They hunted to eat, but they lived to make war.

Their admiration for courage was inbred; to them a man who was not a fearless and brutal warrior was not a man. Made mobile and wide-ranging by their superb mastery of the horses they acquired in the South Plains, they became legendary predators, attacking and retreating before their victims could organize to resist, and killing or savaging women and children along with the men. They often carried off women of child-bearing age, to shore up the low Comanche birth rate and to serve as menials. The Texans responded to the Comanches' savagery with similar no-quarter ruthlessness.

A classic written record of the Indians' contribution to this violence is an impassioned—and one-sided—chronicle published in 1889 by a Methodist minister named John Wesley Wilbarger, who was the brother of one of the earliest victims. Josiah Wilbarger, a teacher and surveyor who lived near the small community of Mina, was shot and scalped by Comanches in August 1833 and survived the experience (*page 166*).

Three decades later, Josiah's brother, fearful that "when the early settlers were all dead their posterity would only know from tradition the perils and hardships encountered in the early settlement of Texas," set about himself to "preserve in history the story of massacres and conflicts with Indians." For 20 years he interviewed survivors and friends and relatives of victims and in 1889 finally published *Indian Depredations in Texas*.

Early in the volume he placed his personal feelings in perspective. "There is a certain class of maudlin, sentimental writers who are forever bewailing the rapid disappearance of the Indian tribes from the American continent," he wrote. "We must confess that we don't fraternize with our brother scribblers on this point. They have evidently taken their ideas of the Indian character from Cooper's novels and similar productions."

To illustrate his book, Wilbarger's publisher selected a young draftsman in the Land Office in Austin, a talented newcomer from North Carolina named William S. Porter, who enjoyed drawing pictures and cartoons and writing fiction more than he did drafting maps. Porter had recently taken to signing his stories O. Henry. The Wilbarger-Porter work became a household volume in Texas and helped to shape the attitudes of generations of Texans.

In a woodcut from a drawing by the artist-writer O. Henry, the wife of Judge Jaynes pulls her dying husband and their wounded son, victims of Indian marauders, into their house, near Austin, as a fellow jurist, Judge Joseph Lee, gallops up too late to help. A slain hired hand lies in the foreground.

An anguished mother, Rachel Plummer, weeps as one of her Comanche captors drags her infant son to death. The Indians had choked the baby and dashed him on the ground but Mrs. Plummer miraculously had managed to revive him just before this scene. She was ransomed after 18 months.

An Indian applies a burning brand to the feet of Matilda Lockhart to keep her from running away. Matilda, about 13, was kidnapped by Comanches late in 1838. Returned in 1840, bruised and burned, she said she had been flogged almost daily.

Jane Crawford, captured in 1837, rescues her infant daughter from Indians who repeatedly hurled the baby into the water. Finally they tried to cut the child's throat, but gave up the plan when Mrs. Crawford pounded the knife-wielder with a club.

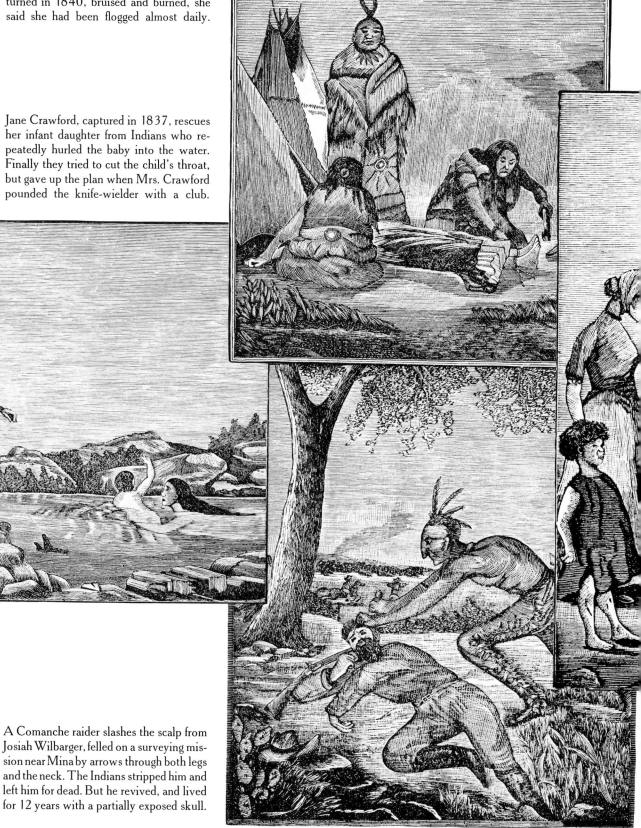

A Comanche raider slashes the scalp from Josiah Wilbarger, felled on a surveying mission near Mina by arrows through both legs and the neck. The Indians stripped him and left him for dead. But he revived, and lived for 12 years with a partially exposed skull.

Starving fugitives, some of 18 who escaped when Indians attacked John Parker's fort in 1836, prepare to eat a skunk. Lacerated by briars, the band traversed 90 miles to Fort Houston in six days. All they had to eat was two skunks and two terrapins.

Everywhere in Texas, game was still plentiful and farmers who once had to hunt to survive were now hunting for sport. Bold groups ventured into the Comanches' plains to hunt buffalo; and behind the frontier, sportsmen went out to bag deer, wild turkey, duck, geese and bear. John Jenkins, who had come to Texas as a six-year-old boy in 1828, wrote lovingly of the lengthy deer hunts he enjoyed with friends two decades later: "Ah, what meat we would have on these excursions, fat and tender and juicy and browned! We had feasting and pleasure better than that of kings, as we rested and chatted, surrounded by everything wild and picturesque and free, relishing as only a hunter can the venison, wild honey, bread and coffee."

Besides game, Texas' bounty still included herds of wild horses—free transportation or valuable merchandise for anyone who bothered to rope and break them. Horse breaking was a primitive, brutal process; Karl Anton Postl, a young Austrian newcomer who later published his memoirs under the pen name Charles Sealsfield, watched with horrified fascination as an expert performed the operation. The rider, with one end of a 30-foot oxhide rope snubbed to his saddle horn, galloped into a mustang herd and dropped the noose end of his rope over the neck of a likely beast. The rider wheeled his horse and, tightening the noose, dragged the struggling mustang until it fell choking to the ground. Next, the mustang's eyes were blindfolded and a huge bit was jammed into its mouth. Then, Postl wrote, "The horse breaker puts on a pair of spurs six inches long and with rowels like penknives, and jumping on his back urges him to his very utmost speed." If the mustang resisted, "One pull at the bit is sufficient to tear his mouth to shreds and cause the blood to flow in streams."

Eventually the mustang was run until it was ready to drop of exhaustion and pain. "The wildness of the horse is completely punished out of him," Postl said, "but for it is substituted the most confirmed vice and malice." This conclusion Postl drew from personal experience with a recently broken mustang; soon after he bought the beast, it tried to kill him.

Ornery or not, horses were the mainstay of overland travel—one thing that improved only slowly. The problem continued to be the terrible muddy roads, which reduced travel to a crawl for everyone but men on

169

horseback. The mud was hard enough on ox-drawn freight wagons, but it was worse for the high-wheeled stagecoaches, which made their Texas debut in the late 1830s and became commonplace after 1850. The stagecoaches always carried long stout poles, which passengers wielded to pry the wheels out of mud holes.

Because roads were bad, the postal service was atrocious. Mail deliveries, made by local freight and stagecoach companies under contract to the government, were not required to be fast or regular, only frequent. But they tended to be so occasional that opportunists hired horsemen and went into business in competition with the government contractors. Andy Yoast, a mere boy left to care for his mother when his father deserted the family, traded some of their land in Bastrop County for a mustang and took a mail rider's job. For about six years Andy carried mail on the dangerous 235-mile run between Austin and Nacogdoches; and when he quit in 1845, he could show an impressive souvenir of his hairbreadth escapes from Indians: a gun with many notches — 35, his mother claimed.

The roads did improve when Texas became a state. In the 1850s a network of roads — some of them graded in places — connected the major Texas towns. Meanwhile the county governments and private transportation firms improved local roads and built bridges or ferries at unfordable streams. And as travel improved, the grip that the land held on the Texas farmer was loosened a little.

Texans got around more. Though they stood stubbornly on their prerogatives, they had always been a social people, eager to party and gossip. They were a hospitable people, too; even the taciturn frontiersmen were known for welcoming wayfarers to their table. Texans had always taken care of their neighbors and shared their produce with newcomers, who had a tough time until they harvested their first crop. Now, as the older farm areas behind the frontier filled in, Texans visited more, developed a deeper sense of community and a keener interest in local affairs.

They attended fairs and patriotic celebrations on the Fourth of July, on Texas Independence Day, March 2, and on San Jacinto Day, April 21. When there was no occasion for socializing, they invented one. A barn raising was not only helpful to a new neighbor, but also an excellent excuse for a community frolic, which usu-

ally featured a rail-splitting contest for the men and a quilting bee for the women. At practically every social function, dancing was the main event; Texans typically loved to dance and young ones often would do so until sun-up. Frontier dancing featured violent stomping; and since this was hard on the feet of men who wore moccasins, they would wait until boot-wearing stompers grew weary and then borrow their footgear. In the towns, dances were more refined but had certain disarming informal touches. Women would bring their blanket-wrapped babies along and, during the dance numbers, deposit them under the benches around the perimeter of the hall.

But the Texans' special passion was horse racing; it combined their itch for gambling with their keen appreciation of good horseflesh. Most towns of any size had at least a rough race course and posted tidy purses to attract horsemen — and business for local merchants. Wealthy sportsmen with fast horses made hefty side bets on match races. An American racing journal reported that wagers of $2,500 were not uncommon around Texas tracks in the late 1830s. One of the biggest bettors was P. R. Splane of Columbia, who offered to match his horse against all comers and to cover all wagers up to $10,000. Betting fever drove otherwise responsible men to wild extremes. Hardworking farmers gambled away livestock they could ill-afford to lose. Colonel Jesse McCrocklin, war hero and prominent citizen of Washington County, wagered his whole veteran's bonus of 4,605 acres on a race — and lost. He packed up his family, left their homestead and began again as a farmer in Blanco County.

Horse racing was considered a sinful sport by pious settlers, but its tremendous popularity suggests that most Texans were no more religious than they had been as nominal Roman Catholics before the revolution. In the hopes of changing all that, hundreds of Protestant ministers flocked into the Republic by 1837 and began building churches. Soon a half dozen sects were systematically campaigning to enroll church members. A Methodist preacher remarked wryly: "The backwoodsman has gone into the forest, and the panther is scarcely more keen scented for his blood than the Methodist preacher is for his soul."

In the race to bring salvation to the Texans, the Methodists took an early lead; by 1850 they had built more than half of the 341 churches in Texas. A good part of the Methodists' success was due to their circuit-riding ministers, who were assigned by their superiors to regular preaching routes that usually took a period of six weeks to cover. These hardy men of God amassed an awesome record of travel. One minister covered an incredible 231 miles in eight days—at least twice the normal rate of horseback travel over the Texas roads. Another circuit rider said of his 36 years of service in Texas and elsewhere, "I have traveled 150,000 miles and preached 7,000 sermons; have lived and worked hard most of the time, and received small allowance for my support."

Religious revivals, usually held in forest glades, were extremely popular, undoubtedly because they offered people a chance to socialize and see a good show in addition to sampling moral uplift. The meetings ordinarily began on a Thursday and ran through Sunday, but if a crowd was well wound up the show might run on for another full week. Farmers and townsmen, equipped with camping and cooking gear, came from 50 miles around to see old friends, to gossip, sing psalms and —of course—listen to well-known preachers.

The ministers also did yeoman service in the cause of secular education. They plumped for book learning and offered their churches as school houses in towns that had none. The need was great; the Texas government, which had mandated public schools in 1836, lacked the funds to create a school system. The Congress did set aside large tracts of public land as an educational resource; the local people might sell all or part of the land to finance school buildings. But education during the Republic remained what it had always been in Texas—a matter for private initiative.

Slowly, church groups, communities and individuals founded all manner of educational institutions: grammar schools, academies, female seminaries, colleges and universities—even charitable schools for the blind and the deaf. Galveston University opened in 1840 with a student body of five. Baptists erected Baylor University in Independence in 1841. The Matagorda Academy, opened in 1839, offered a pupil "all the higher branches of Science and Literature" for nine dollars a month; and for those who could not afford the price, it would teach a basic curriculum for only six dollars a month. Almost everyone in the frontier communities helped to build and equip the local one-room schoolhouse.

By 1850, private enterprise had done a remarkable job with education. Texas then had 446 schools of all descriptions; 8,000 pupils were attending class regularly and, though many more children were part-time students, most of them learned a little reading and writing from time to time. Education in Texas during the Republic reached approximate parity with schooling in similar rural areas of the United States; and it improved still further after Texas became a state. From its newly swelled coffers, the government annually set aside generous sums for public education, and some Texas schools and colleges began to attract students from other states.

In spite of impressive advances in most fields of endeavor, however, the Texans could not solve several major problems. Disease was one—there were sporadic epidemics of yellow fever and cholera—and violence was another. Violence came naturally to a people whose nation was created in war and preserved by constant battle. But organized self-defense was one thing, and civil violence was quite another.

"Henry was cut to pieces in a bowie duel with Rip-roaring Jim Forsyth, a very resolute man." So began an eyewitness account of one incident of random violence in Texas. This particular Henry happened to be Henry Strickland, an infamous bully of Shelby County in eastern Texas, and most people in that backwoods area agreed that he deserved what he got. More to the point, they apparently relished seeing him get it.

According to this eyewitness account, Henry Strickland and Jim Forsyth "swung forward and both struck a chopping lick as their hands met. Forsyth struck Strickland's right a little above the knuckles, cleaned all the flesh off of four fingers clear to the bone, and lodged against his knuckles. Strickland's knife fell and he was at the mercy of Forsyth who only hacked Strickland on his arms, cleaving the flesh to the elbow on both arms. Strickland turned and ran, but Forsyth followed and cut his shoulder blade in two. He then let him go, declaring that Henry was in good condition to behave himself and repent of his evil ways. I thought that a generous act on Forsyth's part. Forsyth told me he could have killed him, but only wanted to cripple him in order to make a pious man out of a rogue,

Charged with "behavior unbecoming a gentleman"— shooting up a Mexican section of San Antonio in 1861 — the long-haired desperado at far

right is about to be hanged by vigilantes. The lynching, which took place in the town square, was sketched from memory by one of the onlookers.

a sponger, a horse thief and a peace disturber."

It was understandable that old backwoodsmen like Strickland and Forsyth would fight and even kill to settle their differences. They were uneducated men, ignorant or neglectful of the law and fiercely proud of their independence. But duels just as vicious were being fought by lawyers and politicians who had pretensions to being gentlemen. Law enforcement was weak, and there seemed to be no way to stop disputes from escalating to mayhem.

A killing put terrible strains on a community and on the Texas system of justice. A speedy trial, especially in the many jailless towns, was essential; but neither the local justice of the peace nor the county court had any jurisdiction over cases of murder and other serious crimes. The judges who did—district court judges—were few in number, had huge territories to cover and usually took weeks to arrive on their regular rounds. So, all too often, law-abiding citizens—frustrated, fearful and believing that only swift and dramatic punishment would deter more killings—acted illegally as vigilantes and lynched the accused.

The Republic saw its worst outbreak of violence and lawlessness in the early 1840s in the notorious Shelby County. It started when a local politician named Charles Jackson shot and killed an old enemy. Revenge was a duty, according to the frontier code, and presently the victim's friends and Jackson's friends were engaged in a series of tit-for-tat killings that spilled over into adjacent counties and lasted four years. The feuding bands, which used the fancy names Regulators and Moderators, killed anyone who got in their way, including a district court judge sent to try Jackson for the original murder. The factions agreed on only one point—that they didn't want outsiders from the Texas government meddling in their private affairs.

"A reign of terror and dread of impending evil spread themselves like a nightmare over the land," a militia colonel wrote. "Men barred their doors at night, nor would they open them unless at the call of a well-known voice. Men were shot from ambush, prisoners were hanged, others were driven from their homes. The most foolish and extravagant infatuation seemed to have seized upon all alike."

The colonel was part of a force of 600 that arrived on the scene and finally put an end to the violence.

The well-disciplined militia undoubtedly did more than any other organization to hold Texas together.

A militia of some sort had existed in Texas since the early days of the Austin colony, when settlers formed local "ranging companies" to pursue Indian raiders. In the 1820s, these informal outfits subdued the small south Texas tribes, and later many militiamen served as volunteers in the war for independence. After the war, the militia was made an institution by act of the Texas Congress. Every able-bodied man between the ages of 17 and 50 joined in his area and spent a day a month drilling; the companies were organized into battalions and regiments. Thus the Texas President could call up any or all of the Republic's fighting men to meet emergencies. Militiamen did most of the fighting for Texas after 1837, when the regular army was disbanded for lack of funds.

As the frontier advanced, militia companies drove out the Cherokees, then met and crushed all other Indian foes. Their last and greatest enemies were the fierce Comanche horsemen, unchallenged masters of the southern plains for more than a century. Early on, the Comanches had aimed most of their raids due south toward San Antonio and beyond, leaving the Texans in the east pretty much alone. But when the Texans won their independence, the Comanches began attacking them on a broad front.

All along the frontier, farmer-militiamen left their fields at a moment's notice from their captain—or at the sound of gunfire in the distance. They were aided by a small corps of flint-hard professionals, which was organized in 1835 expressly to fight the Comanches. This outfit was the Texas Rangers, who later won legendary fame for capturing outlaws and robber bands. But in the beginning, the three 56-man Ranger companies differed from the militia mainly in the fact that each Ranger was paid $1.25 a day. Otherwise the Ranger companies often worked so closely with the militia as to be indistinguishable from it.

In the late 1830s, the militia and the Rangers had more trouble with Comanches than they could handle. Large parties of raiders in their black warpaint easily rode undetected between the widely scattered frontier settlements and attacked communities far behind the frontier. In 1838, their raids on the cotton-growing communities in Bastrop County were so frequent and

By the 1840s a few of the more enterprising Texans had become prosperous
enough to own homes as comfortable as
the frame house of George Allen, a New
Yorker whose brothers founded Houston.

GEORGE ALLEN'S
RESIDENCE
HOUSTON — TEXAS. 1845.

devastating that the settlers fled south, leaving the area virtually depopulated for more than a year. Surveying parties, advancing ahead of the frontier, were attacked with special ferocity by the Comanches, who knew what these white men represented; warriors called the surveyor's compass "the thing that steals the land."

For the most part, the Comanche attacks were small-scale raids on remote settlements. A typical attack hit the Taylor family on Little River, not far from the town of Bastrop. The Taylors later told their story to a veteran Indian fighter, who reported it thus: "A band of 25 or 30 surrounded the house of the isolated settlers, yelling. Mr. Taylor barely had time to bar the doors when they began a persistent assault upon the house. The father, mother and a son of about 14 years composed the force that had to stand up against this savage band. Through portholes they fired out upon them. Charging the little cabin they tried to break down the doors, but Taylor sprang on the table, which had been drawn up against the door, and shot down, killing the leading warrior instantly. While he was reloading his gun, the boy leaped to the table and shot down a second warrior. The Indians soon gave up the fight."

As the Taylor raid suggests, the Comanches relied heavily on the element of surprise and withdrew against a stiff defense; when they succeeded, they would act swiftly—killing, taking scalps and booty, and galloping off before the militia could arrive on the scene. On the rare occasions when a party of militiamen overtook a Comanche band, the warriors would skirmish briefly and then scatter to avoid pursuit. The frontier was simply too vast to be sealed off or defended.

The Texans' savage war with the Comanches reached a critical juncture in January 1840, when three

175

San Antonio's champion of the lively arts

The burgeoning culture of Texas found both a gifted recorder and an enthusiastic contributor in Carl G. von Iwonski, a painter steeped in the traditions of his native Germany. Iwonski had studied art briefly in Breslau before his well-born father, for political reasons, uprooted his family from Silesia in 1845 and immigrated to Texas.

At first, 15-year-old Carl, his parents and a younger brother, Adolph, lived near the Guadalupe River in south central Texas. There, Carl honed his artistic talents by recording—in increasingly detailed drawings, watercolors and oils—this fascinating, primitive land and the structures and activities of his fellow Texans.

In 1858, the Iwonskis moved to San Antonio, where Carl quickly won a reputation as a portrait painter and got commissions to do some of the town's leading citizens, including ex-mayor Sam Maverick. Aside from portraiture, Iwonski shared the passion for music and drama of the German émigrés who were flocking to the area, and he devoted much time to activities centering around the town's newly built Casino Hall and its Casino Club.

Founded by San Antonians of German descent, the club was a cultural and social organization whose members were a mixture of erstwhile aristocrats and newly rich merchants. There were rooms for drinking and dining and reading and card-playing. But the club's most notable feature was a large ballroom, with an elaborate stage and a bal-

Iwonski at his easel, about 1866

cony, that could double as a theater with a seating capacity of 400. The club sponsored its own amateur repertory company and also rented its stage to other thespian groups in the area.

Iwonski's name first appears on the club's records in February 1858, when he was paid $35 for painting stage scenery and sets. He became a full-fledged member and over the years was a leading light in the club's theatrical activities, directing plays and on occasion acting in them. And as an inveterate chronicler, he made certain to paint charming scenes of the Casino Club, showing San Antonio's society attending performances of plays by the earnest amateurs of the repertory company.

The players of the Casino Theater gather for an 1868 portrait. Standing at extreme left is artist Carl Iwonski. Besides producing dramatic works, the Casino imported performers and lecturers from the East.

In Iwonski's highly detailed 1860 painting of San Antonio's Casino Theater during a performance by the repertory company, the artist has painted himself into the audience. He is the spectator at the extreme right.

Comanche chiefs appeared in San Antonio and asked for a treaty conference. Ranger Colonel Henry Karnes agreed to a parley, but only if the chiefs brought in all their white captives, some of whom traders had seen living as adopted Comanches. A second meeting was set for March in the Council House; and Karnes concocted a plan to seize the chiefs in case they failed to keep the bargain.

Some 65 Comanches arrived on the appointed date, including women and children. They brought with them only one captive: she was a 15-year-old girl named Matilda Lockhart, whose nose had been burned off, exposing the bone. According to Mrs. Sam Maverick, wife of the recent mayor of San Antonio, "She told a piteous tale of how dreadfully the Indians had beaten her, and how they would wake her from sleep by sticking a chunk of fire to her flesh, especially to her nose, and how they would shout and laugh like fiends when she cried."

As the chiefs gathered unconcernedly among the vigilant riflemen, Matilda Lockhart told the Texans of at least 15 other prisoners whom she had seen. The chiefs, when asked to explain this, alleged that the missing captives were in the hands of other Indians and would have to be negotiated for separately. Possibly the chiefs were telling the truth; each of the many Comanche bands was autonomous and no chief had anything to say about the conduct of another's band.

In any case, the Texans sprang their trap and a battle erupted in and around the Council House. Among the casualties were seven Texans and more than 35 Indians, including three women and two children. The last feeble chance for a treaty went aglimmering.

That August, the Comanches retaliated with the biggest raid they ever staged. Some 500 warriors from several bands swept past well-defended San Antonio and wiped out Victoria. Then they attacked the coastal town of Linnville, whose citizens fled in boats and watched from the bay as the Indians burned the town and tortured and killed five stragglers. The Comanches, with 2,000 stolen horses, then headed back toward their plains, leaving 24 Texans dead.

Texas fighting men from every direction hurried to cut off the Comanches' withdrawal. The enemy forces collided on August 12 at Plum Creek, and in a long, running battle the Texans killed more than 50 warriors while losing one man of their own. However, the victory was not nearly so important as the action that followed it in October. To press their advantage, some 90 Texans rode deep into Comanche territory. Locating a Comanche village, they launched a surprise attack, killing about 130, including women and children.

The foray established the tactic that eventually defeated the Comanches once and for all: killer raids

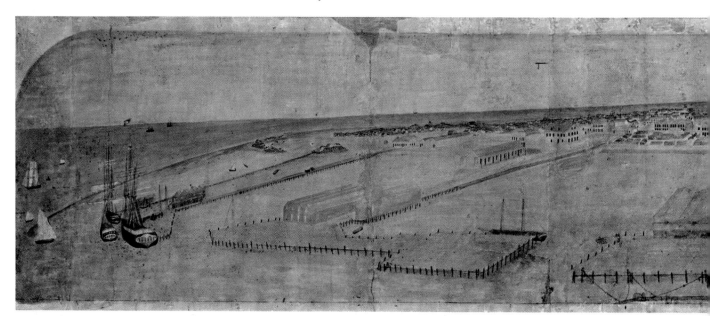

An international fleet of ships, come to carry off cotton and other Texas agricultural products, waits in Galveston's harbor in 1855. Though the

throughout their plains and gorge-cut uplands. The Comanche nation numbered some 20,000 at its peak, but the raids — together with the ravages of white men's diseases — gradually wore the Indians down and broke their will to resist.

At no time during the Republic or early statehood did more than five per cent of the Texans live in communities large enough to be called towns; the frontier and the farmlands behind it kept pre-empting new immigrants. In 1836, there were only a few real towns in Texas; the largest, San Antonio, had about 2,000 citizens. As late as 1860, when Texas boasted more than 600,000 people, fewer than 28,000 were distributed among the five major cities, none of which possessed 10,000 residents. Yet these centers were microcosms of Texas, and their fluctuating fortunes summed up Texas' progress far more dramatically than did the rural areas or the sprawling frontier.

From its founding in 1836, Galveston, made by and for cotton, was Texas' richest and most important town; its population rose — at a typically modest rate — to 4,117 in 1850, then to 7,307 in 1860. San Antonio, the old Spanish capital, remained the largest (8,235 citizens in 1860) and most cosmopolitan center. But because of its out-of-the-way location in the Southwest, it was eclipsed in importance until general

trade with Mexico developed after annexation. Meanwhile, new towns founded along the advancing frontier had a struggle getting established. The northeastern town of Dallas, founded in 1842 by a land speculator named John Neely Bryan, had acquired only 775 inhabitants by 1860.

Land speculators, using every promotional trick in their trade to increase the value of their property, played a vital role in the creation of other important Texas towns, most notably Houston. In the case of Houston, the speculators' strategy was ambitious but simple: since any town that became the seat of Texas government was bound to attract business, with resulting high real-estate prices, they set out to capture that designation for Houston. This was a popular strategy for speculators and promoters throughout the early West, and it made fortunes for more than a few.

When Texas won independence in 1836, its oft-moved capital happened to be located in the small southern town of Columbia. It was obvious to the congressmen, meeting there in September, that Columbia lacked the facilities to house the government permanently; and they began to discuss relocating to various other sites, all of which had self-interested partisans. It was not by accident that many of Texas' most successful speculators were in the government; there they could influence decisions for their own benefit. ◉

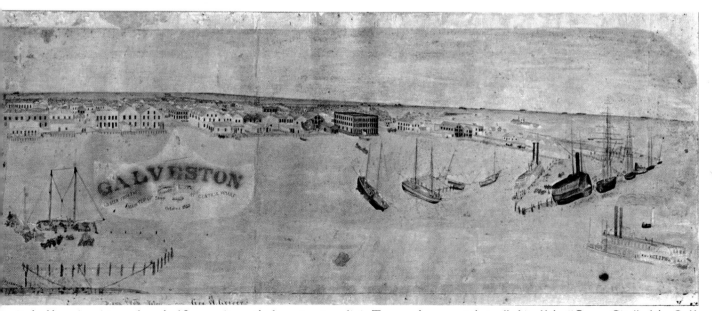

city had been in existence for only 19 years, it was the largest metropolis in Texas and a seaport that called itself the "Queen City" of the Gulf.

The great longhorn—a fortune on the hoof

After the revolution, hundreds of Mexican landowners fled from Texas, abandoning tens of thousands of semiwild range cattle. Lean, mean and possessed of horns that sometimes measured eight feet from tip to tip, these animals were the forerunners of the Texas longhorn. Their long heavy-boned legs and thick hooves enabled them to cover the most difficult terrain without injury; they could go for days without water; and they could survive droughts by grazing on brush and cactus.

They bred prolifically in the wild and by the 1840s at least 300,000 roamed the range, free for the taking. Many landowners set about rounding up whole herds, then began improving the stock by cross-breeding with shorthorns from the U.S.; the result was a still durable but beefier bovine.

By the late 1840s and 1850s beef had become a staple in Texan diets and the longhorn quickly gained value as barter. But the future of the Texas cattle industry lay in selling stock in the north, for cash. At first, New Orleans was the major out-of-state market for Texas beef, but by the 1850s herds had been driven to such distant points as Chicago and California. The drives started on a small scale — no more than 60,000 cattle left Texas in any year prior to the Civil War — but they demonstrated that Texas longhorns could be driven a thousand miles to market with almost no ill effects. Thus began the Old West's trail drive epoch which would, in the 25 years after the war, see some 10 million Texas longhorns delivered in large herds to railheads in Abilene, Wichita and Dodge City.

A mounted Texan holds a longhorn with his lasso while another prepares a red-hot branding iron in this 1867 view of a round-up. Mirages appearing on the horizon attest to the severity of the midday heat.

Dressed much like *vaqueros*, their Mexican predecessors, Texas cowboys guide a herd of longhorn steers across a stream during a trail drive in the 1860s. Their diminutive but sturdy mounts are mustangs, thousands of which ran wild over the Texas plains during the open-range era.

The congressional speculator who invented Houston was a bright and persuasive young senator named John Allen. Allen had arrived from New York in 1832 with his dour brother Augustus, a bookkeeper who provided their partnership with financial expertise. In 1836, the brothers had acquired, for $5,000, some 2,200 acres of land on Buffalo Bayou, about 50 miles by boat above the then-budding port of Galveston. The Allens had already named the swampy site in honor of President Sam Houston, which predisposed him to favor it for the new capital.

Senator John went to work, promoting enthusiastically. In Congress and in newspaper advertisements he declared that "Houston is located to command the trade of the largest and richest portion of Texas," and would therefore "warrant the employment of One Million Dollars of capital" to transform it into "the great interior commercial emporium of Texas." To climax his campaign, Allen offered to erect, at his own expense, a proper capitol building to house the government. The offer was too good for Congress to turn down: unborn Houston was named the capital.

In the fall of 1836, the Allens sent surveyors to lay out a town and hired carpenters to start building the capitol itself. But in January 1837, Francis Lubbock, an eager young merchant from New Orleans, brought a boatload of wares up Buffalo Bayou to the Houston site and found "so little evidence of a landing that we passed by the site, only realizing that we must have passed the city when we struck in the brush. We then backed down the bayou, and by close observation discovered a road or street laid off from the water's edge." There Lubbock found a few tents, one serving as a saloon, and a few workers. He quickly made the first sale ever in the town of Houston: a barrel of flour for $30.

Thereafter, the carpenters made better headway. They erected a two-story capitol building, which the Allen brothers would lease to the government, and a long one-story building of shops, which the Allens would rent or sell to merchants. The capitol building was not quite complete in April 1837, when the government moved from Columbia to Houston; so workmen lashed branches overhead to serve as roof, and Congress convened in May without further delay.

Lured by hopes for government business, merchants and craftsmen began pouring into Houston. They were met by the Allens' agents, who hawked town lots at prices ranging up to $3,000. But Francis Lubbock bought his lot for only $250 and paid another $250 to have a crude shelter erected on it. "There was no window in the house," he said. "When air and light were wanted, a board was knocked off."

Shacks and log cabins were built helter-skelter along unplanned streets, but not nearly fast enough to accommodate all the incoming settlers. The visiting naturalist John Audubon remarked in his diary, "I could not understand where so many people could be lodged. I soon learned that the prairie was dotted with tents." Even legislators slept under canvas—in company with abundant mosquitoes and poisonous water snakes.

The *Telegraph,* whose editor Francis Moore had moved with the government from Columbia to Houston, reported in August of 1837: "This city is increasing with a rapidity unequalled by that of any city in Texas; it contains 12 stores, several taverns, a large and commodious capitol and about 1,200 inhabitants." Predictably, many of the newcomers were not desirable citizens. Opportunists of every stripe—including lawless drifters, prostitutes, card sharps and belligerent former soldiers—arrived in droves and loitered around town, looking for easy money and fighting vicious brawls day after day. They made Houston, in the view of one visitor, "the greatest sink of dissipation and vice that modern times have known." But to Stephen Austin's cousin, Mrs. Mary Holley, it was a blessing in disguise that the riff-raff of Texas were attracted to Houston. The phenomenon, she wrote, "concentrates the rascals, with the Government and its hangers-on, & leaves the rest of the people in peace."

With so many people crowded together, disease in Houston became widespread. People fell sick from drinking the foul waters of the bayou; merchant Lubbock stopped that by persuading Congress to invest $500 in cypress cisterns to collect fresh rainwater. People caught fevers. John Allen, the brilliant young senator and speculator, did not live to enjoy the fortune he and his brother made in Houston; he died of a fever in 1838. The next year, Houston's population reached 2,000, but some 240 citizens perished in a yellow fever epidemic.

Nevertheless, encouraging signs of stability began to appear in 1839. The local typographers formed

Texas' first union, and they also set up in print a help-wanted ad for "A GENTLEMAN capable of undertaking the charge of a SCHOOL." Houston promptly acquired a teacher and its first school. It also acquired a theater, a jail and a court house—but not a single church until October 1840. Countless organizations, from a chamber of commerce to a chapter of the Masons, sprang up. One of these groups was the Philosophical Society of Texas, which 26 intellectuals founded in 1837 for "the collection and diffusion of correct information regarding the moral and social condition of our country."

In 1839, just as things were looking up, Houston was dealt a rude blow: congressmen began talking of moving the capital again. Houston had given them several reasons to abandon it as a capital—the low, marshy site, the humid climate, the prevalence of disease, the inadequate, makeshift accommodations. There were many alternate locations under discussion, but one in particular came with powerful recommendations. Lying far to the north, on a sweeping bend of the Colorado River, this site had been discovered and admired by a party of buffalo-hunting sportsmen led by Mirabeau Lamar, who was then Vice President of the Republic. In 1839, when Lamar succeeded Sam Houston as president, he spoke up for the site to a five-man commission appointed for the purpose of selecting a new capital. The commissioners appraised President Lamar's choice; they liked its elevation as well as its dry, healthful climate. They declared themselves in favor of the location.

Opponents of Lamar's plan protested vigorously, pointing out that the site lay on the edge of the Comanches' territory. The opposition was joined by many citizens of Houston, who were afraid that their town would wither away if it lost its status as the capital. However, Congress eventually voted for the new location and named it Austin in honor of the "Father of his Country."

The government immediately showed that it had learned a good deal from the mistakes at Houston. Edwin Waller, a Virginian who had served Texas with distinction in several government posts, was appointed to take charge of Austin's development, and he did the job with honesty, foresight and taste. With a team of surveyors, Waller carefully laid out a neat, handsome

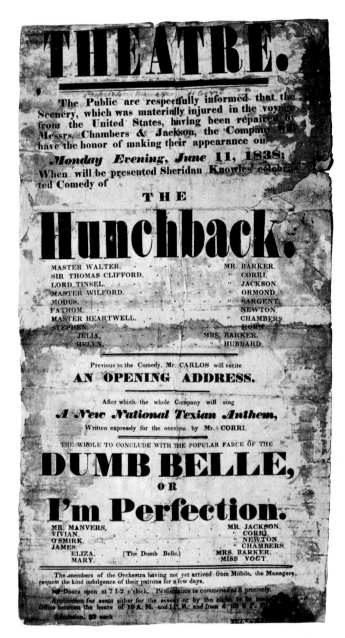

town divided by a broad central boulevard named Congress Avenue; Austin could expand gracefully, without the sprawl and makeshifts that had hampered Houston and the higgledy-piggledy frontier towns. Waller also presided at a proper public auction and sold off 306 building lots—for the benefit of the Republic of Texas, not some speculator.

Under Waller's watchful eye, the construction of the capital commenced in May 1839. As a precaution against attack by Indians, an eight-foot-high stockade

Using a peep sight on a compass, a surveyor establishes a property line in Cas-
troville, near San Antonio, in the 1840s.
French *empresario* Henri Castro settled
2,134 immigrants in the town in a year.

was erected around the capitol building. But Indians
prowled through the wide-open town at night. Occasionally, a late homebound citizen would lose his
scalp, but government officials took no needless risks
after they moved from Houston to Austin in October
1839. As a local politician reported laconically, "You
were pretty sure to find a congressman at his board-
inghouse after sundown."

Austin was duly incorporated by the end of the
year; and in 1840, when the town was spreading outward from Congress Avenue *(page 206),* its 856 citizens rewarded Edwin Waller for his many valuable
services by electing him mayor. Austin went through
its fair share of troubles in the 1840s, and by 1850
its population had dwindled down to 629. In spite of
this, in a general election held during that same year,
the Texans voted Austin to be their permanent capital;
and by the end of the booming 1850s, the population
had risen to a comfortable 3,494. Apparently Austin
never aroused the strong affections—or antipathies
—that Houston had. But, as the Texans eventually
learned, raw passions and good government did not
go hand in hand.

Meanwhile, Houston flourished mightily *(pages
206-209)* in spite of its loss of the government offices.
Business increased apace with the volume of cotton
shipped down the Brazos to Galveston. To facilitate
riverboat traffic, the Port of Houston was created by a
town ordinance in 1841, and work on a shipyard was
begun. The population, swelled by the town's growing
prosperity, rose to 2,396 in 1850 and to 4,845 in
1860. By then, Houston was firmly established as
the "great commercial emporium" that its speculator-
founders wished it to be.

Houston also became known as a center of culture,
boasting more schools and colleges than any other center in Texas. To be sure, its cultural reputation suffered a minor set-back in the late 1840s, when the
members of the Philosophical Society of Texas temporarily lost interest in their pursuits. But that was understandable; all Texans were distracted by the rewards
and opportunities presented by their booming economy. "Times were too pregnant with excitement for
grave pleasure to take strong hold," one Texas lady
wrote, "and consequently the dancing master found
favor with the majority instead of the philosopher."

186

A city where "the chapeau vies with the sombrero"

The great Texas land boom following independence triggered a frantic race to establish and promote new towns. A bemused English observer noted that a landowner had only to stake out some lots, give the place a name and it was "forthwith placed on the list of flourishing and populous localities."

Many of the new "towns" never got past the planning stage. A steamboat traveler on the Trinity River in 1843 passed the time of day by keeping his eye out for all the towns shown proliferating on his map. Their names were impressive: "Trinidad," "Carolina," "Rome," "Pompeii," "Geneva." But the only living soul to be seen where Rome was supposed to stand was a single inhabitant in a run-down cabin.

The towns that succeeded suffered a multitude of woes. Galveston, virtually leveled by an 1837 hurricane, converted beached ships into temporary homes and offices. Houston's dirt streets were so badly rutted that horses and carriages used the board sidewalks until the practice was outlawed in 1839. And as late as 1845, Indians were still raiding the capital city of Austin and lifting an occasional scalp.

Even as new towns were being born in turmoil, the oldest Texas town of all was being reborn. San Antonio, once the capital of Spanish Texas, was already more than a century old in 1836 when it became part of the Republic of Texas. Soon, distinctively American buildings — wood and brick homes, hotels, general stores and saloons — appeared among the adobe structures of an earlier era. In another few years, continental touches appeared as a new generation of Texans, many speaking the French and German of their homelands, revitalized the dormant town into a bustling commercial center.

The views of San Antonio on this and the following pages were recorded in 1849 by William G. M. Samuel, an amateur painter who later became a city marshal. By then, San Antonio was fast turning into a cosmopolitan city where, according to one account, "the chapeau vies with the sombrero."

North Side Main

An American-built hotel dominates the north side of San Antonio's plaza, filled with the carts, wagons and mules of a freight caravan.

za San Antonio TEXAS 1849

190

East Side Main Plaza

The clock tower of the old *cabildo,* or town hall — once the seat of government for Spanish Texas — faces the plaza from the east. At the left, crowned by a giant cypress tree, is the corner where pioneer Sam Maverick and his growing family owned a three-room stone house from 1839 to 1849.

Traffic along the south side of the plaza passes behind a pair of stores constructed of adobe and stone. The popular grocery at left was noted for its delicacies, some imported from as far away as New York, and was run by genial Nat Lewis, known to San Antonians as Don Pelon (Mr. Baldhead).

An American flag, flying in nearby Military Plaza, is visible behind the San Fernando Cathedral on the plaza's west side. The dormered mansion of José Cassiano, a Mexican who supported the Texans in the revolution, is separated from the cathedral by Madame Bustamante's fandango hall.

194

west side Main Pl

San Antonio Texas 1849   WGM Samuel

6 | The furor over statehood

Hardly was the Republic of Texas born when its leaders began campaigning for annexation by the United States. A referendum that year showed Texans favoring annexation by a vote of 3,277 to 93; and when the United States formally recognized the republic early in 1837, most Texans saw the event as the first step toward annexation.

But their hopes were premature; the republic was to wait for a decade as the "Texas question" became one of the most controversial issues in American politics. While the Southern states were prepared to welcome Texas, the Northern states objected that it would upset the balance between the 13 slave states and 13 free-soil states.

When a resolution of annexation was finally presented to Congress in 1838, Representative (and former President) John Quincy Adams of Massachusetts talked it to death in a House speech that lasted 22 days. In 1844 the Texans were turned down again by a Senate unwilling to upset the status quo in an election year.

The Texas question was a central theme of the 1844 Presidential campaign between Henry Clay, whose Whig Party opposed annexation, and Democrat James K. Polk, who came out strongly for what his party's platform referred to as the "re-annexation" of Texas. The campaign was enlivened by highly partisan—and often deliberately misleading—cartoon lithographs used as propaganda by party stalwarts, who posted them on walls.

Polk's victory emboldened outgoing President John Tyler to press Congress successfully for a resolution approving annexation. On February 19, 1846, Texas formally celebrated its hard-earned statehood as Anson Jones—the republic's last president—observed that "the lone star of Texas has passed on and become fixed in that glorious constellation, the American Union."

Symbolized as a triumphant fighting cock in this pro-Whig cartoon, Henry Clay rips into James K. Polk before political figures that include Senator Daniel Webster, far left, and former President Martin Van Buren, center. The artist portrayed kingpin Democrat Andrew Jackson as a bespectacled old man voicing doubts about Polk's Texas stand.

Epitomizing pre-election Whig overconfidence in 1844, Henry Clay and his supporters proceed to a political house cleaning: Jackson, dejected, looks on as the Whigs dispose of the Democratic candidates, Polk and George Dallas, and prepare to do the same for Democrat Van Buren—by dumping his head unceremoniously on the floor. The "mint drops" represent the Democrats' support of a hard money policy: reliance on gold and silver coinage instead of paper currency. The artist for some reason identified the kicking figure as Virginia Congressman Henry Wise. In fact, Wise was one of the few Whigs to come out in favor of the annexation of Texas.

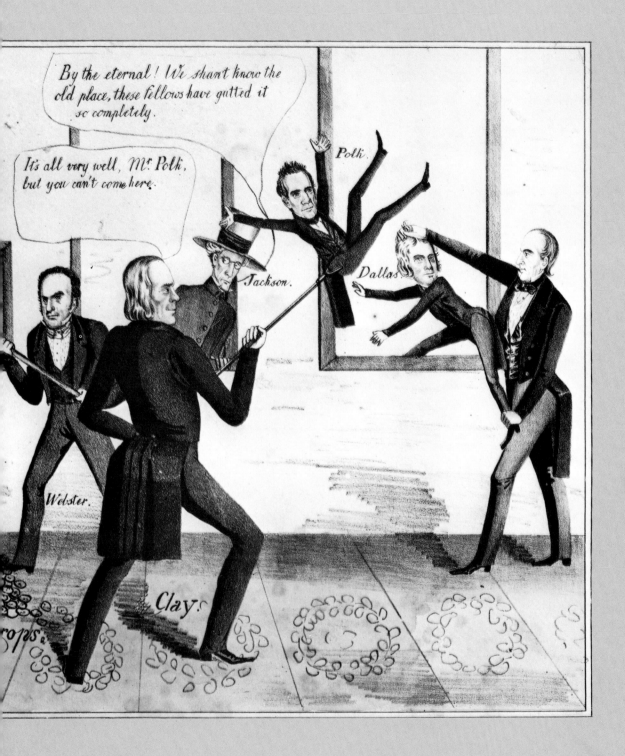

The Democrats' view of annexation is illustrated by this cartoon in which a radiant Texas is welcomed into the Union by the ticket of Polk and Dallas *(left)* but spurned by a cross-armed Clay expressing typical Whig attitudes toward Texan morality. A somber Quaker, representing virtue, gently reminds the high-living Kentuckian that his own reputation is not above reproach. At the last minute Clay equivocated on the Texas issue—which cost him both Northern and Southern votes in the hotly contested election. He lost to Polk by only 38,000 votes.

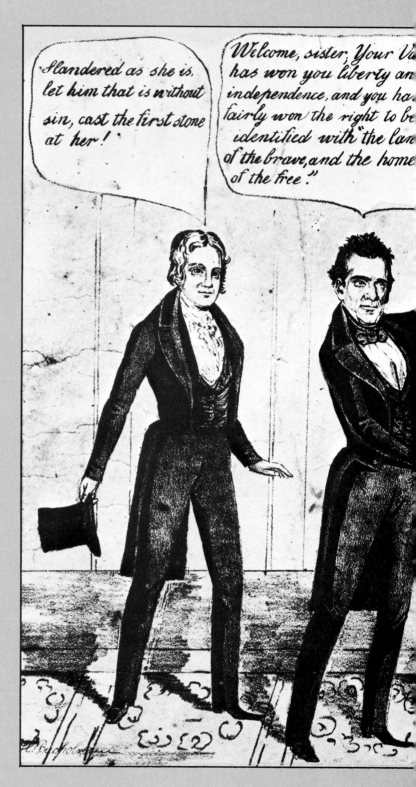

The last great battles of the magnificent barbarian

When Sam Houston came to the presidency in October 1836 for his first term of office — limited under the constitution to two years — Texas was a shambles. The land area claimed by the Republic after the revolution was 242,594,560 acres, stretching from the Sabine and Red rivers in the east to the Rio Grande in the west — although a defeated and resentful Mexico refused to accept the Rio Grande boundary. About 180 million acres were unoccupied and unclaimed, while 62,594,560 acres were settled by some 30,000 Texans. Nearly half of this occupied area had been devastated by Santa Anna's forces. One resident, William B. Dewees, wrote to a friend: "The country has been completely ravaged by the armies. Houses have been robbed, provisions taken, beeves have been driven out of the country, and the game frightened off. We have suffered exceedingly."

With the destruction of the farms, there was a shortage of food, and prices were sky-high. Settler A. M. Clopper wrote, "Provision is very scarce and hard to be got. Flour is selling at $18 pr BBL and I am told $20 on the Brazos. Corn is very scarce, $1.50 pr Bushel on the Brazos." And he added direly: "I am told there is 25,000 Mexicans on the march and will be here early in the Spring."

The threat of attack by Mexico still hung heavily over the Texans, who — even in their euphoria — knew that they could not withstand a well-organized mass invasion. Indian depredations, too, were taking their toll; the Republic was bankrupt, with a public debt incurred during the revolution of about $1,250,000,

and no capital resources; and expected recognition and aid from the United States were not forthcoming.

Yet the government of the Republic began well under President Houston and Vice President Mirabeau Lamar, the dashing Georgian who had fought at Houston's side at San Jacinto. Houston chose his cabinet four days after his inauguration: Thomas Rusk, Secretary of War; J. Pinckney Henderson, a lawyer from North Carolina, Attorney General; Henry Smith, provisional governor of Texas when the revolution was born, Secretary of the Treasury; and Samuel Rhoads Fisher of Pennsylvania, Secretary of the minuscule Texas Navy. For the prize post, that of Secretary of State, Houston picked Stephen F. Austin.

Austin's run against Houston for the presidency had ended in crushing defeat. Ill, humiliated and impoverished, he was preparing to retire to a solitary woodland cabin at Peach Point on the Brazos when his last call to duty came. "I have no house, not a roof in all Texas that I can call my own," he had written an old friend, Joseph Ficklin of Lexington, Kentucky. "The only one I had was burned at San Felipe during the late invasion. I have no farm, no cotton plantation, no income, no money, no comforts. I have spent the prime of my life and worn out my constitution."

If it had not been for the magnanimity of his old antagonist, Sam Houston, Austin might have died embittered and forsaken. Instead, he plunged into difficult and delicate negotiations to secure the recognition of the new republic by other nations, primarily the United States; and for a little while he was revitalized. "The prosperity of Texas," he wrote to a friend, "has been the object of my labors, the idol of my existence. It has assumed the character of a *religion* for the guidance of my thoughts and actions."

The end of Stephen Austin's heroic labors for Texas came in December 1836. On Christmas Eve he

After orchestrating the annexation of Texas in 1846, Sam Houston served nearly 14 years in the U.S. Senate, where he fought to prevent the South — and the state of Texas — from seceding from the Union.

left his office with a severe chill. By Christmas Day he "seemed so much better," a friend said, "that [his cousin] Capt. Henry Austin advised him to be shaved and have his linen changed and brought him out of the little room where his bed was and placed him on a pallet before the fire." Two days later, he lay dying on that floor pallet. His last thoughts were of Texas. Starting up from his near coma he cried out, "Texas is recognized! Did you see it in the papers?" He was 43 years old, and it was 15 years since he had inherited his father's dream of establishing a colony in Mexico.

Houston gave him his due in a public statement: "The father of Texas is no more. The first pioneer of the wilderness has departed. General Stephen F. Austin, Secretary of State, expired this day."

Austin's fantasy, unfortunately, was only that. Texas had not yet been recognized. Houston plucked Henderson from his post as attorney general and appointed him secretary of state with the primary task of prodding the United States toward recognition and subsequent annexation of the fledgling nation.

Progress toward those ends was proving to be a much less simple matter than most Texans had assumed. In the election of September 1836, all but 93 Texan voters had supported annexation. To their astonishment, President Andrew Jackson—whom they had always regarded as Texas' best friend in the United States—not only failed to press for annexation but refused even to extend recognition.

Jackson had good reasons for delaying, although he was personally sympathetic. To recognize Texas before the Mexican government itself had done so could be construed as an unfriendly act and might even drag the United States into war. An even greater barrier to recognition was the question of slavery. Most of the Texans had originally come from Southern states—Alabama, Tennessee, Mississippi, Georgia, Louisiana, the Carolinas—and they had brought with them a tradition of slavery. There were some 5,000 slaves in Texas, most of whom were engaged in growing and ginning cotton, the only important money crop. If Texas was to enter the Union, therefore, it would enter as a slave state. Abolitionist sentiment was growing stronger in the North, and the idea of bringing in a new slave state was repugnant to an increasing number of Americans. Seeing recognition as the first step toward an-

nexation, abolitionists fought it hotly. Furthermore, Jackson had a Presidential election to think about; he himself was preparing to quit the White House, but his friend and Vice President, Martin Van Buren, was running. If Jackson recognized Texas, he would lose Northern votes and possibly the Presidency for Van Buren. So he waited, and Texas waited.

It was an uneasy time. Until the new republic was formally recognized as a full-fledged nation by other nations, it would have to stand apart from the world community. Its land titles would be in question and have no value in attracting immigration; Texas currency and bonds would not be acceptable abroad, nor would there be any hope for infusions of foreign capital. And no nation would recognize Texas until the United States had committed itself.

J. Pinckney Henderson and William Wharton, Texas' minister to Washington, lobbied diligently to secure United States recognition. The tide turned in their favor with the election of Van Buren, which left the outgoing President free to act. On March 3, 1837, the last day of his term, Andrew Jackson extended diplomatic recognition to Texas by appointing a chargé d'affaires to the Republic. But annexation was another matter. The thorny questions of slavery and relations with Mexico still remained; and to the vast disappointment of Sam Houston and Texas, Van Buren rejected all proposals for annexation. There was nothing for the Texans to do but stand on their own feet—a difficult task in view of their critical fiscal situation.

Real money—based on United States denominations and backed by a meager supply of gold and silver—was painfully scarce. To procure government and army supplies from the United States, Houston had to pledge his personal credit; the treasury was bare. The standing army became an intolerable burden—as well as a peril to the nation because of one headstrong man.

When the Mexican troops were driven out of Texas after San Jacinto, they had scattered and then regrouped on the Rio Grande. By early 1837 a Mexican force of some 8,000 was camped across the river from Texas. The main body, under General José Urrea, who had carried out the Goliad massacre in the Texas revolution, was at Matamoros, one of Mexico's major military installations. To the unruly Texas army, no longer under the immediate control of Sam Houston, attack seemed imminent. But one did not materialize, because Mexico was too demoralized and disorganized to mount an offensive campaign.

Houston, cautious as ever, advocated a wait-and-see policy. Not so an aggressive 37-year-old adventurer from Mississippi named Felix Huston, who had arrived in Texas with a force of 500 volunteers from Mississippi and Kentucky in May 1836, too late to help win the revolution but still spoiling for action. In October he became commander in chief of the Texas armed forces, with headquarters at Camp Independence on the Lavaca River 25 miles east of Victoria. Soon afterward he announced his intention of invading Matamoros with the 2,500 ill-trained men under his command to wipe out the Mexicans there before they could attack. To Sam Houston it was an insane idea that could only provoke massive retaliation. He appointed Major General Albert Sidney Johnston, a West Point-trained officer, to take over command from Huston.

When General Johnston arrived at Camp Independence in January 1837, Felix Huston trumped up an excuse to challenge him to a duel. The two men exchanged several shots, one of which seriously wounded Johnston in the thigh. Johnston was obliged to retire for recuperation, and Huston boldly clung to his command.

Sam Houston again bided his time. His chance came in May 1837, when Felix Huston traveled to Houston City, the capital at the time, to lobby for congressional support of his Matamoros expedition. While Huston was buttonholing representatives, President Houston unobtrusively sent William S. Fisher, who had replaced Thomas Rusk as secretary of war, to the army camp with a letter addressed to the men.

Employing considerable irony but admirable tact, Houston's letter congratulated them on the excellent job they had done in defending Texas. Fisher read it to the troops; and while they were still glowing with pride, he offered indefinite furloughs to all who cared to accept, with a choice of free transportation to the United States or liberal land grants in Texas. All but 600 men accepted the offer, and when Huston returned, he found he had little to command.

Sam Houston had managed to reduce the costly army and at the same time end a growing nuisance. If need be, the defense of Texas could be handled by the militia that Congress had established early in Houston's administration. But just to be sure, at Houston's urging Congress turned its attention to the Texas Rangers, and gave the President a month's leave of absence to reorganize the corps.

Veterans of San Jacinto and young brawlers came from all over Texas in answer to Houston's call: such men as Deaf Smith, Ben McCulloch, Edward Burleson, Noah Smithwick, W.A.A. "Bigfoot" Wallace, John Coffee "Jack" Hays, Samuel H. Walker and George Thomas Howard—all of them destined to become enshrined in the hearts of Texans. Houston, back in his role as war horse, was in his element. Without the pressures of war, he quickly organized 600 men into three divisions as a border patrol to guard against Mexican or Indian attack. This done, he returned to his more conventional presidential duties.

Government income remained a problem. In mid-1837 Houston told Congress that in the previous eight months only $500 in cash had come into the treasury. Toward the end of the year he found a partial solution by installing customs houses at all the main ports of entry. Merchants importing goods were required to pay the tariff in specie, bringing sorely needed hard money into the Texas treasury. Duties ranged from 1 per cent on flour to 50 per cent on such luxury items as silks, averaging out to about 25 per cent on total imports. Customs accounted for half the government's revenue for the first five years of the Republic's 10-year life span; property taxes and license fees provided the rest.

But Texas pinned its best hope for sufficient capital on a $5 million bond issue. The bonds carried an interest rate of 10 per cent a year with a maturity date of 30 years. Buyers could, if they wished, redeem them directly for land at 50 cents an acre. The five million dollars thus raised—it was hoped from United States banks and investors—would have paid all of Texas' debts, stabilized its money, and permitted it to get on with the commerce it so desperately needed.

But when the certificates were ready for sale in the latter half of 1837, the United States was deep in a business depression sparked by a bank panic, and the Republic found the bonds impossible to sell. With this failure, hard times fell on Texas too. Real money—gold and silver coin—became scarcer; land values, already low, plummeted. It cost one man a town lot in Galveston to buy a few boxes of cherries for his wife. ◉

A seat of government, a capital of commerce

The hard-won success of the Texas Republic was reflected dramatically in the rise of two new and very different towns, Austin and Houston. Houston, which sprang up in 1836 on swampy land 50 miles from the Gulf, grew without plan into a disorderly sprawl of shops and shacks. But Austin, founded three years later on the banks of the Colorado to the northwest, was carefully designed to be Texas' permanent capital. Its plan, of straight streets and rectangular blocks, was both neat and easy to expand in three directions.

Austin's site was chosen partly to bolster the nearby frontier. When building began in 1839, riflemen stood guard to protect the workers against Indian attack from the west and north. As it turned out, the main threat to Austin came from the south: in 1842, Mexicans invaded Texas, forcing the government to flee eastward. The capital was moved twice before it returned to Austin for good. Later, Texans voted for annexation, and Austin began an era of prosperity and growth.

In the 1850s, elegant public buildings began to replace Austin's first log structures. A handsome capitol was erected, along with a new governor's mansion, a land office and several schools. In 1857 the state started to build Austin's largest structure, a hospital with balconies and a dome. And an unplanned bonus lay in the future. In the 1870s, when the frontier was pushed to its northernmost extent, Austin wound up conveniently located near the center of the giant state.

While government decisions were being made in Austin, Houston pros-

In 1840, Austin's buildings were clustered around Congress Avenue. The imposing structure on the hill *(right)* is President Mirabeau Lamar's house; the long low capitol, at left, is stockaded against Indians.

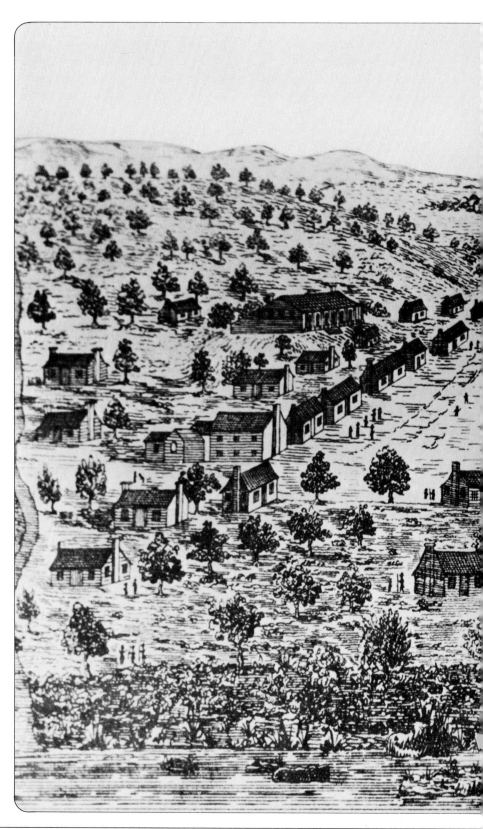

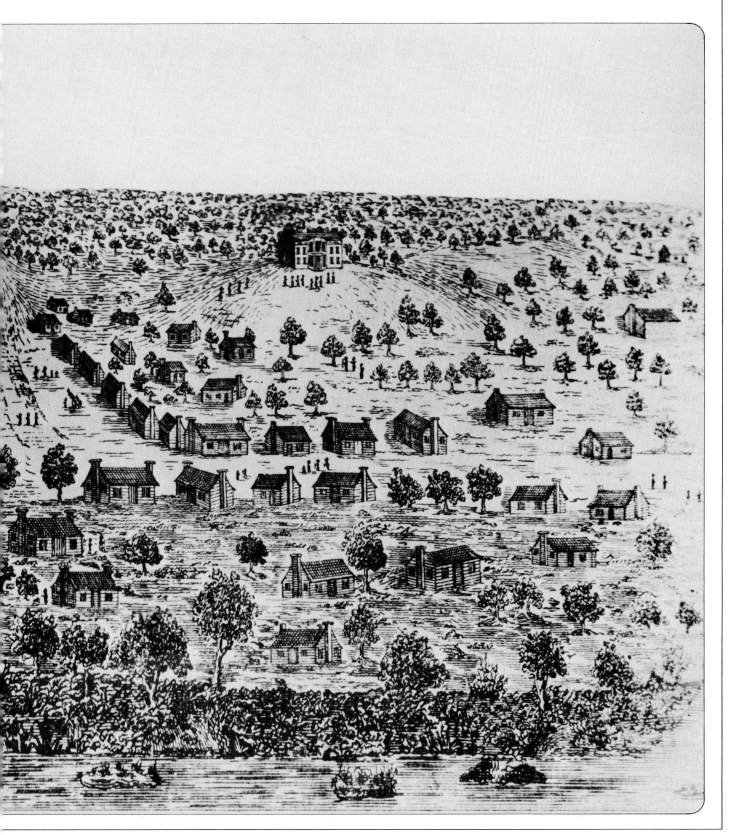

Houston's first railroad station served a seven-mile line south to Pierce Junction. The tracks were laid in 1856 in an attempt to lure profitable trade in hides and cotton from the older city of Harrisburg.

pered as a commercial center, commanding the trade routes between the Brazos River and the Gulf at Galveston. Over a network of roads that converged on Houston, a steady stream of freight wagons trundled to the town docks, where their bales of cotton and bundles of hides were transferred to steamboats bound for Galveston. In the late 1850s, Houston's first railroad station was constructed; a few years later, rail lines connected the town not only to Galveston but also to Columbia in the southwest, Alleyton in the west, Millican in the northwest and Beaumont to the east.

With business booming, a newspaperman, climbing to the top of a new four-story hotel, reported: "Away out on the prairie to the south and west, away over the bayou, the city is spreading out street by street, until it is impossible to find the landmarks as they were even three years ago, while nearby stately brick stores are rising on every bloc."

In 1853, the *Houston Telegraph* boasted, "it is estimated that goods to the amount of over a million dollars have been sent to the interior." Three years later, the same paper summed up Houston's progress with typical Houston gusto: "Boats are constantly arriving and departing, travellers coming and going, everybody working, politicians scheming, Germans smoking, the Irish joking, the ox-drivers cursing and" — poking fun at Houston's semitropical weather — "the clouds are raining."

When the government moved to Austin in 1839 the old capitol building stood like a "banquet hall deserted," lamented the *Morning Star.* But, remodeled and refurbished, it soon became the Capitol Hotel.

The main function of the Houston City Stables was to feed and house horses that pulled the streetcars, but the owner also advertised "orders for weddings, funerals and pleasure parties at reasonable charges."

Miss Brown's Young Ladies' Seminary was one of several small private schools that opened as the city grew. The usual tuition in those days was $3 a month for the three Rs, $6 for philosophy and chemistry.

The Pillot Building, constructed around 1860, was one of the first west of the Mississippi to have a virtually indestructible cast-iron façade. It housed shops on the street level and offices on the upper floors.

Meanwhile, in Washington, new Texan proposals for annexation had been rejected. A disappointed Houston withdrew the offer. It became all the more imperative to seek strong friends in Europe with a view to establishing trade, selling the bonds and securing recognition. In October 1837, Houston sent J. Pinckney Henderson abroad to negotiate with England and France. Henderson was warmly received and in 1838 succeeded in obtaining trade agreements with the two nations. He also opened negotiations with France for a treaty of recognition.

Thereafter a member of the French legation in Washington, D.C., was instructed by his government to make a survey of the Texas economy and soon a peppery mustachioed little man—the well-connected Count Alphonse de Saligny—appeared in Texas and presented himself to Sam Houston. Saligny was wearing on his coat the splendid ribbons and rosettes of his European campaigns. Houston, not to be outdone, exposed his chest, baring his own decorations—the scars of battle. "Monsieur le Comte," he declared, striking his naked breast, "an humble republican soldier, who wears his decorations here, salutes you."

The sophisticated Saligny was, by all accounts, enchanted by his unusual welcome. The meeting marked the start of a new era of international commerce and diplomacy for Texas.

Texas' second national election was held in 1838. Presidential terms were now to last three years instead of two. Under the constitution, Houston could not succeed himself. The political opposition he always aroused by his conservative policies coalesced behind his vice president, Mirabeau Lamar, a colorful personality whose distinguished record as a poet, publisher and war hero made him an appealing candidate. Lamar, sprinkling his campaign with vague but exciting hints of glory for Texas, ran on a ticket calling for vigorous efforts to secure the foreign loan that Houston had failed to obtain; Mexican recognition—obtained by force, if necessary; and the establishment of a strong nation that would extend to the Pacific. His domestic policy promised a national bank, a public system of education, and harsh action against Indians on Texas soil.

Houston's supporters were hard pressed to find a suitable candidate to run against the popular Lamar

and encountered a series of disasters in their efforts to turn one up. Their first choice declined the candidacy and the next two committed suicide—one after being scurrilously attacked during the campaign and the other at the end of a week-long drinking spree. The fourth was an undistinguished and virtually unknown senator named Robert Wilson, who was selected in desperation only three weeks before Texans went to the polls. Lamar swept the election with 6,995 votes to 252 for Wilson.

Houston was undismayed by Lamar's victory. At the inauguration on December 1, 1838, he made a special point of upstaging the new president by appearing in a powdered wig and costume reminiscent of George Washington, and delivering a three-hour farewell address in praise of his own administration. By the time he had concluded his oration the audience was considerably reduced and Lamar, too distraught to speak, had his secretary deliver the inaugural speech. It was an appropriate beginning for a downhill administration that soon jeopardized much of what Sam Houston had accomplished.

Houston retired briefly from public life to attend to his personal affairs. He formed a law partnership with one John Birdsall in Houston, but this was not enough to satisfy his prodigious energy and he devoted much of his time to various business enterprises. One was what he called "city-making"—helping his fellow stockholders in a development company to plan the projected town of Sabine, to be located at the mouth of the Sabine River. Another was part-ownership in a chain of trading posts, called the Torrey Trading Houses, founded by his friends the Torrey brothers of Houston. In time, Torrey posts were established at Austin, San Antonio, New Braunfels and along the Indian frontier, their primary purpose being to buy pelts from the Indians and sell them food staples, tobacco and knives.

In the early summer of 1839 Houston traveled to Mobile, Alabama, to raise capital for his enterprises and buy blooded horses for his own use. While there he was invited to a strawberry festival at the stately home of Mr. and Mrs. William Bledsoe. The occasion was another turning point in his epic life; at the festival he met a young woman named Margaret Lea.

She was 20, less than half his age, possessed of a tranquil beauty and poise that captivated him at once.

Margaret was equally struck by him. She had been on the dock in New Orleans that day in 1836 when he had arrived more dead than alive from his San Jacinto wound and had fainted on his crutches. They spent the rest of the afternoon together. Before the summer was over, Margaret had agreed to marry him.

When Houston returned to Texas, he found that his joy over his betrothal was not shared by friends. At least two, Dr. Ashbel Smith and Colonel Barnard Bee, tried to persuade him that he was not suited to marriage. "I implored him," Bee wrote Smith, "to resort to any expedient rather than *marry.*"

Houston paid no attention. He and Margaret were married on May 9, 1840, at the home of her brother

in Marion, Alabama, and departed together for Texas. Colonel Bee's prognostication was gloomy. "I see with great pain the marriage of Genl Houston to Miss Lea!" he wrote to Ashbel Smith. "In all my acquaintance with life I have never met with an Individual more totally disqualified for domestic happiness — he will not live with her 6 months."

But Houston confounded the cynics. His marriage lasted in happiness to the end of his life. Despite her youth, Margaret was a strong woman. Working with distinctly unpromising material, she set out to cure her husband of his dissolute ways. And Houston, his years of loneliness ended by her radiant company and the children she bore him, found reform pleasing. His drink-

211

The Rangers: saviors to Texans, devils to their enemies

To be a Texas Ranger, it was said, a man had to "ride like a Mexican, track like a Comanche, shoot like a Kentuckian and fight like the devil." If there was something a bit larger than life in that assessment of the Ranger, it was only in character with Texas. For whatever else they were, the Rangers were Texans to the core—and like their land, extraordinary by any standards.

Evolving from Stephen Austin's Indian-battling "ranging companies" of the 1820s, the Rangers were formally organized into a force during the Texas revolution. Constantly on the prowl, alone, in twos or threes, occasionally in companies of a score or more, they functioned as both lawmen and soldiers on the savage frontier. They hunted cattle robbers and bank robbers, pursued Indians, attacked Mexican troops —all with the same single-mindedness. Though they seldom numbered more than 500 men, they had a powerful hand in the shaping of Texas.

One of the early heroes was William A. (Bigfoot) Wallace, a six-foot-two, 200-pound Virginian who epitomized the proud and fearless Ranger spirit. Early in the 1840s, Wallace tracked down a notorious horse thief named Antonio Corao and, invoking the customary Ranger justice, executed the man on the spot. Sometime later, Wallace was in a San Antonio *cantina* when a mean-looking character stomped in, snarling that he was a friend of Corao's and was hunting for his executioner. Wallace drew his bowie knife and bellowed, "I killed Corao and I want to kill all his friends, too." The vengeance seeker took one startled look at the massive Ranger and fled town.

For many years, the Rangers were the only real law along the Texas frontier, and the picture of the lonely Ranger standing firm against one renegade or a hundred engraved itself on the Texas consciousness. A favorite story, possibly apocryphal, is told of the town that was being terrorized by a vicious mob. In desperation, the townspeople sent for the Rangers. Before long, a single Ranger arrived on the scene.

"Where are your men?" asked the Mayor in dismay. "We need a company of Rangers!"

"You've only got one mob, haven't you?" drawled the Ranger. "Let's go."

If Bigfoot and his fellows were the nemesis of lawbreakers, they were no less devastating as scouts and fighters against the Indians and Mexicans.

It was a Ranger captain, John Coffee Hays, who revolutionized mounted warfare in the 1840s by adopting Samuel Colt's new-fangled handgun as a prime cavalry weapon. Invented in 1836, the early Colt five-shot revolver was fragile and prone to misfire. The U.S. Army had rejected the weapon as a mere novelty. But Hays thought differently. The Comanche Indians he was fighting could shoot a dozen arrows in the time it took his men to dismount, muzzle-load their cumbersome rifles and fire a round. Hays dispatched Ranger Samuel H. Walker to help Colt modify the revolver and the result was a durable, quick-firing, easy-to-load, six-shooter known as the Walker Colt. From then on, the Rangers could not only fight on equal terms on horseback but could also generate vastly more fire power than their Comanche enemies.

During the Mexican War, when the Rangers led the U.S. Army into Mexico, the revolver-wielding Texans proved so effective that the Walker Colt was finally adopted as the sidearm for Army cavalrymen. In that short but bitter war, the Rangers operated both as cavalry and as long-range reconnaissance for the U.S. Army. Their ability to penetrate enemy defenses bordered on the uncanny. On one occasion, Ranger Captain Ben McCulloch led 40 men through Mexican lines to find a route from Matamoros west to Monterrey for the invading U.S. Army. In 10 days, he and his men traversed 250 miles and raided several villages and rancheros without once being sighted by the Mexicans.

So fierce and elusive were the Rangers that the Mexicans called them Los Tejanos Diablos—the Texas devils. And after the capture of Mexico City, the Texans earned another name: Los Tejanos Sanguinarios—the bloodthirsty Texans. Quick-triggered at best, the Rangers were enraged when one of their men was murdered in a villainous part of the city, and went on a shooting rampage that left more than 80 Mexicans lying dead in the streets.

The Comanches eventually came to regard the Texans with even greater terror. In the 1850s, the seek-and-destroy missions first staged in the 1820s against the Eastern Karankawas were refined to a bloody art by the latter-day Rangers. In 1858, Ranger Captain John S. (Rip) Ford was given command of all Texas state forces—militia as well as Rangers—and ordered to use whatever means necessary to end Comanche pillaging in northern Texas. Ford gathered 215 men—mostly Rangers, with some militiamen and a number of friendly Indians—and tracked a band of Comanches all the way to the Canadian River in Oklahoma. The trail led to a large Comanche village, defended by 300 warriors. But they were no match for the heavily armed Texans, who lost only two killed and two wounded while killing 76 Indians (including the chief), taking 18 prisoners, capturing some 300 horses and destroying the village's food stores.

In the years to come, the Rangers used their effective mobile assault forces to drive the Comanches out of Texas. And after the Civil War, the U.S. Cavalry adopted their tactic to obliterate Indian resistance in the West.

Bigfoot Wallace gave evidence for his nickname in this late 1870s photo.

ing moderated, and oaths almost disappeared from his conversation—at least in Margaret's company.

A devout Baptist, she steered her husband gradually and with enormous patience toward the church. It took years, but his conversion finally came in 1854. He was baptized in Rocky Creek, near their home in Independence, to the vast astonishment of those who knew anything at all about him. "The announcement of General Houston's immersion has excited the wonder and surprise of many who have supposed that he was past praying for," the religious journal, *America's Own,* reported. As to whether his sins were washed away in the baptism, Houston observed to a friend, "I hope so. But if they were all washed away, the Lord help the fish down below."

The Houstons maintained several beautiful residences in addition to their home in Independence, and traveled between them in a great yellow coach. Their townhouse was on the outskirts of Huntsville, 65 miles north of Houston, with spacious grounds and a log-cabin sanctum in the side yard for Houston's private use. Fourteen miles out of town was a plantation home called Raven Hill, after the name given to Houston by the Cherokees so many years before. Most summers they spent at Cedar Point in a lovely spot on Galveston Bay. Their first child, Sam Houston Jr., was born in 1843, and seven others followed—to Sam Houston's great delight.

Politics, however, cut deeply into the couple's time together. Even before marrying Margaret, Houston had been elected to the lower house of the Texas Congress. President Lamar's policies were leading the country ever deeper into trouble and Houston took it upon himself to head the opposition.

Lamar, 40 years old when inaugurated, had little experience in government but much ambition for himself and the Republic. He scorned annexation and envisioned a powerful independent nation that would be recognized and honored by all the great powers of Europe. One month after he took office the Texas Senate withdrew its offer of annexation to the United States, leaving the Republic to stand on its own feet.

To Lamar, Texas' wisest course was to strengthen its armed forces against possible invasion by Mexico and defend its frontier settlers against Indian raiders. Roads, schools, a permanent national capital and a banking system would have to be established; loans and trade treaties were required to bring prosperity. All these needs were real, and far more compelling than they had been in Houston's term; but the cost of meeting them was beyond the means of the Republic. An impractical if well-meaning man, Lamar launched a grandiose and costly program of government activity that shocked even those who had voted for him.

One of his few positive and truly progressive moves, undertaken early in his administration, was to advocate and obtain passage of the Education Act of 1839, which laid a permanent foundation for public education in Texas. Under the act, three leagues—one league equaled 4,428 acres—were set aside in each county for the establishment of public academies (an additional league was added by later legislation). Fifty leagues of public land were reserved for the eventual founding of two universities.

At the same time, Lamar was laying out the new capital city of Austin—a move that angered a good many Texans, especially Houston and his supporters. But it was a minor irritation compared with some of Lamar's other acts, which his opponents characterized as extravagant, foolish and even cruel. Issuing paper money to pay expenses, he rebuilt the Texas army—not only to forestall attack by Mexican forces and marauding Comanches, but to wage deliberate war on Indians living within the boundaries of Texas. His main objective was to drive the Cherokees—with whom Sam Houston had consistently sought peace—from East Texas, on the grounds that they had no legal title to the lands they occupied.

In July 1839, Texan forces engaged in a series of bloody battles against bands of Cherokees under 84-year-old Chief Bowles, or The Bowl, and drove them relentlessly across the Red River to Indian Territory in the United States. The Bowl, an old friend of Houston's, fell on the second day of fighting. He had refused to retreat. "I stay," he said. "I am an old man. I die here." Pried from his stiffening hand as he lay dead was a sword that Sam Houston had given him. The death of The Bowl turned Houston's hostility toward Lamar into implacable enmity.

The war against the Cherokees cost a great many lives on both sides and far more money than Texas could afford. By September of 1840 Congress had is-

sued almost $3 million in paper money with nothing to back it up, and the value of Texas money sank to 20 cents on the dollar. Outraged by what was happening to his beloved Republic, Houston denounced President Lamar for his "useless extravagance" and "unprincipled profligacy."

The cost of the Cherokee fighting, the building of a new capital and other large government expenditures fell on the debilitated Texas treasury like a sword. The question of recognition by other nations, coupled with the still-unsold $5 million bond issue of Houston's administration, became critically important.

Lamar, at the beginning of his term, had appointed James Hamilton to sell the bonds in the United States and Europe. Hamilton was a New England-educated lawyer and a former governor of South Carolina. A man with useful personal contacts and a talent for making money, he had raised funds for Texas during its revolution. Through his acquaintance with Nicholas Biddle, the influential head of the Bank of the United States in Philadelphia, he sold $400,000 worth of bonds in the United States. He then dashed off to Europe, where he found that France, encouraged by burgeoning trade with Texas, was interested in an official relationship. The Count de Saligny had been impressed by the new nation's prospects and had whetted France's interest with an enthusiastic report. Late in 1839 France formally extended recognition to Texas in a treaty of amity. Saligny was appointed French chargé d'affaires in Texas.

As for the bonds, France was tempted but not yet ready to buy. Hamilton sailed briskly from country to country to obtain recognition and sell the certificates. He had little luck with the latter, but he did successfully negotiate a treaty of recognition with the Netherlands, which was signed in September 1840. Britain, seeing Texas as a buffer against the expansionism of the United States and as a client for its manufactured goods, and also spurred to action by continental Europe's improving estimate of the Republic, granted recognition in November 1840. Belgian recognition followed soon thereafter.

France now looked more favorably upon the Texas bonds. A prestigious banking house agreed to buy them if the French treasury would back them. Hamilton was persuasive in his talks with the government; the Minister of Finance agreed to guarantee the certificates and the matter seemed settled.

It was a tremendous triumph for Hamilton. At last the Republic would have the resources to pay its debts, solidify its currency and build its trade — or so the Texans thought. Unfortunately, France's dandified chargé d'affaires, Alphonse de Saligny, was rapidly becoming disenchanted. The crude manners of the Texans and the rawness of the frontier capital of Austin were particularly appalling to him. An abusive, running battle with an innkeeper over Saligny's hotel bill simmered for months, and came to a head when the innkeeper threw Saligny off his property. In the spring of 1841, the indignant Count Saligny — "No-Count," as the Texans called him — flounced out of Texas forever with epithets ringing in his ears.

Texas laughed, but not for long. France's Minister of Finance was Saligny's brother-in-law — and with the chargé d'affaires' blistering report the government cooled toward Texas, the banking house backed out of its agreement with James Hamilton, and the bond purchase was dead.

With the Republic's government in desperate financial straits, President Lamar plunged into an ill-conceived scheme to garner for Texas a share of the profitable trade being carried over the Santa Fe Trail between Missouri and the Mexican territory of New Mexico. It would be easy, he reasoned, to establish an overland route from Texas ports to Santa Fe, enabling Texas merchants to compete for the New Mexican market and bring plentiful customs revenues into the treasury. He also hoped to plant the Lone Star flag in New Mexico. Texas' old enemy, Santa Anna, had been restored to power in Mexico and Lamar was convinced that the liberal New Mexicans would welcome an opportunity to throw off Santa Anna's dictatorial yoke. In spite of strong congressional opposition spearheaded by Sam Houston, he dispatched an expedition to Santa Fe.

In June 1841, some 300 men led by General Hugh McLeod set off in a caravan of 21 wagons on the 1,300-mile trek from Bushy Creek near Austin to Santa Fe. Many of them were merchants bearing goods for trading; some were soldiers to guard the party against possible attack by the Comanche Indians; and a few were diplomatic envoys empowered by Lamar to invite the New Mexicans to join the Texas Republic.

It was a naive plan that came to a disastrous end. The Governor of New Mexico, a Santa Anna appointee, was waiting for the expedition with a force of dragoons as it crossed the border. He gave a friendly greeting and persuaded the Texans to lay down their arms — then took them captive and seized their wagons. Ignominiously and cruelly, the prisoners were marched to Santa Fe and from there to Mexico City, a journey of 1,500 miles. Those who survived — and many died along the way of hunger, thirst and exhaustion — were flung into the dungeons of Perote Castle.

The needless tragedy was the crowning blow to Lamar's failing administration. Hope of peaceful coexistence between Mexico and Texas virtually vanished. Texas currency was down to three cents on the dollar; the bulk of the bonds remained unsold; and the public debt had risen to more than $6 million.

Sam Houston regarded the condition of the country as "not less gloomy than it was prior to the battle of San Jacinto"; and in the election of 1841 he once more threw his hat into the presidential ring. This time his opponent was David Burnet, Lamar's vice president and a longtime adversary of Houston's.

The campaign was a lively one. Burnet denounced Houston's character; Houston blamed Burnet for Lamar's failures and called his opponent a "political brawler and canting hypocrite." Burnet's supporters attacked Houston's drinking habits, and one said: "The people are becoming more and more afraid of trusting the *righting* of the Ship of State into the hands of a hero who can't *stand upright* himself." Planter James Morgan countered with: "He is still unsteady, *intemperate,* but drunk in a ditch is worth a thousand of Lamar and Burnet." The majority of Texans agreed; Houston received 7,915 votes to 3,616 for Burnet.

Houston appeared for his second inauguration on December 13, 1841, in a linsey-woolsey hunting shirt and pantaloons — fittingly homespun for a time when financial conditions were at their lowest ebb since 1836. "There is not a dollar in the treasury," he told Congress. "We are not only without money, but without credit, and for want of punctuality" — in paying debts, he meant — "without honor."

Houston cut his own salary in half. He refused to live in the two-story president's mansion that Lamar had built in Austin, and took quarters at a modest inn. He abolished positions, consolidated the Navy with the War Department and the Post Office with the State Department, and slashed the government payroll from $174,000 to $32,800 a year. Even the Congressmen cooperated by cutting their pay from $5 to $3 per day. Despite Santa Anna's animosity, Houston would permit no money for a regular army; the militia, he announced, would have to suffice. The bond issue was canceled and Congress suspended the entire public debt: "We have no money," Houston said. "We cannot redeem our liabilities." In the previous three years Lamar had spent $5 million; in the next three Houston would spend $500,000.

Many Texans, hot with rage over the outcome of Lamar's Santa Fe expedition, urged war with Mexico. Houston counseled peace; Texas could not afford another war. "The true interest of Texas," Houston declared, "is to maintain peace with all nations and cultivate the soil."

Both Houston's pacific policy and his hopes for keeping down military expenses were endangered in 1842 when Santa Anna sent strike forces into Texas to show that Mexico had not forgotten that the Republic existed. In March, General Rafael Vásquez crossed the Rio Grande and caught Goliad, Victoria and San Antonio completely by surprise. He did nothing, however, but occupy the cities, raise the Mexican flag, inspect Texan defenses, and withdraw. Congress passed a declaration of war against Mexico; Houston vetoed it. Texas, he said, would defend itself if need be but must not attack.

In September, just as the war talk was subsiding, another Santa Anna force under General Adrian Woll marched on San Antonio with 1,400 men and captured the city. The Mexicans held it for nine days until a force of 600 Texas Rangers headed by Jack Hays decoyed them out of the city and into ambush on Salado Creek. Woll lost 60 men to the Texans' one and retreated toward the Rio Grande.

Houston placed General Alexander Somervell in charge of about 700 volunteers and drafted militiamen with orders to drive Woll out of Texas and patrol the Rio Grande until the danger was over. Somervell followed instructions and Woll withdrew across the river. Late in December Somervell decided it was safe to leave the area and return to camp at Gonzales. But about 300 men, led by Colonel W. S. Fisher, were bent on invading Mexico. They refused to go back to Gonzales, crossed the Rio Grande instead, and attacked the Mexican town of Mier on Christmas afternoon. It was a tragic miscalculation. They did not know that 2,000 Mexican troops were temporarily garrisoned at Mier. The headstrong Texans fought desperately through the night and into the following day, but they had walked into a deadly trap. All who survived the fighting were taken prisoner and force-marched to Mexico City. An attempt to escape along the way was doomed not only to failure but retribution (pages 143-147). Santa Anna sent orders for the execution of every tenth man of the 176 surviving Texans. Those who were left were marched on to the Mexican capital where they joined the survivors of Lamar's ill-fated Santa Fe expedition in the dungeons of Perote Castle.

The Mexican raids and Colonel Fisher's calamitous adventure across the border damaged Houston's prestige both at home and abroad. Texans denounced him for his refusal to make war on Mexico; other nations decried his inability to secure the peace. He also managed to arouse bitter opposition in west Texas by attempting to move the seat of government away from Austin, a town he detested. When his attempt to revive Houston as the capital in mid-1842 met with no success, he compromised by ordering Congress to meet at Washington-on-the-Brazos, where the declaration of independence had been signed in 1836. But the archives, which were the key to government, were still in Austin; wherever they rested was still the capital, no matter where Congress might meet. Therefore, in the late fall of 1842, Houston sent Captain William Pettus to collect them.

But the people of Austin were determined not to lose the capital. When Captain Pettus rode into town, they lopped the mane and tail off his horse and sent him, paperless and half-horseless, back to Washington. Houston then dispatched Captain Thomas Smith to filch the records under cover of night. At midnight on December 30, Mrs. Angelina Eberly—a boarding-house keeper whose business threatened to suffer if the move to Washington proceeded—spotted Captain Smith loading the archives onto a wagon. She hurried

HARDIN RUNNELS

FRANCIS LUBBOCK

ANSON JONES

MICHEL MENARD

SAM MAVERICK

JOSÉ ANTONIO NAVARRO

A gallery of Lone Star statesmen

HARDIN RUNNELS worked his way up the political ladder by serving as state representative, speaker of the Texas house and lieutenant governor. In 1857 he reached the zenith of his career by becoming the only man ever to beat Sam Houston at the polls, defeating him for governor of the state by a vote of 32,552 to 23,628.

FRANCIS LUBBOCK came to Texas from New Orleans in 1836, searching for his brother, a volunteer missing in the revolution. He found him in Velasco, opened a store and later relocated in Houston, where he became a protégé of President Houston. As governor from 1861 to 1863 he supported secession from the Union.

ANSON JONES established a medical practice in Brazoria soon after arriving from New Orleans in 1833. Entering politics after the revolution, he was elected president of the Republic in 1844 and served until annexation. He failed to win a U.S. Senate seat, but became a prosperous planter and bitter critic of Sam Houston.

MICHEL MENARD, a French Canadian, started out as a frontier fur trader and was so highly regarded by the Shawnees in Arkansas Territory that they made him a chief. After several years of trading in Texas, he moved there for good in 1832. Once established, he was elected a delegate to the constitutional convention of 1836.

SAM MAVERICK, a successful rancher, never voluntarily ran for office. But from 1835 to 1867 he was called by his fellow citizens to many public posts — including mayor of San Antonio, seats in the Texas congress and a county chief judgeship. His name enriched the language as the synonym for a dissenting independent.

JOSÉ ANTONIO NAVARRO, a native-born rancher, fought for freedom from the Spanish in 1812 and then sided with Texas against Mexico in the revolution. Taken prisoner by Santa Anna in an 1841 raid, he managed to escape in 1844. He was elected to the 1845 annexation convention and hailed as its only Texas-born delegate.

to Congress Avenue, where a 6-pound cannon stood loaded with grapeshot against possible Indian attack, and let loose a blast that aroused the town. Captain Smith sped off with some of the precious records, but an armed posse followed him and persuaded him to release them. The alert Mrs. Eberly was given charge of the records and an armed guard to protect them. Irate citizens sputtered a warning that anyone else who tried to take the archives from Austin would be shot. In any event, with Smith's failure the Archives War was over and Sam Houston made no further attempt to move the records. He never was reconciled to Austin as the capital, but did not try again to change it.

During the last half of Houston's second term, annexation began to loom again as a distinct possibility. The economy had improved, the frontier was quiet, and British diplomats—whose motives remained not altogether altruistic—were attempting to mediate the lingering quarrel between Texas and Mexico in the hope of negotiating a treaty of recognition.

British interest in Texas was welcome not only for the trade advantages it offered but because it rekindled annexation sentiment in the United States, where there was growing anxiety that Texas might go so far as to become a British protectorate. With John Tyler—a Southerner and a supporter of annexation—now in the White House, Texan hopes for annexation rose.

Nevertheless, abolitionists in the United States were still vigorously opposed to the acquisition of another slave-holding state, and Houston knew that achieving his goal would take the most delicate maneuvering. Sly as ever, he set the stage by pretending utter indifference to annexation. He instructed his minister in Washington, Isaac Van Zandt, to deliberately reject any discussion of annexation on the declared grounds that it might disturb the British, and to make every effort to exaggerate the extent of Britain's trade and other interests in Texas.

Washington was properly alarmed by this carefully fostered impression that Britain and the Republic were on the verge of a major political alliance. Even Andrew Jackson emerged briefly from retirement on September 12, 1843, to declare that the United States must annex Texas—"peaceably if we can, forcibly if we must"—to thwart Britain's supposed designs. On October 16, Minister Van Zandt received a message from Tyler: the administration now believed it could get the two-thirds majority necessary in the Senate to ratify a treaty of annexation and wished to reopen annexation talks. Houston decided to send J. Pinckney Henderson to assist Van Zandt.

While the annexation discussions were in their early stages, Houston wrote to his old friend Andrew Jackson: "Now, my venerated friend, you will perceive that Texas is presented to the United States as a bride adorned for her espousal. But if, so confident of the union, she should be rejected, her mortification would be indescribable." One more rejection by Congress, in Houston's view, would be one too many; if the talks were to come to nothing, Texas would be better off to give up its pursuit of annexation and concentrate on building a better nation.

The conversations went well and a treaty of annexation was finally presented to the Senate in April 1844. It provided for admitting Texas into the Union as a territory, with statehood assumed to come later, and stipulated that Texas' vast public lands would be turned over to the federal government. The United States reserved the right to negotiate with Mexico, and agreed to assume the Texas public debt. Houston was not particularly pleased with most of the treaty's provisions, and both the Texas Senate and the United States Senate failed to ratify it: President Tyler had overestimated his strength. The treaty was rejected by 35 votes to 16, with Henry Clay's Whig Party, seven Northern Democrats and even some conservative slaveowners, who were alarmed by continued agitation of the slavery issue, voting against the treaty. Some Senators abstained from voting because of the approaching Presidential election.

But before Texas could suffer the indescribable mortification that Sam Houston had feared, James K. Polk, a Tennessean who campaigned vigorously for the annexation of Texas, was swept into the United States Presidency. Lame duck President Tyler took the election of Polk as a clear mandate for the annexation of Texas. Instead of waiting for Polk to assume office or reviving the treaty in the Senate, Tyler recommended that Congress annex Texas by joint resolution, a procedure that required only a simple majority of both houses. The resolution passed, and Tyler signed it on March 1, 1845, two days before leaving office.

Tyler's new resolution offered much better terms than the 1844 treaty. Texas would enter directly as a state instead of as a territory, it could keep its own public lands, and it would be assured of United States military protection on its own soil. The United States, as its parent government, would handle the simmering dispute with the Mexican government. The only drawback was that Texas would retain responsibility for its public debt; but that, too, was to be taken over by the federal treasury in time.

A special convention, approved by the Texas Congress, met in Austin on July 4, 1845, to vote on the American offer and draft a state constitution. With a single dissenting vote—by Richard Bache of Galveston, a grandson of Benjamin Franklin—the convention adopted an ordinance of annexation, and on October 13 both the constitution and the ordinance were approved by an overwhelming popular vote. President Polk signed the Texas Admission Act on December 29, 1845, and Texas finally became part of the United States.

The formal ceremony of replacing the government of the Republic with a state government took place on February 19, 1846. Sam Houston, who had worked so hard and with such great skill for annexation, played little part in the formalities; in the Texas election of 1844 he had been replaced as president by Anson Jones—secretary of state in Houston's second administration, and Houston's own choice as successor.

President Jones relinquished the reins of office to the new state's first governor, J. Pinckney Henderson, and shook out the lines on the flagstaff to lower the Lone Star flag of the Republic for the last time. "The final act in this great drama is now performed," he declared. "The Republic of Texas is no more."

As the flag slipped slowly earthward, Sam Houston stepped forward and personally caught its folds.

A commanding figure appeared in the United States Senate in March of 1846. "He was fifty-three years old," reported Oliver Dyer, a member of the Senate's clerical staff, "a magnificent barbarian, somewhat tempered by civilization. He was of large frame, of stately carriage and dignified demeanor and had a lion-like countenance capable of expressing the fiercest passions.

His dress was peculiar, but it was becoming to his style. The conspicuous features of it were a military cap, and a short military cloak of fine blue broadcloth, with a blood-red lining. Afterward, I occasionally met him when he wore a vast and picturesque sombrero and a Mexican blanket."

The magnificent barbarian was Sam Houston, elected by the legislature of Texas to represent the state in Washington, D.C. Talk of war with Mexico was sweeping the capital. Houston urgently counseled peaceful negotiations. But the Mexicans had broken off diplomatic relations with the United States. Annexation, they insisted, was an act of hostility toward Mexico because Texas was rightfully Mexican territory, and in any event they were not prepared to accept the Rio Grande boundary claimed by the Texans after the revolution. If there was a boundary at all—and how could there be if all Texas belonged to them?—then it was not the Rio Grande but the Nueces River.

When a violently anti-American government assumed power in Mexico and openly threatened to retake Texas, President Polk dispatched General Zachary Taylor and a force of 4,000 men to a defensive position a few miles above the mouth of the Rio Grande.

In April, then in May, Mexican forces crossed the Rio Grande and attacked Taylor's army. Twice Taylor drove them back. On May 11, 1846, Polk sent a message to Congress: "Mexico has passed the boundary of the U.S., has invaded our territory and shed American blood upon American soil. We are called upon by every consideration of duty and patriotism to vindicate with decision the honor, the rights, and the interests of our country." Two days later, Congress declared war on Mexico.

Six companies of Texas Rangers added strength to Taylor's force. Nearly 69,000 volunteers, including 8,000 Texans, answered the nationwide call to arms. Generals Taylor, Winfield Scott and Stephen W. Kearny organized them into a three-pronged force.

In Mexico, Santa Anna was recalled from the exile into which he had been sent more than a year before and given command of the Mexican forces, which totaled 35,000 men.

For 16 months the United States and Mexico were locked in conflict. The climax came in the early fall

Sam Houston's family album

After his disastrous early marriage, Sam Houston finally found contentment with Margaret Moffette Lea, who appears as she did when wed in 1840, she at 21 and he 47. (Sam is pictured in his mid-50s.) In the next 17 years, they had eight children. Sam Jr. is shown at about age 25; the girls are depicted in paintings made from an 1850s daguerreotype taken when they were about seven, five and three. After them came another girl and three more sons.

SAM JR.

MARGARET

SAM

NANCY ELIZABETH

MARGARET LEA

MARY WILLIE

of 1847. In August, General Winfield Scott, with 9,000 exhausted, ill-equipped men, reached the outskirts of Mexico City. On the hills above the town loomed heavily fortified Chapultepec Castle, Mexico's military academy; and barricaded in the castle were the academy's cadets and about a thousand of Santa Anna's chosen men.

General Scott camped and worked out his battle plan, deciding to storm the castle before occupying Mexico City. On the morning of September 12 the American Army pulled into position facing the castle and began an artillery bombardment that continued for 14 hours. At daylight on the 13th the gunners resumed fire; and then, at 8 o'clock in the morning, Scott gave the signal to attack. The Americans scaled the devastated walls and grappled hand to hand with soldiers and cadets. An hour later the Mexican tricolor came down, and the Stars and Stripes fluttered over Chapultepec Castle.

In the valley below was Mexico City, garrisoned by Santa Anna and 10,000 troops. Without pausing to rest, Scott and his men went down the hillside and swept through the city's narrow streets. Santa Anna fled, as he had fled the Texans on the day of San Jacinto; and his leaderless army crumbled under the relentless American attack. On September 14, the Mexicans raised a white flag.

With that, the war was over. On February 2, 1848, Mexico and the United States signed the Treaty of Guadalupe Hidalgo. It established the Rio Grande as the boundary between Texas and Mexico, and ceded to the United States the areas of present California, Arizona, Nevada, Utah, New Mexico, and part of Colorado. In return for these vast territories, the United States paid Mexico $15 million.

Texas, at last, was truly freed from Mexico and had in effect brought to the United States an enormous dowry in land. But one internal boundary problem still remained: Texans claimed that New Mexico, as far west as the Rio Grande, was part of the state of Texas, whereas New Mexicans wanted statehood in their own right. After much controversy the matter was resolved by the Compromise of 1850, which established the status of all land won from Mexico. Under its terms, Texas relinquished its New Mexican claims and in return received $10 million from the federal government. The Republic of Texas had been in dire financial straits; now, suddenly, the state of Texas was rich enough to settle all its debts, establish a sound economy and begin a program of public improvement that was sorely needed.

Sam Houston, the chief architect of annexation, might well have felt supremely satisfied. Yet he was uneasily aware that an issue even larger than war with Mexico was looming.

Hardly had Texas joined the Union when the tide of secession began to sweep the Southern states, Texas among them. The issue was not only the abolition or expansion of slavery, but the right of state governments to determine their own course as against the right of the national government to mandate it. If secession was the only way to maintain states' rights, then the slave-holding Southern states would secede.

From the beginning, Houston saw the deadly end of the South's path. As early as 1850 he was delivering impassioned speeches to the United States Senate in an attempt to stave off disaster. "I must say that I am sorry that I cannot offer the prayers of the righteous that my petition be heard," he told the Senate in the first of his anti-secession pleas. "But I beseech those whose piety will permit them reverentially to offer such petitions, that they will pray for this Union, and ask of Him who buildeth up and pulleth down nations to unite us. I wish, if this Union *must* be dissolved, that its ruins may be the monument of my grave."

His fellow Texans resented his words. The idea of bending to pressure from the national government and the powerful Northern states struck at their pride. They had managed to sustain themselves as an independent republic and they had no doubt that they could manage just as well in secession if need be. The Union was less important to them than their slave economy and the sovereignty of the states.

Houston's support in Texas gradually eroded because of his antisecessionist stand, but his status as elder statesman was enough to assure his re-election to the Senate in 1853 for a six-year term. For the next four years he consistently spoke out and voted against measures that threatened the Union.

In 1857, without resigning his Senate seat, he stood for governor of Texas against Hardin Runnels, a Mis-

sissippi-born planter and ardent secessionist. Houston was 64 years old, his body heavy, his hair gray and thinning, his spirit as vital as ever. All during the blazing summer he waged a brilliant personal campaign. He went everywhere in a buggy, often bare-chested against the heat, speaking to informal groups wherever he found them, and hurling his old inspired passion and talent for ridicule against the secessionist radicals. The opposition vilified him as a traitor to Texas. "I, a traitor to Texas?" he roared in return. "Was it for this I bared my bosom to the hail of battle — to be branded a traitor in my old age?"

People turned out in droves to hear Houston and cheered as an act of love, but on election day they voted against him. Hardin Runnels won the governorship by a vote of 32,552 to 23,628.

It was not an overwhelming victory for Runnels, nor was his administration an effective one. Two years later Houston ran again for governor, this time waging a quiet, dignified campaign and winning the post by almost 9,000 votes.

His success seemed to signal an ebbing of the secessionist tide in Texas. However, swelling abolitionist extremism in the United States brought about a reactionary swing in the political temper. After Abraham Lincoln's election to the Presidency in 1860, the secessionist movement in the Southern states became irresistible. Six slave states seceded before the end of January 1861. Secessionists in Texas demanded that Governor Houston order a convention to discuss and vote upon the issue. When he stalled, hoping that the emotionalism of the moment would pass, the state legislature endorsed the convention without waiting for his approval.

The Secession Convention met on January 28, 1861, in the hall of the House of Representatives in Austin. Its presiding officer was Judge Oran M. Roberts, who was well known for his prosecession sympathies. On February 1 the convention passed an ordinance of secession by a vote of 166 to 8, and set February 23 as the date for popular ratification. Meanwhile, the six states that had already withdrawn from the Union formed a new union called the Confederate States of America.

Houston waged the last campaign of his life against ratification of the secession ordinance, stumping the state in a last desperate attempt to keep Texas in the United States. Hostility met him everywhere. At Waco, crowds inflamed by a secessionist speaker threatened his life. In Galveston, on February 18, he stood on the balcony of the Tremont House gazing down upon a crowd so inimical that his friends pleaded with him to leave.

He stood there, a man of nearly 70, still straight as an arrow and majestically self-possessed. "Some of you laugh to scorn the idea of bloodshed as the result of secession," he began, after facing the mob into silence. "But let me tell you what is coming. Your fathers and husbands, your sons and brothers, will be herded at the point of the bayonet. You may, after the sacrifice of countless millions of treasure and hundreds of thousands of lives, as a bare possibility, win Southern independence . . . but I doubt it. I tell you that, while I believe with you in the doctrine of state rights, the North is determined to preserve this Union. They are not a fiery, impulsive people as you are, for they live in colder climates. But when they begin to move in a given direction, they move with the steady momentum and perseverance of a mighty avalanche; and what I fear is, they will overwhelm the South."

Houston's entreaties were of no avail. Texans voted 46,129 to 14,697 — an overwhelming 76 per cent — for secession. On March 5 the convention declared Texas independent of the Union and voted to join the newly formed Confederate States of America. Texas state officials were called upon to take an oath of allegiance to the Confederacy on March 15 and 16. Houston did not appear on the 15th. That evening, an emissary from the convention arrived at the Governor's Mansion with a message ordering Houston to take the oath at high noon the following day. Houston's oldest daughter, Nancy, then 15 years old, later described what occurred at the mansion that night when family prayers had been said:

"After bidding his family good night the General left positive instructions with Mrs. Houston that he must not be disturbed under any circumstances and that no visitors were to be admitted to the mansion. He then went to his bedroom on the upper floor, removed his coat and vest and shoes and remained alone throughout the night, during which he did not sleep. Instead he walked the floor of his bedroom and the upper

hall in his sock feet, wrestling with his spirit as Jacob wrestled with the angel until the purple dawn of another day shone over the eastern hills. He had come through his Gethsemane, and the die was cast.

"When he came down and met Mrs. Houston, he said, 'Margaret, I will never do it.'"

Next day, he told the people of Texas that he would withdraw from office because he loved Texas "too well to bring civil strife and bloodshed upon her." A Presbyterian minister in Austin, William Baker, long afterward recalled: "As I look back into the darkness of those days, the central figure of them all is that of the old governor sitting in his chair in the basement of the capitol, sorrowfully meditating what it were best to do. The officer of the gathering upstairs summoned the old man three times to come forward and take the oath of allegiance to the Confederacy. I remember as yesterday the call thrice repeated — 'Sam Houston! Sam Houston! Sam Houston!' but the man sat silent, immovable, in his chair below."

Lieutenant Governor Edward Clark was sworn in as governor in Houston's place.

Sadly, Houston watched the Union torn apart by secession and the destruction he had been so sure would follow. In the only leisure days he had ever really known, he spent time with Margaret and those of their eight children who were still at home — for Sam Houston Jr., like so many of Texas' best hopes for the future, had gone to war.

The giant who had been a United States Congressman and Governor of Tennessee, Congressman and President of the Republic of Texas, United States Senator and Governor of the only state of the Union to enter as an independent nation, now lived in retirement at Huntsville and Cedar Point by the sea, at 70 an almost forgotten man. He traveled frequently in his buggy to see old friends and talk of Texas, or simply to ponder, in solitude, what would become of the state he had helped create.

In mid-July, 1863, Sam Houston came home to Margaret with a cold that developed into pneumonia. On July 25, 1863, he fell into a deep sleep with his family gathered about him. He slept through the night and stirred briefly the next day. Margaret reached for his hand. "Texas — Texas! — Margaret!" he cried out, and fell back into sleep. He died that day at sunset.

Two pairs of horses pull a wagonload of cotton along Austin's main thoroughfare, Congress Avenue, to the railroad in the 1880s.

King Cotton, leading the way to fabled riches

Cotton was the foundation upon which Texas built its economic wealth — and its Southern political attitudes. Plants of the genus *Gossypium* were native to the area, and the first Spanish explorers and missionaries were quick to see their promise. By 1745 the missions around San Antonio reported the production of several thousand pounds of cotton annually.

When Moses Austin arrived in Texas in 1820 to obtain a colonization grant from the Mexican government, he planned to support himself and his set-

tlers by raising sugar cane and cotton. Within five years, a member of the Austin colony, Jared Groce, had built Texas' first cotton gin — thus earning from later generations the title "Father of Texas Agriculture." That was no mean sobriquet, for by the time the picture below was taken in the 1880s, Texas was turning out more than a million bales of cotton a year and was well on its way to becoming the foremost cotton state in the U.S.

But Texans were not content with even so rich a crop. When the building

of railroads and the removal of the Indians to reservations made it possible to farm vast tracts farther inland, many Texans raised livestock and grew produce other than cotton, and found that in these, too, the earth's bounty was prodigious almost beyond reckoning. With the energy that came to be synonymous with their very name, Texans went on to pile up fabulous fortunes in everything from longhorn cattle and sheep to grain and citrus fruits. Cotton may have been king — but it was a monarch with a rich and versatile court.

Planters with wagonloads of raw cotton line up on the premises of the Austin Gin and Manufacturing Company near the turn of the century. By that time, Texas had become a veritable colossus of cotton, producing a staggering 3.5 million bales yearly on more than seven million fertile acres.

227

Gin hands at William D. Hunter's establishment in Hornsby Bend, near Austin, attend the weighing of a cotton bale in the 1880s. Cotton was being rivaled by another fiber, wool, produced in increasing quantities by sheepherders from the East and from England, Scotland and Germany.

Cotton bales ready to be weighed on scales *(extreme right)* lie along the main street of the town of Rockdale, northeast of Austin. The year was 1879, and similar towns were springing up to the west as railroads spread across the plains, opening the hinterland to Texas farmers and ranchers.

231

Farm wagons from the surrounding countryside jam into the courthouse square of Fort Worth on a market day in 1877. Though most carried cotton bales (which provided prominent perches for farmers who wanted their pictures taken), they also contained a Texan profusion of other produce.

232

TEXT CREDITS

For full reference on specific page credits see bibliography.

Chapter 1: Particularly useful sources for information and quotes in this chapter: Eugene C. Barker, *The Life of Stephen F. Austin,* University of Texas Press, 1969; Noah Smithwick, *The Evolution of a State,* Gammel Book Company, 1900. Chapter 2: Particularly useful sources for information and quotes: Donald Day and Harry Herbert Ullom, eds., *The Autobiography of Sam Houston,* University of Oklahoma Press, 1954; Marquis James, *The Raven: A Biography of Sam Houston,* Bobbs-Merrill, 1929; M.K. Wisehart, *Sam Houston: American Giant,* Robert B. Luce, 1962; 53—Houston quote as Congressman-elect, Barker and Williams, Vol. I, p. 16; 66—Austin to Mary Holley, Barker, p. 4; 68 —Austin letter to San Antonio city council, Barker, pp. 373-374; 70-71—apologetic letter from San Felipe, Binkley, p. 50; 72—Smithwick impressions of Texas army, Smithwick, pp. 109-110; 73—Jones on Bowie and Houston, Jones, p. 12; 75—Milam/Burleson dispatch, Garver, p. 196. Chapter 3: Particularly useful sources for information and quotes: Walter Lord, *A Time to Stand,* Harper & Brothers, 1961; Amelia Williams, "A Critical Study of the Siege of the Alamo and of the Personnel of Its Defenders," *The Southwestern Historical Quarterly,* Vols. 36 and 37, April, July and October 1933, January and April 1934; 93 —Daniel Cloud quote, McDonald, pp. 343-344. Chapter 4: Particularly useful sources for information and quotes: Eugene C. Barker, "The San Jacinto Campaign," *The Southwestern Historical Quarterly,* Vol. 4; Allan O. Kownslar, *The Texans: Their Land and History,* American Heritage Publishing Co., 1972; Frank X. Tolbert, *The Day of San Jacinto,* McGraw-Hill Book Company, 1959; 113—Gray on convention, Shuffler, pp. 325, 327; 115—Noah Smithwick and Uncle Jimmy Curtis, Smithwick, pp. 126-127; 122—survivor quote, Ehrenberg, pp. 199-

204; 123—Smithwick quote, Smithwick, pp. 128-129; 132—Winters quote, Winters, pp. 141-142; 133—Seguin quote, Seguin, pp. 7, 13; 140—Winters quote, Winters, p. 143; 141—Santa Anna quote, Day and Ullom, p. 121; 141—Houston to Santa Anna on massacre, Wisehart, p. 249; Houston on sparing Santa Anna, Barker and Williams, Vol. 6, p. 10. Chapter 5: Particularly useful sources for information and quotes: William Ransom Hogan, *The Texas Republic,* University of Oklahoma Press, 1946; Seymour V. Connor, *Adventure in Glory,* Steck-Vaughn Company, 1965; Joseph William Schmitz, *Texas Culture 1836-1946,* The Naylor Company, 1960; 155—Dilue Harris quote, Tolbert, *The Day of San Jacinto,* pp. 223-224; 159—Goodman quote, Leathers, p. 362; 162—American visitor on raising stock, Sibley, p. 161; 168—Jenkins quote, Jenkins, pp. 201-202; 168—Postl quotes, Anderson, p. 17; 174—Militia colonel quote, Gard, p. 35; 175 —Indian raid description, Jenkins, pp. 182-183; 178—Mrs. Sam Maverick quote, Green, p. 119; 184—Lubbock quote, Lubbock, p. 46. Chapter 6: Particularly useful sources for information and quotes: Llerena B. Friend, *Sam Houston: The Great Designer,* University of Texas Press, 1954; Lowell Harrison, "Houston's Republic," *American History Illustrated,* Vol. 6, December 1971; Marquis James, *The Raven: A Biography of Sam Houston,* Bobbs-Merrill, 1929; Stanley Siegel, *A Political History of the Texas Republic 1836-1845,* Haskell House, 1973; 203—Dewees letter, Dewees, p. 208; Austin to Ficklin, Barker, *The Life of Stephen F. Austin,* p. 449; Austin to a friend, Barker, *Life,* p. 446; 204—Quote from Austin friend, Hogan, "Henry Austin," *The Southwestern Historical Quarterly,* Vol. 37, January 1934, p. 206; 219—Polk message, Billington, p. 579.

PICTURE CREDITS

The sources for the illustrations in this book are shown below. Credits from left to right are separated by semicolons, from top to bottom by dashes.

Cover—Frank Lerner, courtesy of the Texas State Archives. 2—Frank Lerner, from the Showers-Brown Collection at the Star of the Republic Museum, Washington, Texas. 6—H.R. Marks, Austin, Texas, courtesy Rosenberg Library, Galveston, Texas; courtesy William D. Wittliff, The Encino Press, Austin, Texas. 7—Courtesy Rosenberg Library —From *Samuel Maverick, Texan: 1803-1870.* Edited by Rena Maverick Green. 8—Courtesy William D. Wittliff, The Encino Press —courtesy Rosenberg Library. 9—Courtesy William D. Wittliff, The Encino Press—courtesy Private Collection. 10—Courtesy Chicago Historical Society. 11—Bill Malone, courtesy Barker Texas History Center, University of Texas at Austin—Ed Stewart, from the collection of Julia D. Welder and Family, San Jacinto Museum of History. 12—Courtesy Western History Collections, University of Oklahoma Libraries—courtesy Miss Nora Lee Bowen. 13—Courtesy William D. Wittliff, The Encino Press—courtesy Rosenberg Library. 14—Frank Lerner, courtesy James L. Britton. 17—Map by Rafael D. Palacios. 18, 19—J. W. Elicson, courtesy D.R.T. Library at the Alamo. 20, 21—Courtesy Amon Carter Museum, Fort Worth, Texas. 22—Albert Moldvay, courtesy Museo Nacional de Historia, Mexico City. 23—Courtesy The Beinecke Rare Book and Manuscript Library, Yale University. 25—Bill Malone, courtesy Stephen F. Austin Papers, Barker Texas History Center, University of Texas at Austin. 26, 27—Frank Lerner, courtesy The San Antonio Museum Association, Witte Memorial Museum, San Antonio, Texas. 28—Courtesy of the Edward E. Ayer Collection, The Newberry

Library, Chicago. 30, 31—Frank Lerner, courtesy The San Antonio Museum Association. 34, 35—Bill Malone, courtesy Stephen F. Austin Papers, Barker Texas History Center, University of Texas at Austin, except portraits, Frank Lerner, courtesy Fort Bend County Historical Museum, Richmond, Texas. 37—Frank Lerner, courtesy of the Texas State Archives. 38—Courtesy Stone Fort Museum, Nacogdoches, Texas. 40 —Ronnie L. Roese, from the Collection of the Star of the Republic Museum. 42 through 49—Albert Moldvay, courtesy Museo Nacional de Historia, Mexico City. 50—Courtesy of The R. W. Norton Art Gallery, Shreveport, La. 52—Charles Phillips, courtesy of the National Collection of Fine Arts, Smithsonian Institution. 54—Courtesy General Research and Humanities Division, The New York Public Library, Astor, Lenox and Tilden Foundations. 55—Charles Phillips, courtesy Smithsonian Institution, National Anthropological Archives, except left, courtesy General Research and Humanities Division, The New York Public Library, Astor, Lenox and Tilden Foundations. 56, 57—Charles Phillips, courtesy Smithsonian Institution, National Anthropological Archives; courtesy Rare Book Division, The New York Public Library, Astor, Lenox and Tilden Foundations. 59—Henry Beville, courtesy Library of Congress. 60—J. W. Elicson, courtesy D.R.T. Library at the Alamo. 63—F. W. Seiders, courtesy San Jacinto Museum of History Association; inset, courtesy of the Texas State Archives. 64, 65—Courtesy The Beinecke Rare Book and Manuscript Library, Yale University. 67—Bill Malone, courtesy of the Texas State Archives. 69—Courtesy General Research and

234

Humanities Division, The New York Public Library, Astor, Lenox and Tilden Foundations. 72—Courtesy American History Division, The New York Public Library, Astor, Lenox and Tilden Foundations. 74—Courtesy Library of Congress. 76,77—Frank Lerner, courtesy of the Texas State Archives. 78—Bill Malone, courtesy of the Texas State Archives. 79—J. W. Elicson, courtesy D.R.T. Library at the Alamo. 81—Courtesy Barker Texas History Center, Univ. of Texas at Austin. 82, 83—Frank Lerner, courtesy Barker Texas History Center, Univ. of Texas at Austin. 84,85—Courtesy D.R.T. Library at the Alamo. 86 through 89—Charles Phillips, courtesy Library of Congress. 91—Frank Lerner, courtesy of the Texas State Archives. 94,95—Drawing by Don Bolognese. 96,97—Frank Lerner, courtesy The William B. Bates Collection of Texana and Western Americana at the University of Houston. 98, 99—J. W. Elicson, courtesy D.R.T. Library at the Alamo. 100—Albert Moldvay, courtesy Museo Nacional de Historia, Mexico City. 102,103—Courtesy Library of Congress. 104,105—Frank Lerner, courtesy of Brass Door Galleries, Houston, Texas. 108—Frank Lerner, courtesy Barker Texas History Center, Univ. of Texas at Austin. 110,111—Brenwasser, New York, courtesy of The R. W. Norton Art Gallery. 112—Ed Stewart Photography & Associates, Inc., courtesy Collection of San Jacinto Museum of History Association. 116,117—Bill Malone, courtesy Barker Texas History Center, Univ. of Texas at Austin—Frank Lerner, courtesy of the Texas State Archives; Ronnie L. Roese, from the Collection of the Star of the Republic Museum. 118,119—Map by Rafael D. Palacios. 120—Courtesy Barker Texas History Center, Univ. of Texas at Austin. 122—Courtesy Summerfield G. Roberts Collection, Dallas Historical Society. 123—Courtesy Western History Collections, University of Oklahoma Libraries. 124—Courtesy Collection of San Jacinto Museum of History Association; courtesy Western History Collections, University of Oklahoma Libraries. 125—Courtesy Rosenberg Library; Bill Malone, courtesy of the Texas State Archives. 126—Bill Malone, courtesy of the Texas State Archives. 129—Map by Rafael D. Palacios. 130,131—Bill Malone, courtesy of the Texas State Archives. 132—Frank Lerner, courtesy Barker Texas History Center, Univ. of Texas at Austin. 133—Frank Lerner, courtesy Gift of Mr. Frell Albright to the University of Houston Special Collections. 134,135—Frank Lerner, courtesy of the Texas State Archives. 136—Bill Malone, courtesy of Land Commissioner, Bob Armstrong. 137—Bill Malone, courtesy of the Texas State Archives. 138,139—Courtesy of San Jacinto Museum of History Association. 142 through 145—Courtesy American History Division, The New York Public Library, Astor, Lenox and Tilden Foundations. 146,147—Courtesy D.R.T. Library at the Alamo—Courtesy Collection of San Jacinto Museum of History Association; Courtesy American History Division, The New York Public Library, Astor, Len-

ox and Tilden Foundations. 148,149—Bill Malone, courtesy Russell H. Fish III. 150,151—Frank Lerner, courtesy San Antonio Museum Association, San Antonio, Texas. 152,153—Bill Malone, courtesy Russell H. Fish III. 154—Courtesy William D. Wittliff, The Encino Press. 157—Courtesy Sophienburg Museum, New Braunfels. 158,159—Courtesy D.R.T. Library at the Alamo. 161—Courtesy Sophienburg Museum. 163—Courtesy D.R.T. Library at the Alamo. 164 through 167—Courtesy Rare Book Division, The New York Public Library, Astor, Lenox and Tilden Foundations. 168,169—Charles Phillips, courtesy of Susan and Pierce Butler, Nashville, Tennessee. 172,173—Bill Malone, courtesy Charles Adalbert Herf Papers, Barker Texas History Center, Univ. of Texas at Austin. 175—Bill Malone, courtesy of the Texas Memorial Museum, Austin. 176—Lungkwitz & Iwonski, San Antonio, Texas, courtesy James P. McGuire, San Antonio, Texas. 177—Courtesy Mrs. William W. Ochse—Courtesy Sophienburg Museum. 178,179—Frank Lerner, courtesy Rosenberg Library. 180 through 183—Courtesy General Research and Humanities Division, The New York Public Library, Astor, Lenox and Tilden Foundations. 185—The 1838 Houston Theatre Poster is publicly displayed in the Grand Lodge of Texas, A.F. & A.M., Library and Museum, Waco, Texas. 186,187—Frank Lerner, courtesy Mr. & Mrs. Larry Sheerin, San Antonio. 188 through 195—Frank Lerner, courtesy San Antonio Museum Association. 196 through 199—Courtesy Library of Congress. 200,201—Courtesy Prints Division, The New York Public Library, Astor, Lenox and Tilden Foundations. 202—Courtesy International Museum of Photography at George Eastman House. 206,207—Bill Malone, courtesy Barker Texas History Center, University of Texas at Austin. 208,209—Courtesy Texas and Local History Collection, Houston Public Library. 211—Courtesy General Research and Humanities Division, The New York Public Library, Astor, Lenox and Tilden Foundations. 213—Courtesy D.R.T. Library at the Alamo. 217—Courtesy Mrs. Walter Espy, San Antonio; F. W. Seiders, courtesy Collection of San Jacinto Museum of History Association; Frank Lerner, from the Collection of the Star of the Republic Museum—Frank Lerner, courtesy Rosenberg Library; Frank Lerner, courtesy of the Texas State Archives; Bill Malone, courtesy of the Texas State Archives. 220,221—Frank Lerner, courtesy Sam Houston Memorial Museum, Huntsville, Texas, except top left page 220, courtesy Photography Collection, Humanities Research Center, The University of Texas at Austin. 224,225—Courtesy Austin-Travis County Collection, Austin (Texas) Public Library. 226 through 229—Frank Lerner, courtesy Austin-Travis County Collection, Austin (Texas) Public Library. 230, 231—Courtesy Austin-Travis County Collection, Austin (Texas) Public Library. 232,233—From the Collection of The Fort Worth Public Library, Fort Worth, Texas.

ACKNOWLEDGMENTS

The editors wish to give special thanks to Dr. Ernest Wallace, Horn Professor of History, Texas Tech University, Lubbock, Texas, who read and commented on major portions of the book.

The editors also acknowledge the help of the following (cities and towns mentioned are in Texas unless otherwise indicated): Betty Bell, Lubbock; Jerry Bloomer, Secretary-Registrar, The R. W. Norton Art Gallery, Shreveport, La.; Andrea Brown, Photo Services, National Collection of Fine Arts, Smithsonian Institution, Washington, D.C.; Jean Carefoot, Archivist, Texas State Library, Austin; Mary Carnahan, Registrar, Texas Memorial Museum, Austin; John W. Crain, Director, Star of the Republic Museum, Washington; Mrs. Carolyn Ericson, Curator, Stone Fort Museum, Nacogdoches; Mabel Fisher, Dir., Fort Worth Public Library, Fort Worth; Mrs. Virginia Leddy Gambrell, Director of the Museum, Dallas Historical Society; Dorothy Glassner, Houston Public Library; Jack D. Haley, Asst. Curator, Western History Collections, University of Oklahoma Library, Norman, Okla.; Archibald Hanna, Curator, Yale University Western Americana Collection, New Haven, Conn.; Villette Harris, Bethesda, Md.; Jerry Kearns, Head of Reference, Prints and Photographs, Library of Congress, Washington, D.C.; Dr. Chester Kielman, Archivist-Librarian, Robert Tissing Jr., James C. Martin, Asst. Archivists, Robert Martin, Library Asst., Barker Texas History Center, University of Texas, Austin; Dorothy Knepper, Dir., San Jacinto Museum of History Association, Deer Park; Charles Long, Curator, The Alamo, San Antonio; Miss Catherine McDowell, Librarian, Mrs. Martha Doty Freeman, Asst. Librarian, Library of the Daughters of the Republic of Texas, The Alamo, San Antonio; James P. McGuire, Samuel P. Nesmith, Res. Associates, Laura Simmons, Admin. Asst., Betsy Bedell, Library Asst., The University of Texas, Institute of Texan Cultures at San Antonio; Frances Moore, Asst. Curator, Austin-Travis County Collection, Austin Public Library; Frederic Oheim, Archivist, Sophienburg Museum, New Braunfels; Frank Pearson, The Brass Door Galleries, Houston; Jane Pinkard, Houston; Mark E. Price, Dir., Fort Bend County Historical Museum, Richmond; Paula Richardson, Museum Specialist, National Anthropological Archives, Smithsonian Institution, Washington, D.C.; Covington Rodgers, Asst. Curator, Kevin MacDonnell, Special Collections, University of Houston; Elizabeth Roth, Prints Division, New York Public Library, N.Y.; Mrs. Cecilia Steinfeldt, Curator, History, Witte Memorial Museum, San Antonio; William D. Wittliff, Publisher, The Encino Press, Austin; Larry J. Wygant, Archivist, Rosenberg Library, Galveston.

BIBLIOGRAPHY

A Visit to Texas. Goodrich & Wiley, 1834.

Anderson, John Q., ed., *Tales of Frontier Texas, 1830-1860.* Southern Methodist University Press, 1966.

Austin, Stephen F.:
Establishing Austin's Colony. The Pemberton Press, 1970.
"Journal of Stephen F. Austin on His First Trip to Texas, 1821." *The Southwestern Historical Quarterly,* Vol. 7, 1903.

Barker, Eugene C.:
The Life of Stephen F. Austin. University of Texas Press, 1969.
"The San Jacinto Campaign." *The Southwestern Historical Quarterly,* Vol. 4, April 1901.
"The Texas Declaration of Causes for Taking Up Arms Against Mexico." *The Southwestern Historical Quarterly,* Vol. 15, January 1912.

Barker, Eugene C., and Amelia W. Williams, eds., *The Writings of Sam Houston* (8 vols.). University of Texas Press, 1938.

Benjamin, Gilbert Giddings, *The Germans in Texas.* Jenkins Publishing Company, 1974.

Billington, Ray Allen, *Westward Expansion: A History of the American Frontier,* 3rd ed. The Macmillan Company, 1967.

Binkley, William C., *The Texas Revolution.* Louisiana State University Press, 1952.

Bugbee, Lester G., "The Old Three Hundred." *The Southwestern Historical Quarterly,* Vol. 1, 1897.

Burnam, Jesse, "Reminiscences of Captain Jesse Burnam." *The Southwestern Historical Quarterly,* Vol. 5, July 1901.

Castañeda, Carlos E., *Three Manuscript Maps of Texas by Stephen F. Austin.* Privately printed, 1930.

Chabot, Frederick C., *With the Makers of San Antonio.* Privately published, 1937.

Chidsey, Donald Barr, *The War with Mexico.* Crown Publishers, 1968.

Clopper, Joseph C., "J. C. Clopper's Journal and Book of Memoranda for 1828." *The Southwestern Historical Quarterly,* Vol. 13, July 1909.

Connor, Seymour V.:
Adventure in Glory/The Saga of Texas, 1836-1849. Steck-Vaughn Company, 1965.
Texas: A History. Thomas Y. Crowell Company, 1971.

Corner, William, "John Crittenden Duval: The Last Survivor of the Goliad Massacre." *The Southwestern Historical Quarterly,* Vol. 1, July 1897.

Crawford, Ann Fears, ed., *The Eagle: The Autobiography of Santa Anna.* The Pemberton Press, 1967.

Dabbs, Jack Autrey, ed. and translator, "Additional Notes on the Champ d'Asile." *The Southwestern Historical Quarterly,* Vol. 54, January 1951.

Daniell, Forrest, "Texas Pioneer Surveyors and Indians." *The Southwestern Historical Quarterly,* Vol. 60, April 1957.

Day, Donald, and Harry Herbert Ullom, eds., *The Autobiography of Sam Houston.* University of Oklahoma Press, 1954.

Day, W. C., "History of the San Jacinto Campaign." (Pamphlet compiled and published by W. C. Day, Superintendent, San Jacinto State Park, Lynchburg, Texas, 1923.)

Dewees, W. B., *Letters from an Early Settler of Texas.* Compiled by Cara Cardelle, Louisville, Ky., 1858.

Edward, David B., *The History of Texas.* The Pemberton Press, 1967.

Ehrenberg, Herman, *With Milam and Fannin: Adventures of a German Boy in Texas' Revolution.* Tardy Publishing Company, Inc., 1935.

Fehrenbach, T. R., *Lone Star: A History of Texas and the Texans.* The Macmillan Company, 1968.

Fornell, Earl W., *The Galveston Era.* Univ. of Texas Press, 1961.

Frantz, Joe B., and David G. McComb, *Houston: A Student's Guide to Localized History.* Teachers College Press, New York, 1971.

Friend, Llerena B.:
Sam Houston: The Great Designer. University of Texas Press, 1954.
"The Texan of 1860," *The Southwestern Historical Quarterly,* Vol. 62, July 1958.

Gard, Wayne, *Frontier Justice.* University of Oklahoma Press, 1949.

Garver, Lois, "Benjamin Rush Milam." *The Southwestern Historical Quarterly,* Vol. 38, October 1934 and January 1935.

Green, Rena Maverick, ed., *Samuel Maverick, Texan: 1803-1870.* Privately printed, San Antonio, 1952.

Gregory, Jack, and Rennard Strickland, *Sam Houston with the Cherokees.* University of Texas Press, 1967.

Harris, Dilue, "The Reminiscences of Mrs. Dilue Harris." *The Southwestern Historical Quarterly,* Vol. 4, October 1900 and January 1901.

Harrison, Lowell, "Houston's Republic." *American History Illustrated,* Vol. 6, December 1971.

Henry, R. S., *The Story of the Mexican War.* Bobbs-Merrill, 1950.

Hogan, William Ransom:
   The Texas Republic. University of Oklahoma Press, 1946.
   "Henry Austin." *The Southwestern Historical Quarterly,* Vol. 37, January 1934.

Holland, James W., "Andrew Jackson and the Creek War: Victory at the Horseshoe." *The Alabama Review,* October 1968.

Hollon, W. Eugene, and Ruth Lapham Butler, eds., *William Bollaert's Texas.* University of Oklahoma Press, 1956.

James, Marquis, *The Raven: A Biography of Sam Houston.* Bobbs-Merrill, 1929.

Jenkins, John Holland, *Recollections of Early Texas.* University of Texas Press, 1958.

Jones, Anson, *Republic of Texas, Its History and Annexation.* The Rio Grande Press, 1966.

Kendall, Dorothy Steinbomer, *Gentilz, Artist of the Old Southwest.* University of Texas Press, 1974.

King, Irene Marschall, *John O. Meusebach, Colonizer in Texas.* University of Texas Press, 1967.

Kownslar, Allan O., *The Texans: Their Land and History.* American Heritage, 1972.

Kuykendall, James H., "Reminiscences of Early Texans." *The Southwestern Historical Quarterly,* Vols. 6, 7, January, April, July 1903.

Leathers, F. J., ed., "Christopher Columbus Goodman: Soldier, Indian Fighter, Farmer, 1818-1861." *The Southwestern Historical Quarterly,* Vol. 69, January 1966.

Lester, Charles Edwards, *The Life of Sam Houston (The Only Authentic Memoir of Him Ever Published).* G. G. Evans, 1860.

Lord, Walter, *A Time to Stand.* Harper & Brothers, 1961.

Lubbock, Francis Richard, *Six Decades in Texas.* Ben C. Jones & Co., Austin, 1900.

Magner, James A., *Men of Mexico.* Bruce Publishing Co., 1942.

McDonald, Archie P., "The young men of the Texas Revolution." *Texana III,* Winter 1965.

Meine, Franklin J., ed., *The Crockett Almanacks.* The Caxton Club, 1955.

Newcomb, Pearson, *The Alamo City.* Standard Printing Company, 1926.

Pinckney, Pauline A., *Painting in Texas.* Published for the Amon Carter Museum of Western Art, Fort Worth, by The University of Texas Press, 1967.

Potter, Reuben Marmaduke, *The Fall of the Alamo.* Old South Leaflets No. 130, The Directors of the Old South Work, Boston, 1904.

Reese, James V., and Lorrin Kennamer, *Texas, Land of Contrast.* W. S. Benson & Company, 1972.

Reeves, Jesse S., "The Napoleonic Exiles in America." *Johns Hopkins University Studies in Historical and Political Science,* series 23, nos. 9-10. The Johns Hopkins Press, September-October, 1905.

Richardson, R. N., *Texas: The Lone Star State.* Prentice-Hall, 1958.

Roemer, Ferdinand, *Texas, with Particular Reference to German Immigration and the Physical Appearance of the Country,* translated by Oswald Mueller. Standard Printing Company, 1935.

Sanders, Leonard, *How Fort Worth Became the Texasmost City.* Amon Carter Museum of Western Art, 1973.

Schmitz, Joseph William, *Texas Culture 1836-1846: In the Days of the Republic.* The Naylor Company, 1960.

Seguin, John N., *Personal Memoirs of John N. Seguin.* The Ledger Book and Job Office, 1858.

Shuffler, R. Henderson, "The Signing of Texas' Declaration of Independence: Myth and Record." *The Southwestern Historical Quarterly,* Vol. 65, January 1962.

Sibley, Marilyn McAdams, *Travelers in Texas 1761-1860.* University of Texas Press, 1967.

Siegel, Stanley, *A Political History of the Texas Republic 1836-1845.* Haskell House, 1973.

Singletary, Otis A., *The Mexican War.* The University of Chicago Press, 1960.

Smith, Ophia D., "A Trip to Texas in 1855." *The Southwestern Historical Quarterly,* Vol. 59, July 1955.

Smith, Justin H., *The War With Mexico* (2 vols.). The Macmillan Company, 1919.

Smithwick, Noah, *The Evolution of a State.* Gammel Book Company, 1900.

Speiser, Adel, *The Story of the Theatre in San Antonio.* M.A. thesis, The Graduate School of St. Mary's University, San Antonio, 1948.

Tinkle, Lon, *13 Days to Glory: The Siege of the Alamo.* McGraw-Hill Book Company, 1958.

Tolbert, Frank X.:
   An Informal History of Texas. Harper & Brothers, 1951.
   The Day of San Jacinto. McGraw-Hill Book Company, 1959.

Vestal, Stanley, *Bigfoot Wallace.* Houghton Mifflin, 1942.

Wade, Houston, compiler, "Notes and Fragments of the Mier Expedition." *La Grange Journal,* 1936.

Wallace, Ernest, *Texas in Turmoil/The Saga of Texas: 1849-1875.* Steck-Vaughn Company, 1965.

Webb, Walter Prescott:
   Editor-in-Chief, *The Handbook of Texas* (2 vols.). The Texas State Historical Association, 1952.
   The Texas Rangers. Houghton Mifflin, 1935.

Wharton, Clarence, *San Jacinto, The Sixteenth Decisive Battle.* Lamar Book Store, Houston, Texas, 1930.

Wilbarger, J. W., *Indian Depredations in Texas.* Hutchings Printing House, 1889.

Williams, Alfred M., *Sam Houston and the War of Independence in Texas.* The Riverside Press, 1893.

Williams, Amelia, "A Critical Study of the Siege of the Alamo and the Personnel of its Defenders." *The Southwestern Historical Quarterly,* Vol. 36, April, July and October 1933, and Vol. 37, January and April 1934.

Williamson, Roxanne, *Austin, Texas: An American Architectural History.* Trinity University Press, 1973.

Winters, James Washington, "An Account of the Battle of San Jacinto." *The Southwestern Historical Quarterly,* Vol. 6, July 1902.

Wisehart, M. K., *Sam Houston: American Giant.* Robert B. Luce, 1962.